D1031643

Studies in International Economics and Institutions

Springer
Berlin
Heidelberg
New York
Barcelona
Budapest
Hong Kong
London
Milan
Paris
Santa Clara
Singapore
Tokyo

Studies in International Economics and Institutions

H.-J. Vosgerau (Ed.), New Institutional Arrangements for the World Economy
IX, 482 pages. 1989

M. Rauscher, OPEC and the Price of Petroleum
XII, 206 pages. 1989

F. Gehrels, H. Herberg, H. Schneider, H.-J. Vosgerau (Eds.), Real Adjustment Processes under Floating Exchange Rates
VI, 302 pages. 1990

T. Tivig, Flexible Wechselkurse aus der Sicht des Finanzmarktansatzes
IX, 226 Seiten. 1991

S. Berninghaus, H. G. Seifert-Vogt, International Migration Under Incomplete Information
VIII, 116 pages. 1991

H. Kräger, K. F. Zimmermann (Eds.), Export Activity and Strategic Trade Policy
VI, 190 pages. 1992

J. Hentschel, Imports and Growth in Highly Indebted Countries
XVI, 210 pages. 1992

H.-J. Vosgerau (Ed.), European Integration in the World Economy
VII, 819 pages. 1992

Assaf Razin
Hans-Jürgen Vosgerau (Eds.)

Trade and Tax Policy, Inflation and Exchange Rates

A Modern View

With Contributions by
Gil Bufman, Alex Cukierman, Bernd Genser, Gene M. Grossman, Andreas Haufler, Elhanan Helpman, Arye Hillman, Manuel Hinds, Nikolaus K. A. Läufer, Leo Leiderman, Branko Milanovic, Assaf Razin, Efraim Sadka, Albert Schweinberger, Peter Birch Sørensen, Srinivasa Sundararajan, Heinrich Ursprung, Hans-Jürgen Vosgerau

With 32 Figures
and 11 Tables

Springer

Professor Assaf Razin
Tel Aviv University
The Eitan Berglas School of Economics
Faculty of Social Sciences
Ramat Aviv
Tel Aviv 69978
Israel

Professor Dr. Hans-Jürgen Vosgerau
University of Konstanz
Faculty of Economics and Statistics
Postfach 55 60
78434 Konstanz
Germany

ISBN 3-540-63120-8 Springer-Verlag Berlin Heidelberg New York

Library of Congress Cataloging-in-Publication Data
Trade and tax policy, inflation and exchange rates: a modern view / Assaf Razin, Hans-Jürgen Vosgerau (eds.); with contributions by Gil Bufman ... [et al.]. p. cm. – (Studies in international economics and institutions)
Includes bibliographical references.
ISBN 3-540-63120-6 (hardcover: alk. paper)
1. Economic stabilization. 2. International economic relations. 3. Commercial policy. 4. Foreign exchange rates. 5. Taxation. I. Razin, Assaf. II. Vosgerau, Hans-Jürgen, 1931– III. Bufman, Gil. IV. Series. HB3732.T73 1997

Hardcover-Design: Erich Kirchner, Heidelberg

SPIN 10075772 42/2202-5 4 3 2 1 0 – Printed on acid-free paper

TABLE OF CONTENTS

Introduction

Assaf Razin and
Hans-Jürgen Vosgerau

The eight chapters of this volume have been grouped into two parts. Part A contains chapters which are mainly monetary in character, whereas real aspects of international economics are treated in Part B. It goes without saying that this is only a device for structuring the field. In substance most chapters reveal the close connections between real and monetary aspects.

Part A on "Inflation, Exchange Rates, and Macro-Economic Adjustment in the Global Economy" consists of four papers.
In recent years, an inflation targeting framework for monetary policy has been adopted by New Zealand, Canada, the United Kingdom, Finland, Sweden, Australia, and Spain (in chronological order). The use of inflation targeting can be viewed as a further step in the evolution of monetary policy techniques adopted by central banks. A common feature of the countries that have adopted inflation targets is the relatively poor inflation record over the last 30 years compared with other industrial countries such as Germany, Switzerland, Japan and the United States. Because of their relatively good inflation record, this latter group of countries has not explicitly adopted inflation targeting. With, or without, explicit inflation targeting the monetary policy credibility hinges on the independence of the central bank. *Alex Cukierman* addresses the issue of central bank independence by surveying alternative ways to characterize independence. His chapter highlights the proposition that the design of policy making institutions matters for the inflation performance of a country. Central bank independence is viewed as a device which can offset a policy bias that is driven by the short-term low cost of using monetary policy to quickly, but only temporarily, achieve various goals like high employment, financing budget deficits, attainment of balance of payment objectives, through low interest rates.

Israel's economy has had, in the last 25 years, inflation and sharp disinflation episodes and massive waves of immigration that can put to test old and new theories of the role of fiscal policy. *Assaf Razin* and *Efraim Sadka* provide an overview of the main policy lessons emerging from this experience. Among the key lessons are: (1) deficits lead to inflation and stopping inflation requires elimination of deficits; (2) inflation has a major effect on the composition of the tax burden falling on labor and capital income; (3) inflation-induced and disinflation-induced redistributions of the tax burden between capital and labor generate a post-stabilization output-employment cycle; (4) absorption of large labor supply budges without worsening government finances depends critically on how market-based government absorption policy is, and on the flexibility of the housing and labor markets. New theories of tax smoothing and expansionary fiscal deficits are confronted with the experience in Israel, an economy which has been the subject of large external and domestic shocks.

Following inflation stabilization programs which use the exchange rate as a rigid nominal anchor, a number of countries have gradually shifted towards a more flexible regime with wider bands. The question whether the regime shift, and in particular the shift from fixed to crawling bands, is perceived as a signal of a tilt towards policy relaxation is addressed by *Elhanan Helpman, Leonardo Leiderman,* and *Gil Bufman.* The evidence collected in the chapter supports the view that instead of being a signal of policy relaxation, the new regime provided a way of restoring external competitiveness after a period of real appreciation.

The international transmission of shocks, for a three-country world economy consisting of a fixed exchange rate among two of the leading members of the EU (the French economy and the German economy) and a flexible exchange rate system towards the economy of the rest of the world, is the subject of an analytical treatment by *Nikolaus Läufer* and *Srinivasa Sundararajan*. They highlight a new channel by which a negative international transmission of real shocks may occur. This channel is generated by the flexible rate which links the two relatively small economies and the large (rest of the world) economy. A positive real shock in one of the two small economies raises the real rate of interest both in the source and the other small economy, and causes an appreciation of the real exchange rate vis a vis the large economy. Consequently, the world demand to the small economies' output will decline. This indirect negative effect on the small country to which the shock is transmitted cannot happen in the standard Mundell-Fleming two-country world economy.

A common feature of the first three chapters of ***Part B*** is the endogenous treatment of trade policy. Whereas the first two chapters accomplish this by using public choice arguments, the third chapter is mainly normative in character; its novelty consists in incorporating international capital ownership. The fourth chapter is devoted to the analysis of trade distortions by different indirect taxation schemes in the European Union.

Gene Grossman and *Elhanan Helpman* are using the framework of a two-stage game to model the complex interactions between factor owners represented by lobbies and the government on the one hand and between the trade partners' governments on the other hand. Whereas the game within each country links the vector of trade taxes and subsidies to the actions of the lobbies, the game between the two governments is characterized by a non-cooperative Nash solution (trade wars) which via negotiations can be transformed into a cooperative solution (trade talks).

The chapter by *Arye Hillman, Manuel Hinds, Branko Milanovic* and *Heinrich Ursprung* links trade policy to the transition process from socialism to a market economy. In the center of the latter is privatisation by sales to foreign investors and distribution of property via vouchers to the population. There is a twofold contradiction. Firstly, the foreign investor has an interest in protection possibly shared by domestic owners and workers, which is in conflict with the efficiency objective and consumer interest in liberalization. Secondly, the government aims at restructuring the economy, but is constrained by a minimum of social consent. Formally these interactions are modelled as a game between governments and foreign investors, which produces a rich variety of outcomes, describing many phenomena observed in the countries of the former Comecon.

Starting from the optimal tariff argument, *Albert Schweinberger* and *Hans-Jürgen Vosgerau* allow for capital ownership by home country residents in the foreign country and vice versa. Depending on whether the international capital ownership is in the export or the import sector, the optimal tariff may be higher or lower - or even negative - compared with the standard case. The reason is of course the influence by changes in the terms of trade on foreign capital income. In addition to this relatively simple case a second best optimal tariff and a general optimal tariff are derived. The analysis is conducted in terms of a factor specific model; possible generalisations are indicated.

The attractiveness of indirect taxation via a value added tax rests on its ultimate incidence with final consumption. Therefore in an international framework the destination principle is usually preferred to the origin principle. But with different national tax rates the destination principle presupposes border controls, which are increasingly abolished within the European Union. *Bernd Genser, Andreas Haufler* and *Peter B. Sϕrensen* in the last chapter are analyzing the resulting trade distortions, allowing for international capital mobility, and discuss ways to achieve non-distortionary indirect taxation under the origin principle and allowing for differentiated tax rates and taking into account practical and administrative complications.

The volume has grown out of the cooperation between the Departments of Economics of the University of Tel Aviv and the University of Konstanz. The chapters are written by members of one of these departments; some are coauthored by other colleagues. The underlying research has been supported by various Israeli, German and other institutions. Several chapters have been prepublished in professional journals. This is documented at the beginning of each chapter. The cooperation between the Universities of Tel Aviv and Konstanz and the preparation and publication of the volume including mutual visits and a workshop were supported by the Lion Foundation, Konstanz and Kreuzlingen. This is gratefully acknowledged by the authors and the editors.

A. INFLATION, EXCHANGE RATES AND MACRO-ECONOMIC AJUSTMENT IN THE GLOBAL ECONOMY

Central Bank Independence, Political Influence and Macroeconomic Performance: A Survey of Recent Developments

Alex Cukierman*

Abstract

Monetary policy usually enables policymakers to quickly but temporarily achieve various real goals like high employment, financing of the budget deficit, attainment of balance of payments objectives and low interest rates. In the process, high-powered money is increased fueling inflation. To offset this policy bias, various institutional mechanisms that reduce the ability of governments to freely expand the money supply have been tried. Among them, an important device, which is gaining popularity recently, is the granting of sufficient independence to the Central Bank in conjunction with an unequivocal mandate to focus on the attainment of price stability.

This paper surveys alternative ways to characterize independence and also can be considered as validating the more general proposition that the design of policy-making institution matters.

---

* This survey is an expanded version of an invited lecture presented to the Twelfth Latin American Meeting of the Econometric Society, August 1993, Tucuman, Argentina. It was first published in Cuadernos de Economía, No. 91, Año 30, December 1993, pp. 271-291, and is reproduced here with the permission of Instituto de Economía, Pontificia Universidad Católica de Chile, Santiago, Chile.

1. Introduction

Monetary policy usually enables policymakers to quickly but temporarily achieve various real goals like high employment, financing of the budget deficit, attainment of balance of payment objectives and low interest rates. In the process, high-powered money is increased fueling inflation and inflationary expectation and creating an inflationary bias which persists long after the desirable effects of monetary expansion have vanished.[1] To offset this policy bias, various institutional mechanisms that reduce the ability of governments to freely expand the money supply have been tried. Among these are the gold standard and various forms of partial commitments to fixed exchange rates like the Bretton Woods system and the European Monetary System.

Another device, which is gaining popularity recently, is the granting of sufficient independence to the Central Bank (CB) in conjunction with an unequivocal mandate to focus on the attainment of price stability. Countries like New Zealand and Chile have recently expanded the autonomy of their central banks[2], and other countries like Mexico, France and the United Kingdom are seriously considering various reforms of their central bank laws that would make them more independent of government. A likely reason for this trend is the success of the Bundesbank (Germany's CB) in maintaining one of the lowest rates of inflation for several decades. The Bundesbank is one of the most independent central banks in the world. It also is directed by its charter to elevate the objective of price stability above all other objectives. The law does specify that the Bundesbank should support the general economic policy of government, but hastens to add that in case of conflict between this goal and the Bundesbank's primary objective (i.e. stability of the currency) the bank's main responsibility is to its primary objective.

How does the degree of central bank independence (CBI) affect price stability, growth and other important macroeconomic variables? These are questions to which any country considering institutional reform of the CB should pay serious attention.

---

1 A non-technical introduction to the various mechanisms that induce the inflationary bias appears in chapter 2 of Cukierman (1992).

2 Details appear in Swinburne and Castello-Branco (1991).

In particular, how effective is CBI in achieving price stability? Do more independent central banks reduce the long-run rate of growth of the economy by being less activist? Until very recently there were no systematic answers to such questions due to the absence of measures of CBI.

This paper is a survey of recent advances and ongoing work in the systematic characterization of the degree of CBI and of the effects of independence on macroeconomic performance. Granting more or less independence to the CB is a way to organize the institutions that (at least partially) decide on, and implement monetary policy. Does the structure of these institutions matter for the choice of policy and economic performance? The broad answer of this survey is: for many issues it does. This paper can, therefore, be considered as validating (in one area) the more general proposition that the design of policymaking institution matters.

The paper surveys several alternative ways to characterize independence. One measure is the degree of independence granted by law. There often are serious gaps, particularly in LDCs, between the letter of the law and its application. Indices that reflect some of these gaps are the actual (as opposed to the legal) term of office of the CB governor and responses of experts on monetary institutions to a questionnaire on CBI. Independence often has many dimensions, some of which are not easily quantified. Nonetheless, the combination of these measures for different groups of countries provides, I believe, a lot of pertinent information.

Even the most independent CB is subject to political influence. But this influence varies from subtle and largely hazy influence like in the U.S.[3] to gross and obvious political influence in which new political masters routinely replace the head of the CB as in some Latin American countries. The paper briefly surveys recent advances in the measurement of gross political influence on the CB and in the identification of the effect of such influence on macroeconomic performance.

---

3 A recent description of these channels appears in Havrilesky (1992).

The paper is organized as follows. Section 2 describes existing measures of legal and of actual independence. Section 3 relates these measures to inflation performance in both developed and less developed economies. A subsection provides theoretical underpinnings for the finding that, past a certain threshold, inflation is higher the lower the probability that the chief executive officer of the CB will remain in office. Section 4 discusses recent advances in the measurement of gross political influence over the CB. Section 5 reports cross country and over time evidence on the relationship between CBI, on the one hand, and growth and investment on the other in both developed and less developed economies. Section 6 briefly discusses the empirical interconnections between the intra-country variability of growth, CBI, and the level of development. The relationships between CBI and the distribution of interest rates are discussed in section 7. This is followed by concluding remarks.

Except for one subsection in Section 3, the paper's focus is empirical. To facilitate the life of quick readers major empirical regularities are highlighted in a series of "conclusions" throughout the paper.

2. Recent Developments in the Measurement of Central Bank Independence (CBI)

Central bank independence is believed to be an important determinant of policy choices and - through them - of economic performance. This belief has eluded systematic verification due to the absence of obvious quantitative measures of CBI. The first attempt to quantify CBI is due to Bade and Parkin (1980) who used a number of *legal* attributes from Central Bank charters to create measures of economic and of financial independence for a subset of industrial countries. Subsequent attempts to quantify independence extended those measures to more countries and proposed alternative ways of aggregating specific *legal* features of the law. But they followed in a similar mould by focussing on legal independence *within industrialized* economies[4]. Broadly based measures of legal independence for over sixty countries have recently been developed in Cukierman (1992) and Cukierman, Webb and Neyapti (1992).

Legal proxies for independence have two problems. First, the laws are incomplete in the sense that they do not specify explicitly the limits of authority between the central bank (CB) and the political authorities under all contingencies. These voids are filled by tradition or power politics. Second, even when the law is quite explicit, actual practice may deviate from it. To address these problems more behaviorally, oriented proxies for actual independence have recently been developed. One is the actual (as opposed to the legally prescribed) turnover of CB governors. This proxy is available for over sixty countries including all industrial countries and over forty LDCs. A second proxy is derived by aggregating the responses of experts on monetary policy to a questionnaire on CBI. This proxy is available for a group of over twenty countries.

This section briefly surveys the procedures used to characterize legal independence as well as the other two, more behaviorally oriented, proxies of independence. It draws on materials from chapter 19 of Cukierman (1992) and Cukierman, Webb and Neyapti (1992).

2.1. Legal Independence

Legal independence is one, but certainly not the sole, determinant of CBI. It also suggests the degree of independence that legislators meant to confer to the CB.

The specific features of legal independence, used to obtain an aggregate index of legal independence, are constructed in the following manner: a code of independence is assigned to each central bank for each characteristic based on a limited number of narrow but relatively precise legal characteristics. Only the

4 Among these are Skanland (1984), Parking (1987), Alesina (1988, 1989), Swinburne and Catello-Branco (1991), Grilli, Masciandaro and Tabellini (1991), and Eijffinger and Schaling (1993). In addition, Leone (1991) presents information on legal limitations on lending by the central bank to government for an extensive sample of industrial and less developed countries.

written information from the charters is used. Additional information on how the law is applied in practice is deliberately left out because it is reflected by the other behavioral indices.

The coded legal characteristics or "variables" can be divided into four groups: (1) variables concerning the appointment, dismissal, and term of office of the chief executive officer (CEO) of the bank (usually the governor); (2) variables concerning the resolution of conflicts between the executive branch and the CB and the degree of participation of the CB in the formulation of monetary policy and in the budgetary process; (3) final objectives of the CB as stated in its charter; and (4) legal restrictions on the ability of the public sector to borrow from the CB. Such restrictions take the form of various limitations on the volume, maturity, rates, and width of direct advances and of securitized lending from the CB to the public sector.

In coding various central banks by the degree of independence within each group of characteristics, the following criteria are used: central banks in which the legal term of office of the CEO is longer and in which the executive branch has little legal authority in the appointment or dismissal of the governor are classified as more independent on the CEO dimension. By the same logic, central banks with wider authority to formulate monetary policy and to resist the executive branch in cases of conflict are classified as more independent on the policy formulation dimension.

Central banks in which the only or main objective of policy (as specified in the charter) is price stability are classified as being more independent in this dimension than central banks with a number of objectives in addition to price stability. These banks are, in turn, classified as being more independent than banks with a large number of objectives or banks in whose charter price stability is not mentioned as an objective at all. This classification of the "objectives" variables is designed to capture the legal mandate of the bank to single-mindedly pursue the objective of price stability. (One of the few central banks in which such an unequivocal legal mandate exists is the Bundesbank).

It does not, therefore, reflect (as the previous two groups of variables) the general level of independence from government. It indicates, instead, the legal mandate of the CB to elevate the target of price stability above other objectives. In Rogoff's (1985) terminology, it measures how strong the "conservative bias" of the CB, as embodied in the law, is.

Similarly, banks in which the limitations on lending from the CB to the public sector are stricter are classified as more independent to pursue the objective of price stability. These limitations encompass a number of more detailed variables such as separate limitations on advances and securitized lending and restrictions on maturities and on interest rates. Generally, the stricter the limitation, the higher the independence coding given to the bank on that dimension. The comparability of various types of limitations is complicated because different countries specify limitations in terms of different reference variables. A few countries specify limitations in absolute cash amounts, and others use a percentage of CB liabilities. The most prevalent type of limitation is formulated as a percentage of revenues, and in a minority of cases as a percentage of government expenditures. The "bite" of these limitations obviously depends on the magnitudes of the reference variables. Other things the same, however, absolute cash limits are more binding than limits in terms of government revenues. The most accommodative limits are those specified in terms of government expenditures. These considerations are embodied in a "type of limit" variable and also influence the coding of the severity of limitations on loans to government via advances and securitized lending.

Limitations on lending are also classified as stricter, the nearer the rates paid by government to market rates and the shorter the maturities of the loans from the CB to the public sector. They are also stricter, the narrower the circle of institutions that are allowed to borrow from the CB and the smaller the discretion of the executive branch in deciding to whom the CB will lend and how much. In addition, central bank laws that prohibit the CB from buying government securities on the primary market are considered, ceteris paribus, stricter than laws that do not contain such a prohibition.

Altogether, sixteen different legal variables are coded using a scale between 0 (smallest level of independence) to 1 (highest level of independence). The number of independence levels generally varies across legal variables depending on the fineness of data on alternative legal characteristics. Using a two-step procedure, the sixteen legal variables are aggregated into a single overall measure of legal independence. This overall index is basically a weighted average of the sixteen legal variables. It varies during the 1980s between a maximum of 0.69 (for Germany) and a minimum of 0.10 (for Poland). The median level of legal independence is about the same in developed countries and in LDCs. Further details on the coding of the legal variables appear in Table 19.1 of Cukierman (1992) or in Table 1 of Cukierman, Webb, and Neyapti (1992).

2.2 The Turnover Rate of Central Bank Governors as a Proxy of Actual Independence

As most practitioners in the area of monetary policymaking are well aware, the legal status of a central bank is only one of several elements that determines its actual independence. Although there are important variations in the degree of completeness of different CB laws, many are highly incomplete and leave a lot of room for interpretation. As a result, factors such as tradition or the personalities of the governor and other high officials of the bank at least partially shape the actual level of CB independence. Even when the law is quite explicit, it may not be operational if there is a tradition or understanding within government that things should be done in a different way. A striking example is Argentina, where the legal term of office of the governor is four years. But there was also an informal tradition that the governor of the CB offers his resignation to the executive whenever there is a change of government or even of the finance minister. Argentinean governors invariably adhered to this tradition. As a consequence, the average actual term of office of the governor in Argentina during the 1980s was about ten months. Obviously, the actual degree of independence of the Argentinean CB was substantially lower than the one implied by measures of legal independence including, in particular, the four-year legal term of office.

There are no obvious indicators of actual, as opposed to legal, CB independence. This is not because the matter is not important, but because it is hard to find systematic indicators of actual independence when it diverges from legal independence. The extreme case of Argentina, though, suggests that at least above some threshold the turnover rate of central bank governors is a proxy of (lack of) actual independence. The average yearly turnover rate between 1950 and 1989 ranges from a minimum of 0.03 (average tenure of 33 years) in Iceland to a maximum of 0.93 (average tenure of about thirteen months) in Argentina. Turnover rates in LDCs tend to spread into a range that has not been experienced in the developed countries (DC). The highest turnover among the DC is 0.2 (average tenure of five years) for Spain and Japan. More than half of the LDCs have turnover rates exceeding this. Table 1 presents turnover rates for selected LDCs during the 1980s.

Low turnover does not necessarily imply a high level of CB independence - a relatively subservient governor may stay in office longer precisely because he does not stand up to the executive branch. This may be true for countries with exceptionally low turnover rate such as Iceland, Denmark, Britain, and the United States. In such countries, turnover is probably unrelated to independence. On the other hand, it is very likely that above some critical turnover rate CB independence is the lower the higher the turnover rate of CB governors. One reason is that for sufficiently high turnover rates the tenure of the CB governor is shorter than that of the executive branch. This makes the governor more susceptible to influence by the executive branch and discourages him or her from trying to implement longer-term policies the lower the expected tenure. Since in most countries the electoral cycle is at least four years, it is likely that the threshold turnover is somewhere between 0.2 and 0.25 (average tenure of four to five years). In addition, for very short terms of office such as three years or less (turnover rates of 0.33 or larger), it is generally more difficult to implement long-term policies for any electoral cycle. It is therefore unlikely, a priori, that turnover is a proxy (lack of) independence in LDCs but that it is largely unrelated to it within industrial countries. The evidence reviewed in the next section is consistent with this conjecture.

TABLE 1: Turnover Rates of the Central Bank Governor 1980 - 1989

(Average number of changes a year)

Country	*Turnover*
Thailand	0.10
Hungary	0.10
Honduras	0.10
South Africa	0.20
Philippines	0.20
Israel	0.20
Greece	0.20
India	0.30
Uruguay	0.30
Portugal	0.30
Pakistan	0.30
Turkey	0.40
Nicaragua	0.40
Poland	0.50
Venezuela	0.50
Singapore	0.60
Chile	0.80
Brazil	0.80
Argentina	1.00

Source: Adapted from Table 3 of Cukierman, Webb, and Neyapti (1992).

2.3 Questionnaire on Central Bank Independence During the 1980s

The other group of indicators of central bank independence is based on responses to a questionnaire that was sent to a non-random sample of specialists on monetary policy in various central banks. Some questions involve the same issues that underlie the legal variables, but they focus on the practice rather than the law - for example, central bank objectives, their importance in practice, and the strictness of limitations on lending in practice. Some questions refer to additional issues, such as subsidized credits from the bank to the private sector, quantitative targets for the money stock, the determination of the bank budget, and the degree of actual tenure overlap between the governor and high officials in the executive branch. One question focusses on the actual practice followed in the resolution of conflicts between government and the CB.

Although the judgements of those responding to the questionnaire are subjective and not entirely uniform, the responses help to identify divergence between actual and legal independence, particularly when the divergence is large.

Answers to the questionnaire sufficed for coding nine questionnaires variables for 23 countries. As with the legal variables, the range of codes is in the zero-one interval with one standing for the highest level of independence and zero for the lowest level. Aggregation of the questionnaire variables indicates that central banks in developing countries are less independent than those in industrial countries. Only two industrial countries - Ireland and Belgium - are below the median of 0.60, and only four developing countries - the Bahamas, Costa Rica, South Africa, and Zaire - are above it. This contrasts with the findings for legal independence, where the two country groups do not differ widely, but it is similar to the finding for turnover. Further detail appears in chapter 19 of Cukierman (1992) and in Cukierman, Webb, and Neyapti (1992).

2.4 Relationship between Indices of Independence

The correlations between legal independence, the turnover rate, and the questionnaire-based index are low, which suggests that each of them contains information about different aspects of CBI.

Only the correlation between the legal independence index and the questionnaire-based index of independence for the industrial countries is even marginally significant, which suggests that the law is a more important determinant of actual independence in the industrial countries. Since the correlation across these indexes is not high, they can be usefully combined to obtain a better measure of overall central bank independence. Such a measure is described in the next section.

3. Inflation and Central Bank Independence

Conventional wisdom is that, by insulating the CB from short-run political pressures, independence enables the central bank to put a stronger emphasis on price stability and to achieve, therefore, a lower rate of inflation. For industrial economies, this hypothesis is, by now, supported by evidence from a number of studies. In particular, it is found that for those economies there is a negative association between inflation and legal independence [Alesina (1988), Grilli, Masciandaro and Tabellini (1991), Cukierman, Webb, and Neyapti (1992), Eijffinger and Schaling (1993b) and Alesina and Summers (1993)].

No similar relationship between inflation and legal independence emerges in LDCs. But there is a strong positive association between inflation and the turnover rate of CB governors. Interestingly, no such association between turnover and inflation is found for industrial economies. These and other findings lead to the conclusion that legal independence is a more appropriate proxy for actual independence within industrial economies and that turnover is a more appropriate proxy for actual independence within LDCs. This conclusion is supported by two additional considerations: First, when both groups of countries are lumped together and the turnover variable broken down into a high and a low range, only the former is found to be significantly related to inflation. It will be recalled from the previous section that turnover within industrial countries is usually in the low range. Second, legal independence is more likely to reflect actual independence within industrial countries than in LDCs since there is more respect for the law in the first group[5].

[5] There is evidence that the relationship between the legal and the actual term in office of the CB governor is stronger for industrial countries than for LDCs [(Pal 1993)].

Further detail and discussion appear in chapter 19 of Cukierman (1993) and in Cukierman, Webb, and Neyapti (1992). The main conclusions are summarized in what follows:

Conclusion 1: *Within industrial economies inflation is negatively related to legal independence and unrelated to CB governors turnover.*

Conclusion 2: *Within LDCs there is no relation between inflation and legal independence. But there is a strong positive association between inflation and CB governors turnover.*

3.1 Inflation and the Questionnaire-based Index of Central Bank Independence

For the sample of twenty-three countries for which a questionnaire-based index of CBI is available there is a significant negative relationship between inflation and the questionnaire-based proxy of independence[6].

3.2 Governor's Turnover and Inflation - Some Theoretical Underpinnings

A higher average turnover rate of CB governors is equivalent to the probability of replacement of the governor being higher. This subsection briefly describes a conceptual framework in which the policy chosen by the CB governor is the more inflationary, the higher the probability that he is removed from office. The intuition underlying this result is that a positive inflationary surprise produces immediate benefits like (temporarily) higher employment and lower interest rates. But the full costs of this policy (in terms of lower credibility and higher inflation) appear later. Central bank governors with shorter horizons in office are therefore more likely to succumb to inflationary temptations. Hence, there should be a positive association, at least above some threshold, between inflation and

---

[6] The countries are (in decreasing order of their questionnaire-based index of independence): Germany, Costa Rica, Finland, Austria, Italy, Denmark, the Bahamas, Luxembourg, France, the United Kingdom, South Africa, Zaire, Lebanon, Ireland, Barbados, Uganda, Uruguay, Belgium, Turkey, Tanzania, Peru, Yugoslavia and Ethiopia.

turnover. Similarly, once high inflation has been unleashed, the benefits of a stabilization accrue only after a while whereas its unemployment and high-interest rates costs occur upfront.

The formal model is an extension of the model of a policymaker with an (extended) information advantage from chapter 10 of Cukierman (1992). As long as he is in office, the governor possesses an objective function with a changing but persistent relative emphasis on the creation of surprises versus price stability. In the present context, this shifting weight can be thought of as originating in changes in the extent of political pressures on the CB. The public never gets to observe these pressures directly but can draw noisy inferences about their current and future state from past inflation rates. These inferences are noisy because the CB does not have perfect control over the rate of inflation.

Let s be the probability of survival of the governor in office in period t given that he has remained in office until period $t-1$.[7] In states of nature in which he is not in office, the governor does not care about either price stability or surprise creation[8]. The relevant part of the governor's objective function is

$$E_0\left\{\left[\Pi_0-\Pi_0^e\right]x_0-\frac{\Pi_0^2}{2}+\sum_{i=1}^{\infty}(s\beta)^i\left[\left(\Pi_i-\Pi_i^e\right)x_i-\frac{\Pi_i^2}{2}\right]\right\}+\sum_{i=1}^{\infty}s^{i-s}(1-s)K \quad (1)$$

where $x_i = A + p_i$, $p_i = \rho p_{i-1} + v_i$, $A > 0$ and $0 < \rho < 1$. v_i is a normal variate with zero mean and variance σ_v^2. Here Π_i is actual inflation in period i and Π_i^e the rate of inflation expected for that period at the beginning of the period. β is the discount factor and x_i is a stochastic variable whose realisations are restricted to the positive orthant. It reflects the potency of political pressures on the CB. The larger x_i the stronger are the pressures of the political establishment on the governor to

---

[7] I assume for simplicity that this probability is constant and independent from events in other periods.

[8] This somewhat extreme assumption is used for simplicity. The main result would go through even if he cared but less than in periods in which he is in office.

expand the money supply. x_i is private information. Its positive serial correlation reflects the presumption that when pressures are above their mean level, they tend to remain above it for some time. K is the *constant* level of utility experienced by the governor when not in office. s^i is the probability that the governor survives in office until the end of period i, and $s^{i-1}(1-s)$ is the probability that he terminates at the beginning of that period after having survived until the end of the previous period. Equilibrium is of the Nash variety; taking the (rational) process of expectation formation by the public as given, the governor plans rates of monetary expansion and inflation so as to maximize the objective function in equation (1); taking the behavioral rule of the governor as given, the public forms expectations so as to minimize the mean (square) forecast error.

Application of the results in chapter 10 in Cukierman (1992) to this case reveals that equilibrium inflation is given by

$$\Pi_i = \frac{1-s\beta\rho}{1-s\beta\lambda}A + \frac{1-s\beta\rho^2}{1-s\beta\rho\lambda}p_i + \psi_i \tag{2}$$

where ψ_i is a normal variate with zero mean and variance σ_ψ^2. ψ_i characterizes the (lack of) precision of monetary policy in controlling inflation. λ is function of ρ, σ_v^2 and σ_ψ^2, and satisfies the inequality $\lambda \le \rho$.

Note that since s, β, ρ and λ are all smaller than one, the coefficients of A and p_i are positive. How does an increase in the governor's survival probability affect equilibrium inflation? The following proposition provides an answer to this question.

Proposition 1: *For any given realization of the political pressure shock (p_i) and of the control error (ψ_i) the rate of inflation is the higher, the lower the survival probability, s, of the central bank governor.*

Proposition 1 provides precise underpinnings for the intuitively plausible notion that a governor with a low probability of survival in office will inflate at a higher rate than a governor with a higher probability of survival. The reason is that part of the cost of *currently* more expansionary monetary policy takes the form of higher *future* inflationary expectations. A governor who is less sure of being in office in the future is obviously less sensitive to this cost. He, therefore, inflates at a higher rate.

Two facts are worth noting. First, due to the dynamic nature of his optimization problem, the governor's policy while in office is influenced by what he perceives to be his future survival probability. Second, a lower survival probability raises the CB inflationary response to any given level of political pressure.

3.3 Two-way Causality between Inflation and Governor's Turnover

The previous subsection shows that there are theoretical reasons to believe that a lower survival probability of the CB governor induces him to follow more inflationary policies. This is consistent with the empirical positive association between turnover and inflation reported earlier in this section. But this association may also be due to reverse causality from inflation to turnover. High inflation is partly blamed on the CB, which tarnishes the bank's public images and makes it more likely that the governor will not persist in office. By the same token, the successful stabilization of inflation is often followed by an increase in the prestige of the CB, which may reduce the likelihood of instability at the bank.

The possibility of reverse causality raises the issue of potential simultaneity bias in the estimated relationship between inflation and turnover. But reestimation of this relation using instrumental variables supports the view that at least part of the significant association between inflation and turnover (in LDCs) is indeed due to causality running from the latter to inflation.

A related issue concerns the causality, in the Granger sense, between turnover and inflation. Estimation of bivariate autoregressive processes for inflation and turnover in broad periods (decades) shows that (Granger) causality operates in both directions. More precisely, lagged turnover affects current inflation and lagged inflation affects current turnover. Further detail appears in subsection 6 and 7 of chapter 20 in Cukierman (1992).

4. Measures of Political Influence on the Central Bank

All central banks are probably subject to some degree of political influence. This influence may be subtle and covert or blunt and quite obvious. The first type of influence is typical of countries like the U.S. in which the CB enjoys a relatively high degree of legal independence. Havrilesky (1992) has recently described some of these channels of influence. Among those are public signalling from the administration to the CB about the "desirable" path of interest rates, the power of appointment and periodic proposals by Congress to enact legislation that would limit the Fed's authority in various ways. Those pressures are only partially successful probably because the law and the way it is implemented sufficiently shield the Fed's high officials from direct retribution when they resist pressures. U.S. presidents usually appoint Board members who they believe will support the economic orientation of the administration. But the long and secure term in office of a Board member (fourteen years) gives him a lot of leeway. The fact that a tenure of a Board member usually spans that of several administrations also increases his freedom of action.

At the other end of the spectrum we find gross political influence, which, like in Argentina or Brazil, results in the removal from office of the CB governor following a change of regime or even of prime minister. This section describes a test for the existence of gross political influence of this type as well as measures of political influence that are based on the extent to which the term in office of the CB governor depends on political changes.

4.1 A Test for the Existence of Gross Political Influence on the CB

The test is based on a comparison of the frequency of governor changes shortly after political transitions with the same frequency in other "non-political" periods. In the absence of gross political influence, we should expect those frequencies to be similar magnitudes. On the other hand, a significantly higher frequency shortly after political transitions would point to the existence of political influence.

Cukierman and Webb (1993) have performed such a test for a sample of 64 countries during the 1950-89 period[9].

In order to compare the frequencies of governor changes between political and non-political periods, it is necessary to find: how long is the time lag following a political transition within which a governor change is identified as political. The cut-off lag is estimated in two steps. First, the first nine months following all political transitions are divided into a number of short (two- or three-months) intervals and the frequency of changes at the CB is calculated within each such interval as well as in the "ten months or more" interval[10]. The cut-off between political and non-political periods is then found by taking the largest lag interval for which: 1) There is a significant difference between the frequency of changes at the CB within this interval and the frequency of such changes at lags of ten or more months, and 2) the frequencies in all intervals beyond this one do not significantly differ from the frequency in the ten-or-more months interval. The demarcation line between political and non-political periods is then estimated to be at the upper bound of this lag interval.

Cukierman and Webb (op. cit.) find that the probability of a CB governor turnover is highest in the first lag interval and that it decays gradually as the time elapsed since the latest political transition increases. The main conclusions reached are summarized in what follows:

Conclusion 3: (i) *There is strong evidence of gross political influence on the CB during the 1950-1989 period.*

(ii) *The cut-off between political and non-political period is at six months following a political transition for the entire sample.*

(iii) *The probability of a CB governor turnover within six months of a political transition is three times larger than the same probability in non-political periods (seven or more months) after a political transition.*

---

[9] The data start later for countries that achieved political independence or established a CB after 1950.

[10] This interval is considered a priori as non-political.

When the sample is broken down into industrial and developing countries, the same qualitative results obtain within each subgroup. Interestingly, there is evidence of gross political influence on the CB even within industrial countries. But the probability of a political turnover within that group of countries is substantially smaller than this probability in LDCs.

Within LDCs the probability of a political turnover at the CB within the same or one month following a political transition is highest in countries that have switched between a democratic and an authoritarian regime (mixed regime), second-highest in countries which had only authoritarian regimes and lowest in countries which were democratic throughout the period of the sample. Further detail appears in Cukierman and Webb (1993).

4.2 The Political Vulnerability of the Central Bank and Related Measures of Dependence

A central bank whose chief executive officer is frequently replaced following political transitions is likely to be more dependent on the political authorities than a central bank in which the governor outlives most political changes. This notion is captured by using an index of political vulnerability of the central bank. The index is defined as the fraction of times that a political transition is followed within six months by a replacement of the central bank governor. The index ranges between a minimum of zero for a number of countries (including the United States, Canada, and Austria) and a maximum of 1.375 (for Argentina).

Central bank vulnerability is generally lower in developed economies than in LDCs. Within LDCs, it is highest in countries that alternate between democratic and authoritarian regimes and lowest in countries with authoritarian regimes. It also tends to increase in periods characterized by a change of regime, i.e., replacement of a democratic regime by an authoritarian one or vice versa.

Given the time profile of political transitions, it is possible to decompose governor's turnover into political and non-political turnover. The latter is defined as CB governor's changes which occur in periods that are seven or more months following a political transition. Political turnover at the CB and vulnerability are largely substitute indices of independence. But non-political turnover and CB vulnerability are probably complementary indices of CB independence. The first is a measure of general instability at the CB whereas the second is a measure of vulnerability of the governor's office to political change.

4.3 Inflation, Political Instability and Instability at the Central Bank

Political instability and inflation tend to be positively related [see for example Cukierman, Edwards, and Tabellini (1992)] or chapter 4 of Cukierman (1992)). An important question is how much of this relation is due to a direct effect from political instability to inflation and how much to (politically induced and non-politically induced) instability at the CB. Cukierman and Webb (1993) examine this question and find that both types of instability have positive effects on inflation. In particular, inflation is higher, the higher the CB vulnerability, and the higher non-political CB turnover. But it is also higher, ceteris paribus, the higher the frequency of high- and low-level political changes[11]. This leads to the following conclusions.

Conclusion 4: *(i)* *High-level political instability raises inflation directly as well as by raising the political vulnerability of the CB.*

(ii) *Non-political turnover at the CB has an additional positive effect on inflation.*

It is well known that inflation and its variance display a strong cross-sectional positive relationship. Cukierman (1992, ch.18) proposes a causal theory in which those two variables are linked because of their common link to CBI. By using CB vulnerability and non-political turnover as measures of CB dependence, it is possible to examine how much of the positive relation between inflation and its variance is due to their common relation with CBI. Cukierman and Webb (1993) find that about one third of the association between inflation and its variability is due to their common association with CBI.

---

[11] A high-level political change is a change in regime. A low-level political change is a change of head of government only.

5. Central Bank Independence, Growth, Investment and Productivity Growth

A priori considerations do not produce a clear-cut hypothesis about the relationship between CBI and growth. On the one hand, by reducing inflation and the associated nominal uncertainty, CBI may enhance the efficiency of resource allocation and encourage investment. We would, therefore, expect more CBI to lead to higher growth on average. But, by reducing the scope for policies to maintain full employment and to encourage investment directly, more independence of the central bank may reduce the average performance of the economy and the long-run rate of growth[12]. Thus it is ambiguous a priori which way central bank independence will affect real growth.

The first attempt to examine the relation between CBI and growth is due to Grilli, Masciandaro, and Tabellini (1991). They examined the cross-sectional relation between average growth and legal independence in a sample of industrial countries and found no association between the two. Using a slightly different coverage of (industrial) countries and another index of legal independence, Alesina and Summers (1993) reach a similar conclusion. Since these studies do not control for other determinants of growth, this finding may reflect an omitted variables bias rather than a lack of association between growth and CBI. But for the industrial countries, this lack of association persists even after controlling for other determinants of growth like initial GDP and the initial levels of primary and of secondary education [Cukierman, Kalaitzidakis, Summers, and Webb (1993)].

Conclusion 5: *Average real growth is unrelated to (legal) CBI within industrial economies.*

When similar experiments are repeated for LDCs, again, no association is found between *legal* independence and growth. But this may well be due to the low association between actual and legal independence in LDCs rather than the lack of

---

[12] Those who advocate such policies probably believe that nominal contracts and/or informational asymmetries produce sufficiently long-lasting effects of money on the economy.

association between growth and CBI. To handle this problem, Cukierman et al. (op. cit.) have used several *behavioral* measures of CBI like governor's turnover and the index of CB political vulnerability as proxies for CBI in LDCs. Barro (1991) has recently uncovered a number of cross-sectional determinants of growth like initial levels of GDP and initial primary and secondary education levels. Using pooled cross-section time series[13] and controlling for those cross-sectional determinants of growth as well as for decade effects and terms of trade shocks, Cukierman et al. find a *ceteris paribus* positive association between growth and CBI. In summary,

Conclusion 6: *After controlling for other determinants of growth (like initial GDP and terms of trade shocks) CBI is found to have a positive effect on growth in LDCs.*

The coefficient of turnover is –3.58. This implies that a 0.1 increase in turnover (one more per decade) reduces the average rate of growth, other things the same, by about 0.36 percent per year. To illustrate the orders of magnitude involved, consider Chile with an average yearly turnover of 0.54 and Indonesia with a turnover of about 0.22 over the 1960–89 period. Taken literally, this implies that about 1.15 percentage points of the difference in average yearly growth rates between these two countries is attributable to the difference in turnover.

One should not interpret this to imply that a reduction of 0.1 in turnover *without any other change* will raise average yearly growth by 0.36 percent, but it is usually the case that a lower turnover of Central Bank governors is associated with a more stable macroeconomic policy environment. When this, and other related factors, change in conjunction with the lower turnover, it seems reasonable to expect an increase in the average rate of growth of the order of magnitude implied by the regression results. A parable may sharpen the argument. Measuring turnover is analogous to taking the temperature of a sick patient. A high temperature is a signal that something is wrong. This does not mean that a reduction of temperature by means of aspirin without taking care of the root cause is going to cure the patient. However, after treatment of the root cause, a reduction in temperature is usually taken as a genuine signal of

---

[13] The data consists (at most) of three-decade-wide observations (1960s, 1970s, and 1980s) on each variable in each country.

recovery. Similarly, the reduction of turnover at the central bank without doing anything else is tantamount to the treatment of a symptom only. However, when the central bank is given more authority to pursue stable policies, this is normally accompanied by a reduction in turnover. In such cases, turnover is a good proxy for the quality of policymaking institutions.

When growth equations using turnover as *proxy* for (lack of) independence are re-estimated for the combined sample of industrial and of developing countries, the coefficient of turnover is again negative, quite significant and even larger than the corresponding coefficient for LDCs alone. This suggests that, controlling for other variables, turnover may also capture differences in growth between the two groups of countries. This conjecture is also supported by the fact that CBI is substantially higher in developed than in developing countries and that the variability of independence within the second group is much higher (see section 3). The conjunction of these findings is consistent with the hypothesis that low independence retards growth in *all* countries but that this effect is not detected within industrial countries because of the smaller variability of CBI and the smaller number of countries in that group. Another possibility is that independence has a detectable effect on growth only above a sufficiently high threshold[14].

5.1 Inflation as a Proxy for Unstable Macroeconomic Policies in Growth Equations

The commonly held view of policy-oriented economists - that unstable macroeconomic policies retard growth - evolved from the experience of high-inflation Latin American economies, and is kept alive by recent developments in some Eastern European economies and the former Soviet Union. This view has been tested by adding inflation or its variability as regressors to growth equations. When this is done, inflation and its variability are found to have a significant negative impact on growth. See for example equation (7) in Fischer (1991) and the literature quoted therein. One problem with this way of testing for the effect of unstable

---

[14] Within industrial countries alone turnover is insignificant. It is possible that this insignificant effect also reflects the lack of association of turnover with actual independence in that group of countries.

macroeconomic policies is that inflation itself is an endogenous variable. It is affected by monetary policy but is also influenced by other non-policy variables. In particular, a negative supply shock will lower the rate of growth and, given policy, raise the measured rate of inflation. Hence the negative coefficient of inflation in the growth equation may be at least partly due to reverse causality – from growth to inflation.

To address this problem, Cukierman, Kalaitzidakis, Summers and Webb (1993) have reestimated growth equations with inflation as a regressor by means of instrumental variables. The political vulnerability of the CB and non-political turnover are used (alternatively) as instruments. Since they represent long-run institutional features of a country, those variables are unlikely to be directly affected by growth. We also saw in section 4 that both of them do affect inflation. They qualify, therefore, as good instruments for inflation in growth equations. The basic result is that, although its effect is less significant, inflation still has a *ceteris paribus* negative effect on growth.

When political vulnerability of the central bank is used as a measure of unstable macroeconomic policies *instead* of inflation, it also has a negative partial effect on growth. In summary,

Conclusion 7: *Unstable macroeconomic policies as proxied by instrumented inflation or central bank vulnerability have a ceteris paribus negative effect on growth.*

5.2 Central Bank Independence, Private Investment and Productivity Growth

One of the channels through which the positive association between growth and CBI may arise is that macroeconomic instability, which is caused by or reflected through low CBI, deters private investment. Cukierman et al. (op. cit.) test that possibility by estimating investment equations for developing countries between 1970 and 1990. After controlling for some of the same variables that appear in the growth equations, they find that central bank turnover has a significant negative impact on private investment as a share of GDP. So does the political vulnerability of the central bank.

When the Barro-Wolf proxies for political instability[15] are added as regressors, the significance of turnover and vulnerability is reduced but their effects remain negative.

The summary conclusion is:

Conclusion 8: *Less CBI as proxied by a higher governor's turnover or by more political vulnerability at the central bank has a negative impact on the share of private investment in LDCs. This effect weakens but does not totally disappear in the presence of proxies for political instability.*

Another channel through which CBI could affect growth is productivity growth. Cukierman et al. find a weak partial negative association between productivity growth and central bank independence as proxied by turnover in LDCs. But this effect vanishes in the presence of measures of political instability.

6. The Intra-Country Variability of Growth, CBI, and the Level of Development

Countries with more dependent central banks normally conduct more activist monetary policies in order to affect aggregate demand. It is an open issue, though, whether such activism actually dampens or increases the amplitude of business cycles. Political authorities are more likely than the central bank to pursue a variety of objectives besides dampening of the cycle. For instance, they might produce a political cycle [for a recent empirical survey see Alesina, Cohen, and Roubini (1992)] Even when they aim to dampen the cycle, politicians may exacerbate it, along the lines of Friedman's long and variables lags argument [see also Meltzer (1987)]. Hence, there are conflicting theoretical predictions about the relationship between a country's growth rate variability and the independence of its central bank[16].

---

[15] Those variables are counts of political assassinations, revolutions and coups.

[16] But theory *does* imply that, other things the same, policy is the more activist, the more dependent the central bank [Cukierman (1992) p. 355].

The type of relationship, if any, between the variability of growth and the level of CBI is, therefore, an empirical matter.

Cukierman et al.(op.cit.) find, after controlling for the effect of terms of trade shocks, that there is a negative relationship between the variability of growth within a country and CBI as proxied by turnover. But when one controls for initial GDO, this variable turns out to have a significant negative impact on the variability of growth, and turnover becomes insignificant. Hence,

Conclusion 9: *The over time variability of growth within a country is negatively related to its level of development and unrelated to the independence of its central bank as proxied by turnover.*

7. CBI and Interest Rates

The first attempt to investigate the relationship between the distribution of interest rates and CBI is in Alesina and Summers (1993). Their results pertain to a sample of 18 industralized countries. Using the Alesina (1988) legal measure of CBI, they find that: (1) there is no (cross-country) association between the level of export real rates and CBI; (2) the (intra-country) variability of real rates is inversely related to CBI. They attribute this finding to the negative association between the variability of inflation and CBI.

Using their own measure of legal independence, Cukierman, Kalaitzidakis, Summers, and Webb (1993) replicate the second result and find no association between the variability of export real rates and legal independence in LDCs. On the other hand, they find a strong positive association between this variability and central bank turnover in LDCs. These results are consistent with the view that legal independence is an appropriate proxy for actual independence in industrial countries and that turnover is the appropriate proxy in LDCs.

They also find that there is a negative relationship between CBI and the variability of nominal rates but no similar relationship between CBI and the variability of long-term nominal rates. In summary,

Conclusion 10: (i) *The variabilities of ex-post real rates and short-term nominal rates are negatively related to (the appropriate respective measures of) CBI in both developed and less developed economies.*

(ii) *There is no relation between the variability of nominal long-term rates and CBI.*

Contrary to Alesina and Summers, Cukierman et al. find a positive relationship between the level of the ex-post real return to savers in industrial economies and legal independence.

A similar qualitative result emerges for LDCs when Argentina is included in the sample. More precisely, there is a significant negative association between the average real return to short-term financial savings and turnover. When Argentina is excluded, the coefficient of turnover becomes insignificant but remains negative. In summary,

Conclusion 11: (i) *The ex-post average real return to deposits is positive associated with legal independence in industrial economies.*

(ii) *The ex-post average real return to deposits in LDCs is negatively associated with the turnover of CB governors. But when Argentina is excluded from the sample, this effect becomes insignificant*[17].

A likely explanation for the positive association between the real deposit rate and CBI is that in most countries the real return to savers in short-term financial assets is below its competitive equilibrium level because of government regulation and periodic inflationary surprises. As a consequence, the quantity of short-term financial savings is supply-constrained. The lower the degree of CBI, the farther below its equilibrium value is the real return to savers because of higher interference with the short-term return to nominal savings through regulations and inflationary surprises.

[17] Further detail appears in Cukierman et al. (op. cit.).

This view is consistent with the McKinnon and Shaw notion of financial repression [McKinnon (1973)].

In addition, conclusion 11 implies that the level of financial repression is higher, the lower CBI. This view is further supported by the observation that the real return to savers in LDCs is substantially lower than in industrial countries in conjunction with the fact (section 3) that overall independence in the second group is higher on average.

8. Concluding Remarks

The evidence surveyed in this paper leads to the conclusion that, over the long term, CBI and the absence of gross political influence on the central bank improve, or at least do not reduce, macroeconomic performance. Higher levels of independence are associated with lower inflation without discernible effects on growth and its variability in developed economies. In LDCs, higher CBI and lower levels of (gross) political influence are associated with lower inflation, more growth, and more private investment without any discernible effect on the variability of growth. In addition, higher levels of independence are associated with higher returns to financial savings, less variability of these returns and most likely a more efficient allocation of financial capital.

Central bank independence (CBI) is one of several ways to *partially* commit politicians to pay relatively more attention to price stability. In the absence of *some* commitment device, adverse shocks to the economy or to the political system may induce a policy response that allows the development of high inflation. CBI should be viewed mostly as a *preventive* rather than a remedial device. Once high inflation has been allowed to develop, independence alone does not suffice to eradicate it.

As many recent successful stabilizations have clearly demonstrated, an ongoing inflation can be stabilized only with the full and determined participation of the highest levels of government. But once price stability has been restored, CBI can play a useful, long-term, preventive role. The recent tendencies toward granting more independence to the central banks in countries like Chile, Mexico, and Argentina are, therefore, pointed in the right direction.

But an important lesson from the findings reported here is that more legal independence *alone* does not suffice. When actual practice is allowed to substantially depart from the written law, even a highly independent charter does not function as an effective commitment device. The experiences of Argentina and Chile in previous decades are living proof of this principle. A general climate of respect of the rule of law, of the kind found in some developed democracies, enhances the effectiveness of legal independence as a commitment device.

It seems that having an independent central bank is particularly important in situations in which the authority for deciding on fiscal expenditures is relatively decentralized as is the case in Brazil, the former Socialist Republics, and may be the case in Western Europe if and when a European monetary union comes into being. As the number of players that have the authority to commit government spending increases, each player pays less attention to the effect of the expenditures he advocates on the general rate of inflation. As a result, the rate of inflation increases[18]. Effective constraints on the ability of politicians to tamper with the money supply seem particularly important in such cases.

---

[18] A recent analytical formulation of this idea appears in Aizenman (1992).

APPENDIX

Proof of Proposition 1: totally differentiating equation (2) with respect to s and rearranging

$$\frac{d\Pi_i}{ds} \equiv -K\left[(1-s\beta\lambda\rho)^2 A + (1-s\beta\lambda)^2 \rho p_i\right] \tag{A1}$$

where

$$K \equiv \frac{\beta(\rho-\lambda)}{(1-s\beta\lambda)^2 (1-s\beta\lambda\rho)^2} \tag{A2}$$

Since $\rho - 1 > 0$, K is positive. Since $A \geq p_i$ and $(1-s\beta\lambda\rho)^2 > (1-s\beta\lambda)^2 \rho$, it follows that the expression in square brackets on the right-hand side of (A1) is positive. Hence

$$\frac{d\Pi_i}{ds} < 0$$

which establishes Proposition 1.

References

Aizenman, J. (1992), "Competitive Externalities and the Optimal Seigniorage", *Journal of Money, Credit and Banking,* 24, pp. 61-71.

Alesina, A. (1988), " Macroeconomics and Politics", in: Stanley Fischer (ed.), *NBER Macroeconomics Annual,* MIT Press, Cambridge.

Alesina, A. (1989), "Politics and Business Cycles in Industrial Democracies". *Economic Policy*, 8, pp. 57-98.

Alesina, A., G. D. Cohen, and N. Roubini (1992), "Macroeconomic Policy and Elections in OECD Democracies", in: Alex Cukierman, Zvi Hercowitz, and Leonardo Leiderman (eds.), *Political Economy, Growth and Business Cycles*, MIT Press, Cambridge.

Alesina, A. and L. H. Summers (1993), "Central Bank Independence and Macroeconomic Performance: Some Comparative Evidence", *Journal of Money, Credit and Banking*, 25, pp. 151-162.

Bade, Robin and Michael Parkin (1980), "Central Bank Laws and Monetary Policy". Manuscript. Department of Economics, University of Western Ontario.

Barro, R. J. (1991), "Economic Growth in a Cross-Section of Countries" *Quarterly Journal of Economics*, 106, pp. 407-443.

Cukierman, A. (1992), *Central Bank Strategy, Credibility and Independence: Theory and Evidence*, The MIT Press, Cambridge, Massachusetts.

Cukierman, A., S.B. Webb, and B. Neyapti (1992), "Measuring the Independence of Central Banks and its Effect on Policy Outcomes", *The World Bank Economic Review*, 6, pp. 353-398.

Cukierman, A. and S. B. Webb (May 1993), "Political Influence on the Central Bank - International Evidence", Manuscript, Tel-Aviv University.

Cukierman, A., P. Kalaitzidakis, L. H. Summers and S. B. Webb (1993), "Central Bank and Independence, Growth, Investment, and Real Rates". *Carnegie-Rochester Conference Series on Public Policy,* Autumn.

Eijffinger, S. and E. Schaling (1993a), "Central Bank Independence in Twelve Industrial Countries", *Banca Nazionale del Lavoro Quarterly Review*, 184, pp. 49-89.

Eijffinger, S. and E. Schaling (1993b), "Central Bank Independence: Theory and Evidence", D. P. No. 9325, Center for Economic Research, Tilburg University.

Fischer, S. (1991), "Growth, Macroeconomics and Development", *NBER Macroeconomics Annual*, pp. 329-379.

Grilli, V., D. Masciandaro, and G. Tabellini (1991), "Political and Monetary Institutions and Public Financial Policies in the Industrial Countries", *Economic Policy* 13, pp. 341-392.

Havrilesky, T. (1992), *The Pressures on American Monetary Policy*, Kluwer Academic Publishers, Norwell, MA.

Leone, A. (1991), "Effectiveness and Implications of Limits on Central Bank Credit to the Government", in: Patrick Downes and Reza Vaez-Zadeh (eds.), *The Evolving Role of Central Banks*, IMF, Washington, pp. 363-413.

McKinnon, R.I. (1973), *Money and Capital in Economic Development*, the Brookings Institutions, Washington, D.C.

Meltzer, A. (1987), "Limits of Short-Run Stabilization Policy", *Economic Inquiry*, 25, pp. 1-14.

Pal Noga (1993), "The Effect of Statutory Laws on Turnover at the Central Bank", Graduate Term Paper, Dep. of Economics, Tel-Aviv University.

Parkin, Michael (1987), "Domestic Monetary Institutions and Deficits", in: James M. Buchanan et al. (eds.), *Deficits*, Basil Blackwell, Oxford, pp. 310-337.

Rogoff, Kenneth (1985) "The Optimal Degree of Commitment to an Intermediate Monetary Target". *Quarterly Journal of Economics* 100, pp. 1169-1190.

Skanland, H. (1984), *The Central Bank and Political Authorities in Some Industrial Countries*. Norges Bank, Oslo.

Swinburne, M. and M. Castello-Branco (1991), "Central Bank Independence and Central Bank Functions"; in: Patrick Downes and Reza Vaez-Zadeh (eds.), *The Evolving Role of Central Banks*. IMF, Washington, pp. 414-444.

Fiscal Balance During Inflation, Disinflation, and Immigration: Policy Lessons

Assaf Razin and
Efraim Sadka*

Abstract

The paper provides an overview of the role of the fiscal imbalances and the ensuing public debt in explaining major episodes in Israel's recent economic developments. The main conclusions from the Israeli budgetary developments may have more general validity: (a) deficits lead to inflation and stopping inflation requires elimination of deficits; (b) a major effect of inflation is a large shift of the tax burden from capital to labor; and (c) shocks to labor supply, such as massive labor inflow through immigration, can be absorbed without worsening government finances, when the labor and the housing markets are sufficiently flexible.

---

* This chapter was written as an IMF Working Paper in April 1996, while Assaf Razin was visiting the Fiscal Affairs Department at the International Monetary Fund. The views expressed are those of the author(s) and do not necessarily represent those of the Fund.
The authors wish to thank Nils Gottfries for useful comments. This chapter was first published in the *Swedish Economic Policy Review*, Vol. 3, No. 1, Spring 1996, and is reprinted here with the publisher's permission.

Summary

This paper outlines the role of the fiscal deficit and the ensuing public debt in Israel's contemporary economic history. Its focus is on the inflation and disinflation episodes of the 1980s and on the massive labor inflow in the form of the wave of immigration in the 1990s. These episodes serve as a testing ground for old and new theories of the role of fiscal policies in economies that are subject to various external and domestic shocks.

The following main policy lessons emerge from Israel's budgetary developments: (1) deficits lead to inflation and stopping inflation requires elimination of deficits; (2) a major effect of inflation is a large shift of the tax burden from capital to labor; (3) in low-debt cases, the aggregate demand effects of fiscal stabilization are not large because of debt neutrality; (4) aggregate demand may rise with severe fiscal contractions in high-debt cases; (5) when the exchange rate is used as a nominal anchor, in the presence of international capital movements, the economy typically ends up with an overvalued currency, which eventually leads to recession; (6) inflation-induced and disinflation-induced redistributions of the tax burden between capital and labor cause a poststabilization output-employment cycle; (7) shocks to the labor supply, for example, through massive immigration, can be absorbed without worsening government finances when the labor and the housing markets are sufficiently flexible; and (8) productivity increases with a significant lag, however, in the presence of large inflow of skilled labor.

The main policy implication that can be drawn is that the absence of budget discipline, coupled with an almost inevitable monetary accommodation, will eventually fuel an inflationary process that could run out of control. The huge budgetary expansion in Israel and the associated monetary expansion were initiated by wars and severe terms of trade shocks (the oil crises). At the same time, subsidies, other transfers, cheaper public education, as well as some "supply-side economics" measures were maintained. The emergent inflation proved in the end to be detrimental to income distribution objectives, to factor productivity, and to economic growth. Inflation undermined the tax system and tilted income distribution in favor of capital and against labor. Even worse, the inflation-induced tax concessions to capital were highly distortionary without having any positive effect on growth.

The budgetary expansion associated with the absorption of the massive immigration from the countries of the former Soviet Union did not increase the public debt in a relative sense even though the tax burden was not raised. This surprising outcome occurred because output was capable of responding swiftly to the increased aggregate demand, through the use of excess capacity of capital (residual of the poststabilization recession) and high labor force participation rates among the newcomers.

1. Introduction

This paper provides an overview of the role of the fiscal deficit and the ensuing public debt in explaining major episodes in Israel's contemporary economic history. We focus on the inflation and disinflation episodes in the 1980s, and the more recent experience of massive immigration in the 1990s. These episodes can serve as a testing ground for old and new theories concerning the role of fiscal policies in economies which are subject to various external and domestic shocks. The main questions addressed in the paper are: What is the relation between deficits and inflation? How do inflation and disinflation affect effective tax burdens and the distribution of income between capital and labor? Is there evidence of debt neutrality and tax smoothing? Can a fiscal contraction be expansionary? What factors caused the immediate boom and the subsequent real appreciation and recession observed in Israel after the 1985 stabilization program? How are government finances affected by massive immigration and why is the recent Israeli experience so different from the German unification experience in this respect?

The paper is organized as follows. Section 2 overviews the theoretical underpinnings of the macroeconomic effects of fiscal policies. Section 3 highlights the main features of the inflation process in Israel. Section 4 analyzes the links between fiscal contractions and aggregate demand. The income distribution issues associated with inflation and disinflation are considered in Section 5. Post-disinflation cycles are considered in Section 6. The roles of tax smoothing and the labor market in the successful absorption of immigrants are analyzed in Section 7. Section 8 contains a summary and concluding remarks.

2. Macroeconomic Effects of Debt: Theory

There are a number of ways to model the macroeconomic impacts of the government deficit and its accumulation into government debt. We argue that the Israeli experience can best be cast within two main frameworks, which we now sketch briefly.

The first is the traditional Mundell-Fleming model, which emphasizes short term, cyclical effects of macroeconomic policies (fiscal and monetary) on inflation, the real exchange rate, employment, external imbalances, and the like.[1] In this framework, government deficits lead to inflation if money creation is used to finance them. The second framework emphasizes long-term intertemporal considerations pertinent to economies with forward-looking individuals, as in Barro, 1974. Within this framework, issues such as tax smoothing, debt neutrality, the effect of government deficit on private savings and interest rates, public consumption versus public investments, policy credibility, fiscal contraction and consumption boom, and the like, can be usefully analyzed. In the general equilibrium analysis, fiscal shocks affect the path of prices if they change the present value of current and future government surpluses at the pre-existing equilibrium prices.

The small economy version of the Mundell-Fleming model is suitable for assessing the impact of government deficits and the associated monetization on the short-run adjustment to equilibrium. The model consists of four key elements.

---

1 The real exchange rate measures the relative price of foreign-produced goods in terms of home-produced goods.

The first is the demand-supply equation for the domestic product. (Its mirror image states that the current account deficit is equal to investment minus savings, both private and public.) The second is a standard market-clearing equation for domestic money. The third states that international mobility of financial capital must yield interest parity: the nominal rate of interest is equal to the world (nominal) rate of interest plus the expected rate of depreciation of the domestic currency. The fourth key element is a slow short-run adjustment of wages and prices, due to pre-set nominal contracts. The model predicts that a government deficit would lead to a higher real rate of interest, an appreciation of the real exchange rate, an increase in the current account deficit, higher aggregate demand and employment, and higher domestic prices. When, as is typically the case, the government deficit is at least in part monetized (in the current as well as expected future periods), prices, employment and the external deficit grow even higher, while there is an offsetting effect on real interest rates and the real exchange rate. The real effects of monetary policy, however, dissipate in the longer run when wage and price contracts adjust fully.[2]

Now, when more long-run driving forces of individual optimization behavior à la Barro are taken into account, some of the conclusions of the above, a more traditional framework, are modified. Economic agents with a long horizon may well realize that higher government deficits today will eventually necessitate surpluses in the future, so as to keep government solvency intact. As a result, private savings may offset government dissavings,

---

2 Under a flexible exchange rate, a current transitory fiscal expansion (which does not alter expectations about the future path of the exchange rate) induces a rightward shift of the IS schedule, raising both the level of output and the domestic interest rate. To maintain interest parity, the rise in the interest rate must result in appreciation of the domestic currency. Under a fixed exchange rate, interest arbitrage ensures equality between the domestic and foreign interest rates. Consequently, a fiscal expansion that induces a rightward shift of the IS schedule gains full potency in raising the level of output, because there is no currency appreciation to offset it. Monetary policy is only weakly effective under exchange rate targeting since a tight monetary policy which puts upward pressure on the domestic interest rate induces capital inflow from abroad, which has to be monetized given the commitment to the exchange rate target. The monetization of the capital inflow neutralizes the initial monetary tightness.

thereby mitigating the Mundell-Fleming effects of government deficits on the real rate of interest and the real exchange rate.

Nevertheless, with slow-adjusting prices, the associated monetary expansion may still be effective, as in the Mundell-Fleming framework.

Since taxes cause deadweight losses, with an increasing marginal burden, it may not be optimal for the government to increase taxes each time its spending rises. Consequently, it may be optimal to smooth taxes over time, by allowing deficits in high-spending and/or low-output years, and surpluses in low-spending and/or high-output years. This tax pattern will then equate the marginal excess burden over time, thereby minimizing the sum total of excess burdens over time. Thus, a balanced-budget rule, which is in direct conflict with tax smoothing, is bound to involve significant deadweight losses.

Interestingly, if the deadweight loss is expected to rise with fiscal pressure, then a drastic fiscal consolidation may untraditionally generate a rise in aggregate private demand. The reason for the increase in aggregate private demand in this case is twofold. First, when the growth of public debt comes to a halt through the fiscal contraction program, consumers realize that future debt service is considerably less distortionary. The fiscal contraction which accordingly helps restore balance in the intertemporal allocation of the tax burden will increase consumers' lifetime wealth. Consequently, private consumption will then expand as well, contrary to the prediction of the traditional model. Second, private investment may rise as a result of the expected future decline in capital income (especially corporate income) taxes. Thus, a fiscal-based disinflation program is plausibly expansionary under these circumstances, raising aggregate demand and employment (see Giavazzi and Pagano, 1990).

All in all, in practice, persistent government deficits typically generate inflationary processes. The latter have significant real effects on the distribution of income, the tax system, and growth.

3. The Inflation Process: Fiscal and Monetary Fundamentals

Israel's flirtation with inflationary cycles can ironically serve as a good testing ground for macroeconomic theories. Following the Yom Kippur War of October 1973 and the pursuant oil crisis (OPEC I), Israel's fiscal and monetary disciplines were significantly weakened. A key factor in this process was a sharp increase in military expenditures with an associated slowdown in economic growth and, consequently, a low growth of the tax base. Government deficits persisted, resulting in a growing public debt. Figure 1 describes the public sector deficit as a percentage of GDP. It shows a sharp increase in the deficit to a level of 12 percent to 20 percent of GDP following the 1973 war. These deficits accumulated to generate a peak public sector debt of 175 percent of GDP at the end of 1984, just before a sharp disinflation policy was implemented. (See Figure 9a for the development of the public sector net debt.) Eventually, the public deficit was partly monetized. Also, weak fiscal discipline must have pushed up wages well above productivity increases (see Figure 2), a trend which was accompanied by an accommodating monetary policy. Furthermore, controls on capital imports were largely relaxed in October 1977. This occurred when domestic rates of interest were significantly higher than their world counterpart and the exchange rate, though officially flexible, was in practice still severely managed at a rate of depreciation which fell short of purchasing parity. The deviation from purchasing parity favored domestic financial investments. This generated a massive capital inflow which was largely monetized by the managed exchange rate mechanism. The growing public debt gave rise to expectations of future monetization of budget deficits, thereby raising current inflationary pressures (see Sargent and Wallace, 1981). In sum, under the apparently managed exchange rate system, the central bank could not control the money supply: higher interest rates only generated capital inflow and sterilization of the capital flows was to a large extent ineffective. At the same time, with growing budget deficits, any anti-inflation monetary policy would have been severely contractionary, which made this kind of policy politically infeasible. In a nutshell, these factors are the fundamentals behind the eruption of high inflation in Israel in the late 1970s, lasting until mid-1985 (see Figure 3).

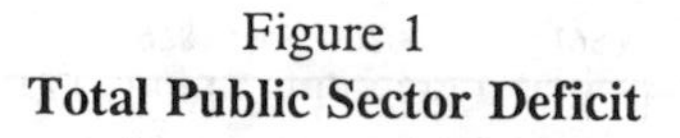

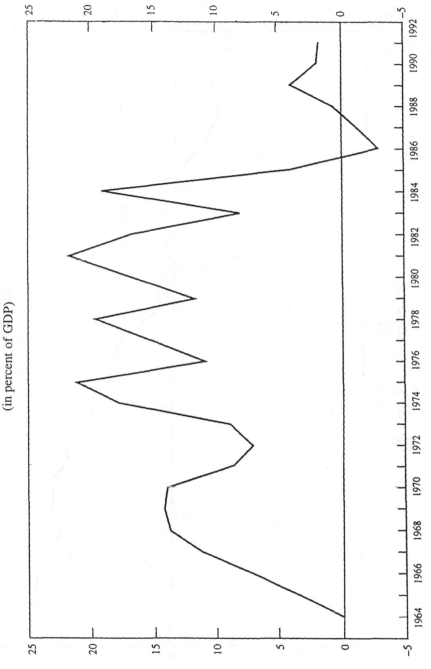

Figure 1
Total Public Sector Deficit
(in percent of GDP)

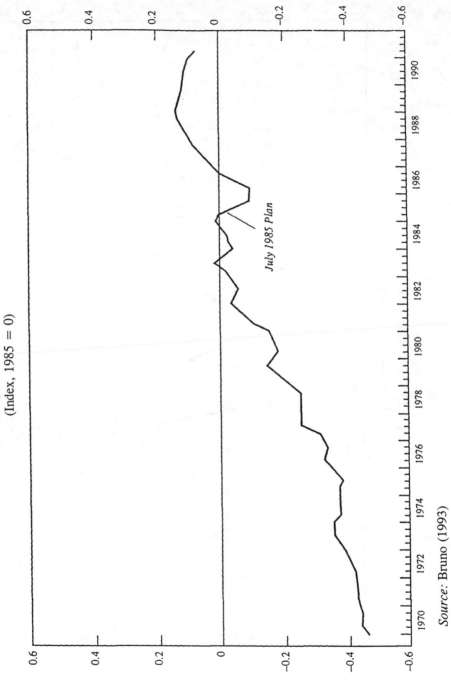

Figure 2
Real Wage in Manufacturing
(Index, 1985 = 0)

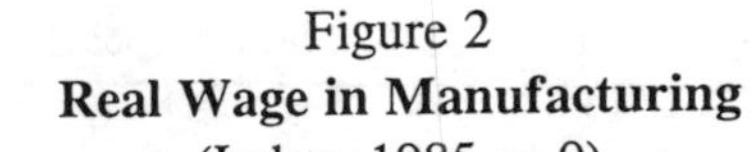

Source: Bruno (1993)

Figure 3
Annual Inflation Rate, 1960 - 89
(percentage change)

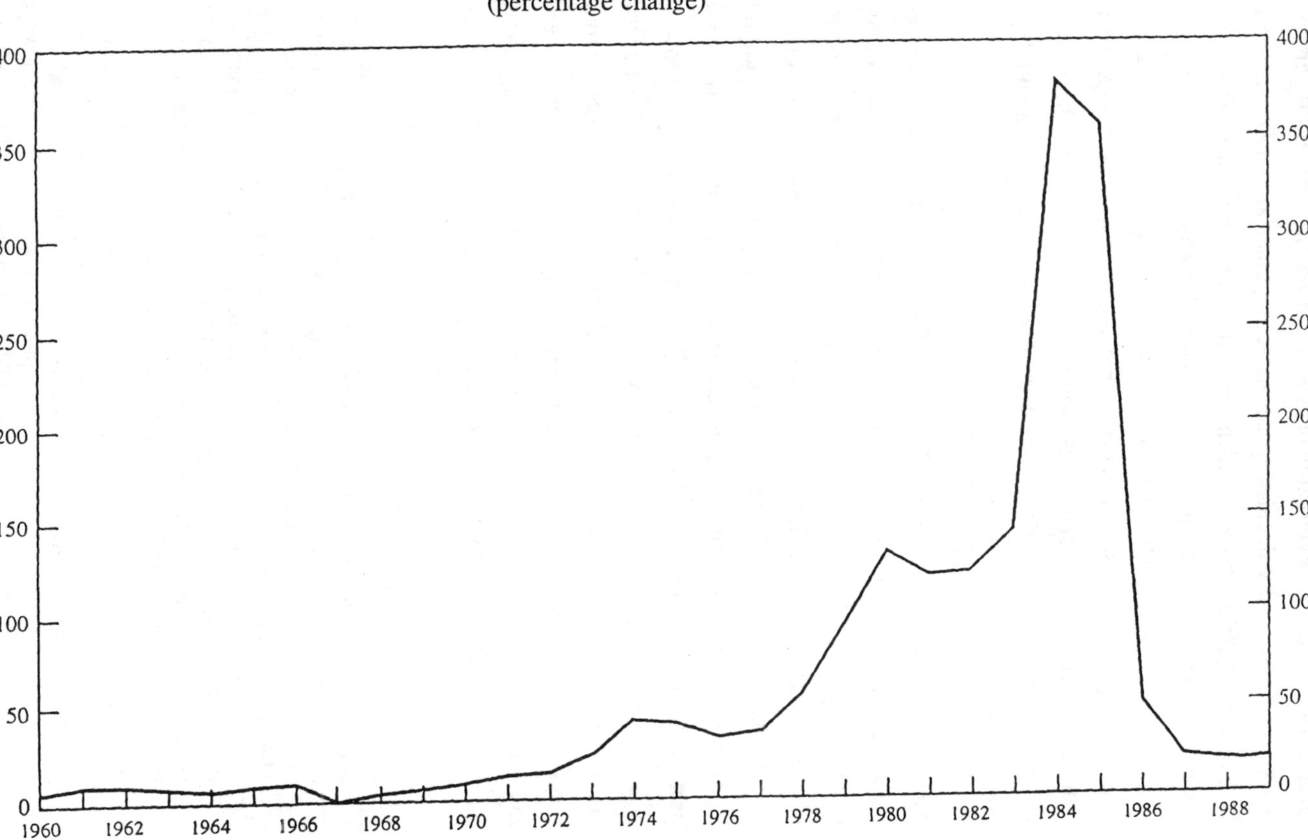

In mid-1985, with the external debt reaching a record high of 80 percent of GNP, the government finally decided to get its act together and embarked on a comprehensive stabilization policy which proved remarkably successful. Before that, several attempts had been made at slowing the rate of inflation. These were based on holding back devaluations and/or using administrative measures aimed at restraining price increases or actually freezing prices, even though it was evident that the economic fundamentals were not in line with the "anti-inflation" measures. Most importantly, none of these attempts included a significant budget consolidation.[3]

The distinct feature of the mid-1985 disinflation program was major and severe fiscal and monetary restraint, coupled with a major realignment of key prices. Government subsidies of basic food products and public transportation were severely slashed. In addition, there was a cut in domestic defense spending (following the pullout of the Israeli army from Lebanon).[4] In addition to the significant expenditure cuts, tax revenues increased substantially. A significant part of the increase in tax receipts was a direct consequence of the lower inflation rate. Indeed, when inflation rates are high, the time lapse between accrual of the tax liability and actual payment of that liability erodes the total amount of tax revenue collected in real terms (the so-called Tanzi effect). Thus, when inflation rates drop, real tax collections automatically rise. Another reason for the growth in tax revenues was the adoption of a Blue-Ribbon Commission's recommendations

---

3 Ruge-Murcia (1995) addressed the issue of credibility of disinflation programs from an econometric perspective. In his application to Israel, he provided evidence as to the lack of credibility of the failed stabilization programs of 1984 and early 1985. The skepticism about the content of spending cuts in the disinflation package explains, in part, the volatility of inflation in this period. In contrast, his estimates show that for the July 1985 program, individual agents correctly inferred that a major shift in regime drives the spending process. Thus, his estimates confirm that the fiscal regime shift was indeed credible and effective.

4 Wage and price controls were used in the first few months, immediately after the stabilization program. However, price controls were partial and relatively ineffective. Wages were renegotiated, on a national level, to sacrifice the first cost of living adjustment but to pick up most of the price increases later on. Real wages, which suffered a short-term reduction in the immediate aftermath of the program, increased significantly in the following two years.

for taxing the business sector under conditions of inflation that tightened the indexation procedures for calculating real income in the business sector for tax purposes. Also, a temporary surtax was levied on the income of self-employed.

Figure 4 shows the effects of the ensuing fiscal restraint. The public sector domestic deficit fell to 0 to 2 percent of GNP, from about 12 percent prior to stabilization. Together with a total of about 1.8 percent of GNP in emergency aid (over a two-year period) provided by the United States Government, this helped to generate an overall budget surplus amounting to some 2 percent of GNP. Despite the pegged exchange rate policy, tight restrictions on international capital movements enabled the monetary authorities to exercise severe restraint. (For instance, a surcharge was levied on financial capital imports.) The effects of the monetary restraint are shown in Figure 5. A curbing of the M3 monetary aggregate (which includes means of payments, interest-bearing unindexed assets, and resident deposits linked to foreign currencies) became immediately apparent after the stabilization program was implemented. The sharp decline in the rate of growth of the money supply came at a time when the demand for money grew drastically due to lower inflation expectations. As a result, monetary restraint also manifested itself through a sharp rise in real interest rates, immediately after the program was implemented (see Figure 6). These measures naturally contributed to a drastic fall in inflationary pressures, and consequently, to an almost immediate economic stabilization.

The realignment of some key prices included, in addition to the cut in subsidies, a remedial adjustment in the exchange rate. The Israeli sheqel was devalued by 42 percent up front. In fact, the exchange rate at that point reached a real level that was not experienced again until recently, 10 years later. Indeed, the deficit cut facilitated the sharp real depreciation in the immediate aftermath of the program. The direct effects of the devaluation and the cut in subsidies on the CPI were initially sterilized from the cost of living adjustment (COLA) to wages. Real wages later recouped this decline within one year (see also Figure 2).

Following the stabilization program, the Government used the exchange rate as a nominal anchor. Together with a fairly tight monetary policy which was reflected in high interest rates (see Figures 5 and 6), the exchange rate peg generated,

Figure 4
Budget Deficit (positive) or Surplus (negative), 1980 - 1988
(in percent of GNP)

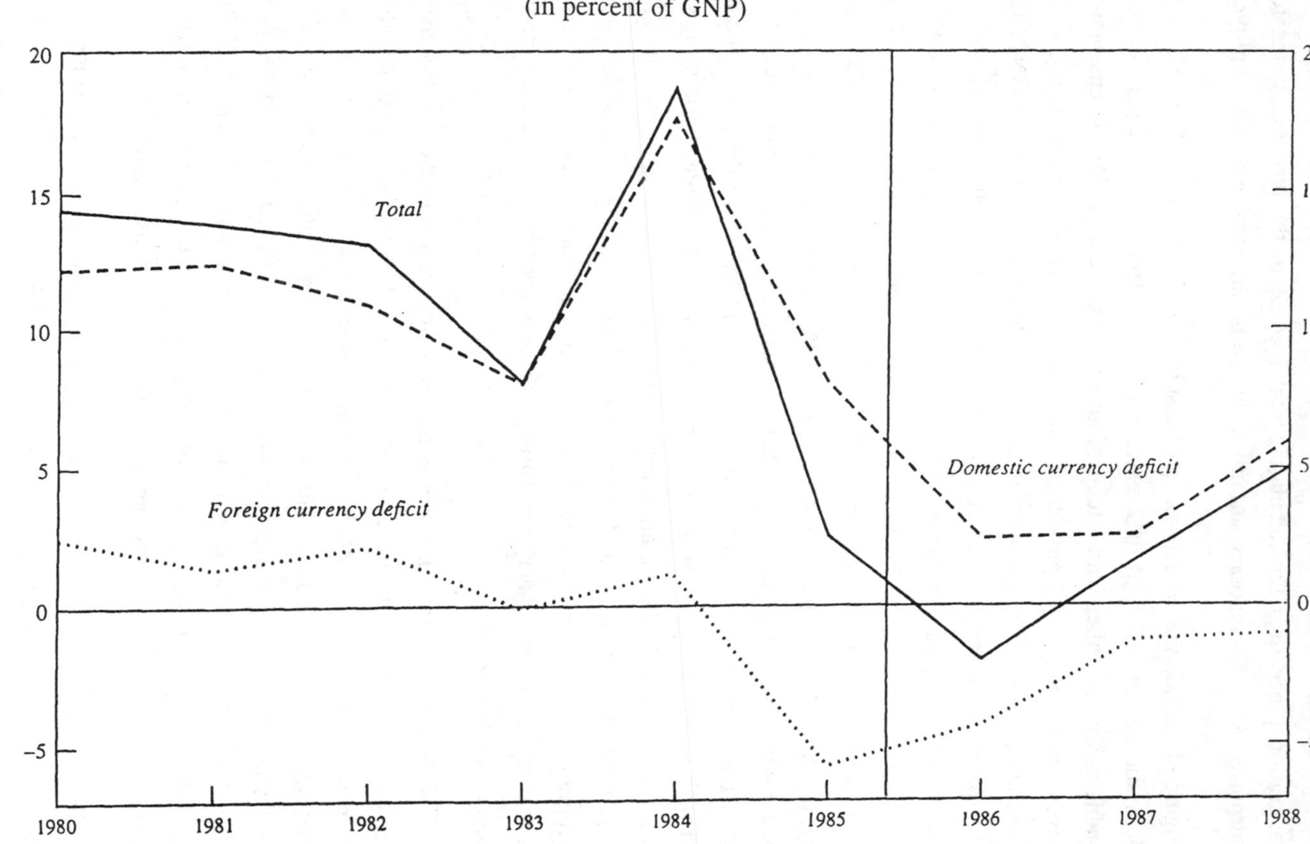

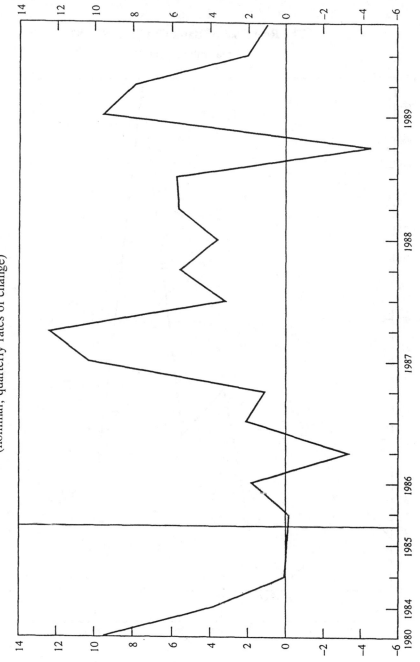

Figure 5
M_3 Developments, 1980 - 89
(nominal, quarterly rates of change)

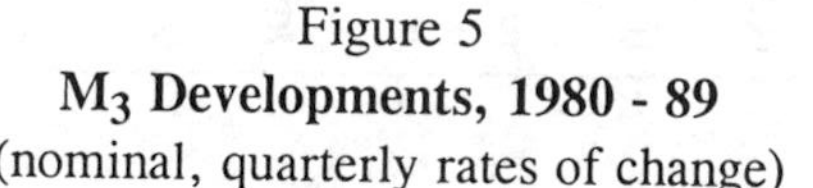

Figure 6
The Real Cost of Bank Credit, 1980 - 87
(real interest rate)

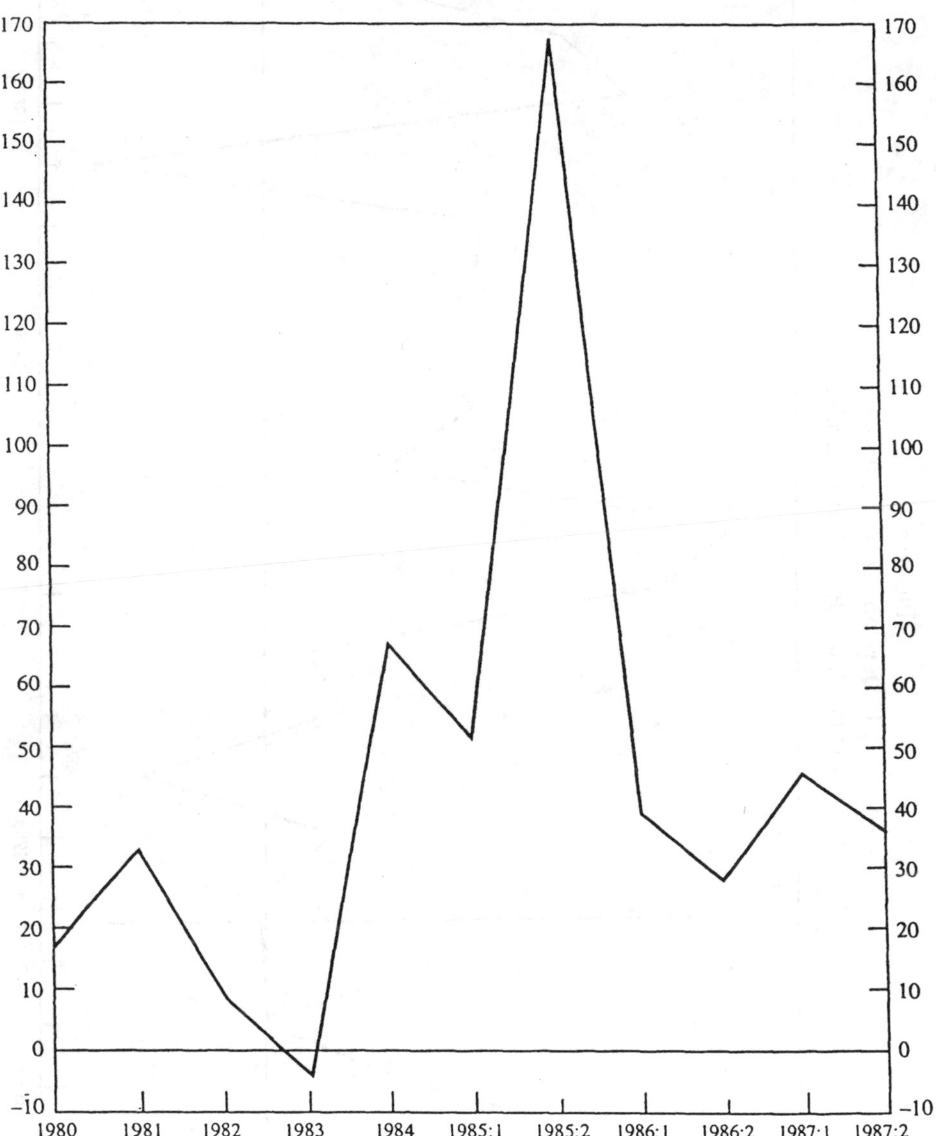

in line with the Mundell-Fleming hypothesis, a continuous process of real appreciation of the Israeli sheqel. Thus, in the poststabilization phase, tight monetary policy and high interest rates supported the pegged exchange rate in the presence of capital inflows and generated a loss of competitiveness (real appreciation). With a lag of about two years, the policy mix of fiscal and monetary restraint and real appreciation of the Israeli sheqel led the economy into a recession and rising unemployment, very much like the experience of Sweden, Italy, and the United Kingdom prior to the ERM currency crisis of 1992.

4. Fiscal Contraction and Aggregate Demand

In this section, we analyze the relationship between public and private savings and the effect of fiscal contraction on aggregate demand.

4.1 Private and public saving rates

The possibility of public debt neutrality has gained renewed interest since Barro's (1974) seminal contribution, "Are Government Bonds Net Wealth?". Specifically, assume a given path of government expenditures. Now, suppose the government cuts taxes and issues new bonds in order to finance the resulting deficit. Naturally, the current disposable income of the private sector rises. The question then is whether the entire current increase in disposable income will be saved by the private sector in anticipation of higher taxes (and the consequently lower disposable income) in the future, needed to finance the larger government debt service. If the answer is in the affirmative, that is, additional private savings completely offset the additional government dissavings, then national saving must remain intact, a phenomenon dubbed "debt neutrality". In this case, government bonds in a nonmonetary economy as in Barro (1974) are not net wealth in the hands of the private sector, since the latter immediately capitalizes the future tax liability generated by increased government debt. Indeed, if capital markets are well functioning (so that there are no liquidity constraints), taxes are nondistortionary, prices are market clearing, and the private sector does not suffer from myopia, debt neutrality is expected to prevail: a debt-financed tax cut has no effect on national saving.[5] This is in contrast to the more traditional Keynesian notion that such a fiscal measure stimulates private sector consumption and pushes interest rates upward.

As already mentioned, Israel's disinflation program of 1985 involved a sharp reduction in the public deficit. Thus, it can provide a testing ground for the validity of the debt-neutrality hypothesis. Indeed, Figure 7 reveals that when government savings rose after the stabilization, private savings fell so that national savings increased only moderately. Furthermore, this figure shows that the national saving rate, defined relative to a broad measure of income (which includes, in addition to GNP, unilateral transfers from abroad), is fairly trendless; the private saving rate is almost a mirror image of the public saving rate. It can be seen, however, that there was some increase in national saving in 1985-86, after the sharp fiscal contraction which was the backbone of the disinflation program. In other words, the associated decline in private saving was smaller than the increase in public sector saving.

An econometric study of the neutrality of public debt by Leiderman and Razin (1988) centers around the stabilization episode. They implemented a model with two deviations from debt neutrality (consumers with finite horizon and liquidity constraints, but not tax distortions) on monthly data from Israel during the first half of the 1980s. They found some econometric support for the debt-neutrality hypothesis, but only after proper adjustment was made for liquidity constraints. Furthermore, the proportion of liquidity constrained individuals in the population was found to be small (but significant).

---

5 Strict debt neutrality holds under the assumption that each family has an operational bequest motive, based on equating the marginal utilities of all generations. Rising real wages in the future may, however, render the bequest motive nonoperational for some families, since parents are likely to want to receive transfers from their children although such transfers may not be enforceable.

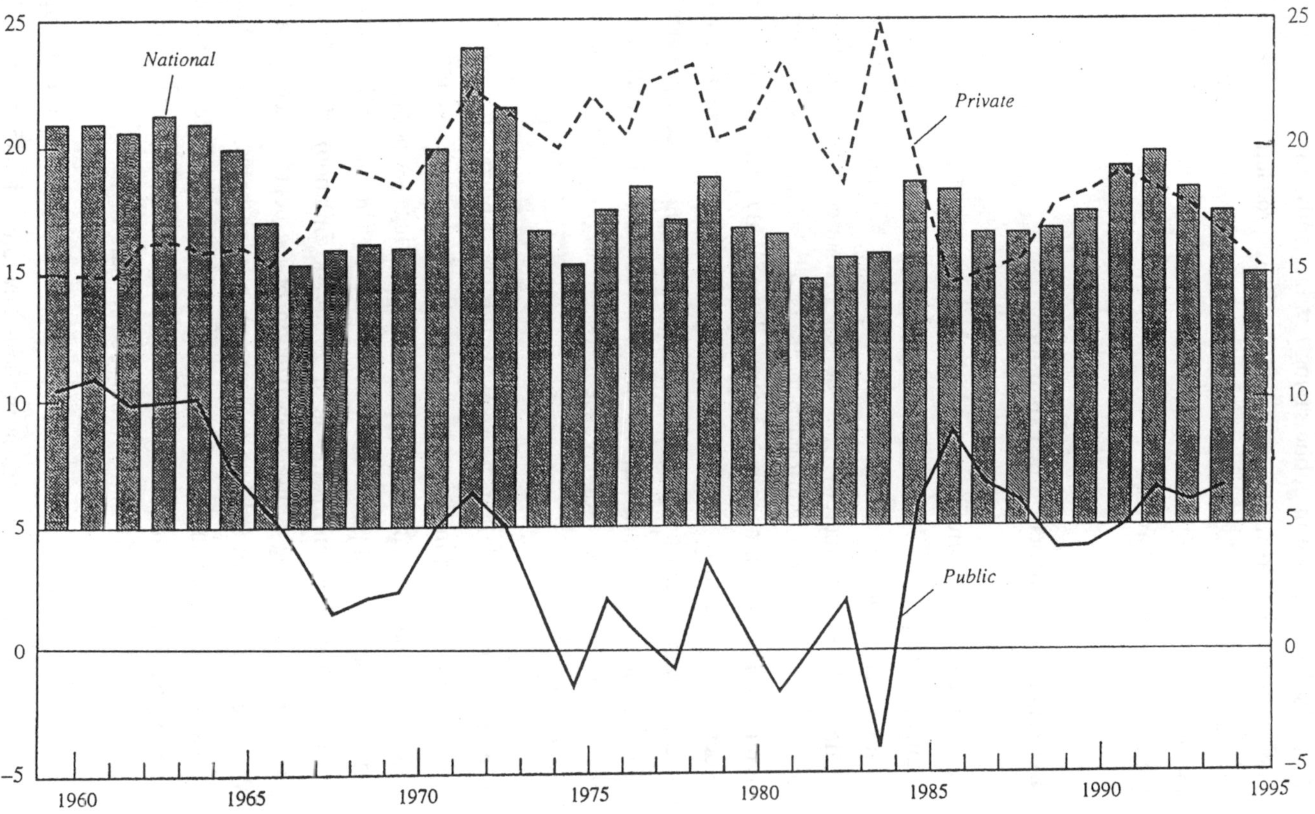
National
Private
Public
25
20
15
10
5
0
−5
1960
1965
1970
1975
1980
1985
1990
1995

Why was the sharp rise in public saving less than fully offset by changes in private saving? We think that the sharp increase in productivity that followed the disinflation program, despite the resulting consumption boom (see below), was the major reason why private saving did not fall to an extent that would fully offset the increase in public saving.

4.2 Can fiscal contraction be expansionary?

In the presence of significant deadweight losses of taxation, sharp fiscal policy changes could potentially be expansionary (see Giavazzi and Pagano, 1990). Such policy changes generate expectations regarding a future decline in the excess burden of taxes and, thereby, raise current private consumption. This was indeed the case in the fiscal consolidation in Israel, which was accompanied by a significant increase in aggregate private demand. By bringing the fiscal situation under control, stabilization produced a wealth effect that generated a boom. This occurred even though taxes increased in the short run, especially since the success of stabilization came as a surprise that was counter to the expectations which had been ingrained by past divergence between the expenditure path and the tax revenue path.

The sharp cut in the deficit, as a key part of the stabilization program, apparently had a direct effect on inflation, both current and expected, even though by itself it had only a relatively small effect on national savings. A partly monetized current deficit and accelerated public debt, accompanied by an already high tax burden (on a base which was shrinking as a result of inflation) must have generated expectations regarding future monetization of the debt service (à la Sargent and Wallace, 1981) which fed into the current inflation process. Consolidation of the public budget halted this process. Also, the fiscal consolidation put the government squarely into its intertemporal budget constraint, with a low inflation path of prices in the present and in the future (see Woodford, 1996).

The elimination of the public deficit, which was partly achieved through spending cuts, was indeed a key ingredient in the policy to halt inflation - even though it led to growth in private consumption, so that national saving did not change much.[6] An increase in unilateral transfers from abroad, induced mostly by a special grant from the United States, and a sharp fall in domestic investment (driven down by an increased tax burden on capital; see the next section) also helped to eliminate the external current account deficit.

5. Inflation-induced Shift in the Composition of Tax Revenue

The Israeli experience unequivocally suggests that sudden stabilization of the economy generated an automatic increase in tax revenues which, by itself, helped reduce the public deficit. Furthermore, such a stabilization shifted a tax burden from labor to capital. Since the capital stock is fixed in the short run, such a tax shift generated a short-lived consumption-based boom in economic activity (à la Giavazzi and Pagano). However, in the medium (and long) run, the higher tax burden on the accumulation of new capital had a significant negative effect on growth and productivity.

In this section, we uncover a marked shift in the functional distribution of disposable income in the sudden transition from high to low inflation in Israel. As mentioned before, the massive fiscal adjustment, which provided the backbone of the stabilization policy package, reflected an increase in tax revenues and a fall in subsidies as well as some spending cuts. The increase in the overall real burden of taxes was not shared equally among income groups and across various tax bases. An effective subsidy to capital that characterized the high inflation period had been switched to a relatively high tax burden on capital in the aftermath of disinflation. At the same time, the real tax burden on labor income declined sharply. Moreover, a large portion of the revenue increase was due to a significant rise in consumption rates (mostly VAT) which, like a wealth tax, entails an equal burden on laborers and capitalists.

---

6 Alesina and Perotti (1996) show that successful fiscal contractions are typically those that manage to cut the most politically sensitive budget items: government wages and transfers.

Economists have long been interested in the inflation tax, defined as the real depreciation of money holdings. The revenue (seigniorage) obtained by the government is generated because the public holds zero interest-bearing assets in the form of cash, and the government requires commercial banks to hold reserves at much below market rates of interest. Eckstein and Leiderman (1992) found that while inflation fluctuated between 40 percent and almost 500 percent per annum, the ratio of seigniorage to GNP remained between 2 percent and 3 percent.[7]

Tanzi (1977) identified another important and practical aspect of inflationary finance which operates to reduce real tax revenues when inflation rises in the opposite direction to the seigniorage effect. Due to collection lags, defined as the time that elapses between the date when the tax liability accrues and the time when the tax payment is received by the government, inflation causes erosion of the real tax revenue. The collection lag can be shortened to lessen the effect of inflation on the tax system, but such measures are themselves not without costs. For example, when inflation reached triple digits, the filing period for the VAT was shortened from three to one month, thereby increasing both bookkeeping costs and government collection costs.[8]

The experience with inflation in Israel emphasizes yet another aspect of the effect of inflation on the tax system: the difficulty of properly defining taxable income in the business sector. Taxable income in the business sector is calculated according to standard accounting procedures which are nominal in nature. In other words, one sheqel is treated as one sheqel regardless of the date on which it was paid or received. Nominal business income (or profit), that is, revenues (or sales) minus costs, is calculated by adding together sheqalim received

---

7 See also Bruno and Fischer (1986). Nevertheless, the welfare costs associated with this relatively small revenue were quite significant and rising with the rate of inflation.

8 The Bank of Israel's annual report for 1984 estimated that before shortening the collection lag, the loss of tax revenues due to the Tanzi effect had reached about 10 percent of overall tax revenues (see Bank of Israel, 1984, p. 103).

at different dates (and having different real values) and subtracting from them sheqalim paid at different dates (and having different real values). When inflation rates are 100 percent to 500 percent per annum, a beginning-of-the-year sheqel may be worth, in real terms, as much as 2-6 end-of-the-year sheqalim. As a result, nominal income cannot serve as even an approximation of the real income of a business firm in a period of high inflation rates, such as those existing in Israel during the late 1970s and the first half of the 1980s.

Inflation creates several deviations of nominal income from real income. Some of these deviations (or biases) are negative and some are positive, but the main point is that they do not offset each other. Furthermore, their incidence and magnitude are not independent of the taxpayer's behavior. In other words, a typical taxpayer will take certain tax-avoidance actions that will reduce his calculated nominal income even though his real income remains unchanged. In such a case, a higher inflation rate reduces real tax revenues; the tax system thus fails to serve as an automatic stabilizer.

The deviations (or biases) of real income from nominal income that are caused by inflation may be briefly classified into four main categories (for more details see Sadka, 1991, or Razin and Sadka, 1993):

a) Nominal capital gains on an asset have two components: an artificial or inflationary component that merely reflects an increase in the general price level of all goods and services, and a true, real component that reflects the appreciation in the value of the asset resulting from fundamentals such as increased demand for, or scarcity, of the asset. Thus, nominal income overstates real income by the sum of the inflationary component of capital gains.

b) Analogous to the distinction between the inflationary and real components of nominal capital gains is the distinction between the inflationary and real components of the interest rate. Thus, allowing deductibility of nominal interest accumulations causes nominal income to understate real income by the sum of the inflationary component of the interest accumulations.

At first glance, one might argue that (a) and (b) above offset each other. On the one hand, inflationary capital gains on an asset are included in taxable income, but on the other hand, the inflationary interest charges incurred for the purpose of acquiring the asset are tax deductible. This argument is invalid on two grounds. First, the purchase of an asset may be financed by equity rather than by debt. Second, capital gains are taxed upon realization whereas interest is deductible on an accrual basis. Thus, the inflationary component of the interest charges is deductible annually, while the inflationary capital gains on the asset purchased will not be taxed until the asset is sold.

(c) The depreciation allowance on a physical asset is calculated on the basis of the nominal (historic) cost of the asset. In this respect, nominal income overstates real income. When the monthly inflation rate reaches double digits, an additional major factor causes nominal income to deviate significantly from real income. This factor, which affects operating income, relates to the nature of the production process, which takes place over time.

(d) Output is usually sold at the end of the production process, while the costs of labor, raw materials, and other inputs are incurred earlier. Thus, output is sold at high (inflated) nominal prices, relative to the low nominal prices of the inputs. As a result, the nominal operating income overstates the real operating income.

One might conclude that since the various deviations of nominal income from real income are not all of the same sign, the effect of inflation on nominal taxable income, vis-à-vis real income, is ambiguous. However, such a conclusion ignores the long-run response of the taxpaying firm to the effect of inflation on nominal income. In the long run, firms will take various tax-avoidance measures in order to reduce nominal taxable income. For instance, they will rely to a lesser degree on equity capital and invest more and more in buildings and real estate. Such tax-avoidance activity is further fueled by changes that are made in tax laws in the wake of inflation - changes that are typically partial, unbalanced and usually aimed at relieving the burden on those sectors negatively affected by the tax treatment of inflation. Indeed, one of the first measures taken in Israel was to exempt from tax (or tax very lightly) inflationary capital gains without, at the same time, disallowing the deductibility of nominal interest charges.

Quantitatively, therefore, the deductibility of nominal interest charges combined with light taxation of capital gains (for example, real estate investments were effectively subsidized) was a main reason for the understatement of capital income. Furthermore, the law permitted self-employed individuals and proprietorships to manipulate the timing of their cash receipts and payments (vis-à-vis some sectors of the economy which were indexed and thus indifferent to such manipulations) in a way that reduced taxable income to ridiculously low levels. In fact, this sector of the economy benefitted the most from inflation.

Unlike taxpayers in the business sector, wage earners cannot maneuver the time schedule of their wage payments in order to reduce their real tax burden because of the withholding system. This system ensures that any manipulation of the timing of cash receipts for wages earned will have a negligible - if any - effect on real tax payments.

The bottom line is that inflation stabilization is expected to raise the burden of taxes such as income taxes on the business sector and the VAT, and to reduce the tax burden on wage earners. To confirm this hypothesis, we computed effective average tax rates during and after the inflation stabilization period.

Our computation was based on a stylized tax model in which the economy is aggregated to have three goods: consumption, labor, and capital (see

Razin and Sadka, 1993, for details).[9]

Table 1 describes the evolution of effective average tax rates from the high-inflation period to the low-inflation period. The table reveals that the effective average tax rate on consumption went up from 6-12 percent during the period of high inflation to 22 percent in 1990. This is due to VAT rate hikes, cuts in subsidies to necessities (mostly food and public transportation), and the curbing of the Tanzi effect. The effective average tax rate on labor went down from 31-32 percent during the high-inflation period to 19 percent in 1990. The effective tax rate on capital, which was negative in the high-inflation period, went up and exceeded the labor income tax rate in 1990. As explained above, this is due mostly

---

9 Tax revenue is classified according to taxes on labor income, capital income, and excise taxes. In our three-good economy the transfers, b, government good purchases, g, and taxes, t, should be understood as (three-tuple) vectors in line with the three-good disaggregation. For example, the first component of the b-vector, b_1, denotes government transfers in terms of the consumption good, while the second and third components, b_2 and b_3, are transfers in terms of labor and capital. In the case of transfers, however, the last two components of b are typically zero. Similarly, on the expenditure side, g_1 denotes purchases of the consumption good, g_2 denotes government hiring of labor services, and g_3 denotes government hiring of capital services from the private sector. The tax vector, t, consists of rate of excises, t_1, rate of labor income tax, t_2, and rate of capital income tax, t_3. We denote the consumer price vector by p (that is, the posttax price) and the producer price vector (that is, the pretax price) by q. The tax rates are computed from the good-by-good percentage difference between the price vectors p and q. For example, the excise tax rate (in percent) is given by $[(p_1 - q_1)/q_1] \times 100$.

Using this notation, the household budget constraint is specified as follows:

$$px - pe - pb - qy - q_1 B_1^P + p_1 D_1 \leq 0$$

where x, e, b, and y denote consumption, endowments, government transfers,and production, respectively; $B_1{}^P$ denotes the private sector current-account deficit, and D_1 denotes the public-sector deficit. Note that by convention, the first component of the production vector, y_1, which denotes the private sector gross output, is positive, while the second and third components, y_2, and y_3, denoting, respectively, labor and capital inputs, are typically negative. Note also that under the assumption of constant returns to scale in production, the value of the output vector in producer prices, qy, must equal zero. Otherwise, there are infinite profits to be made and this is inconsistent with competitive equilibrium.

An immediate implication of this simplification is that in the single-period model, saving (which is equal to future consumption) must be added to current consumption in order to obtain a meaningful indicator of the economy (lifetime) consumption. Similarly, government deficit (representing future taxes) is lumped together with current taxes to get a meaningful measure of the overall tax revenue.

to the fact that inflation erodes the real tax base in the business sector.[10] In fact, taxes on wage earners accounted for approximately two thirds of all income tax revenues on the eve of the stabilization program, compared to only about one third nowadays.

Table 1: Effective Average Tax Rates
(in percent)

Type of Tax	1980	1985	1990
Consumption	6.4	12.1	22.3
Labor income	31.0	31.6	19.2
Capital income	-4.4	-34.8	34.5

6. What Factors Cause the Postdisinflation Immediate Boom and Subsequent Recession?

An interesting issue is why, in the aftermath of the 1985, stabilization program, there was first a boom and later a recession. In this section, we offer two possibly reinforcing explanations: (1) a shift inthe tax burden from labor to capital; and (2) exchange rate policy. Interestingly, the first explanation has to do with a long-term, credible restructuring of the tax system, while the second, associated with an unsustainable overvaluation of the exchange rate, is based on the policy not being fully credible.

10 This change occurred even though statutory tax rates on business income were sharply reduced.

6.1 A tax-based cycle

Recall the shift of the tax burden from labor to capital as a consequence of drastic disinflation. The lighter tax on wage income could have helped fuel the consumption boom, together with the wealth effect emanating from the elimination of inflation-based distortions. The effect of the shift towards a high capital income tax rate can explain why a recession came later, since the capital formation which is directly affected adversely by this tax is typically a slow process. But the tax burden on capital could eventually have caused the decline in the rate of growth of capital and recession. Indeed, while disposable wages showed a sharp increase (after a very short decline in the first quarter after the mid-1985 program), the capital income tax effect (along with the detrimental effect of a high short-term interest rate) seems to be the reason, along with the high short-term rates of interest, behind the fall in the investment-output ratio. The fall in investment spending led to a sharp decline in the capital-output ratio of the business sector, which went down from about 1.8 before 1985 to about 1.5 in 1990.

6.2 An exchange rate-based cycle

Using the exchange rate to accomplish further disinflation after the stabilization program led to persistent real appreciation. An examination of similar episodes in high-inflation countries suggests the possibility of a common pattern for exchange-rate-based stabilization programs. (See Kiguel and Liviatan, 1992; and Calvo and Vegh, 1993.) Those countries which rely on the exchange rate as a nominal anchor experience a poststabilization boom in economic activity, a large real exchange rate appreciation, and a rise in real wages. Later on in the programs, real appreciation of the domestic currency and a rise in real wages eventually lead to a sharp economic contraction.

One possible explanation is that the private sector may regard the appreciating path of the exchange rate as unsustainable, because it generates persistent current account deficits, which at some point in the future will call for a policy reversal.

But an overvalued currency which is perceived to be temporary could generate a consumption boom because it creates incentives to shift consumption from the future to the present, that is, a consumption cycle which drives the postdisinflation business cycle. However, the 1985 stabilization started with a large real depreciation so that the 1986-87 consumption boom took place when the real exchange rate was relatively low (see Figure 8). With this as a background, it is not very plausible that strong expectations regarding exchange rate policy reversals in the near future could have been developed so as to sustain significant intertemporal substitution in consumption. Thus, in the case of the Israeli stabilization episode, the exchange-rate-based explanation is not convincing.

6.3 Fiscal discipline

It could be argued that while fiscal discipline was very tight immediately after stabilization, it gradually became more lax later on. The Mundell-Fleming model predicts that this pattern of the fiscal stance can deliver a gradual process of real appreciation. This could have contributed to the emergence of the recession down the road.[11]

---

[11] According to Frenkel, Goldstein, and Masson (1991) and Giavazzi and Pagano (1988), fixed exchange rates afford more fiscal discipline than flexible exchange rates, because by adapting a lax fiscal policy under the fixed exchange rate system, international reserves will eventually be exhausted; thus putting an end to the peg. The collapse of the system is costly for the authorities. Therefore, the fear of suffering political punishment will discipline the fiscal authorities under the fixed exchange rate system. However, as argued by Tornell and Velasco (1995), there is also a similar flip side to a lax fiscal policy under a flexible exchange rate system. Unsound policies lead to an immediate depreciation of the currency (hence inflation). Since inflation is costly for the fiscal authorities, forcing the political costs up-front in the flexible system can provide more fiscal discipline.

Figure 8
Unit Labor Costs and Real Effective Exchange Rate*
(in US dollars, 1980 = 100)

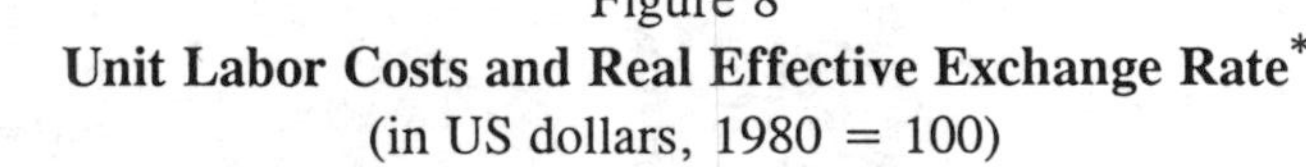

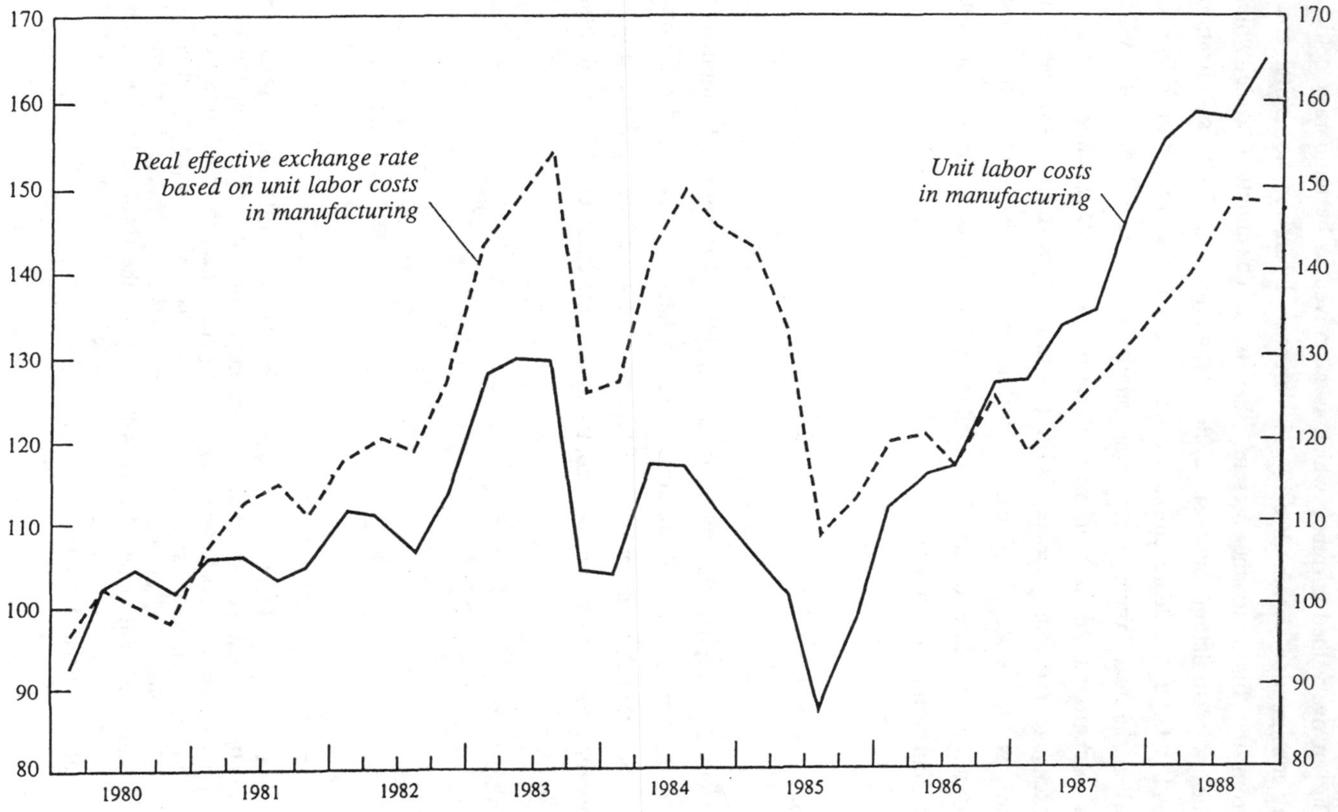

* Real effective exchange rate compares Israel's unit labor costs to a trade-weighted average for 17 trading partners.

6.4 Another effect

As we describe in Razin and Sadka (1995a), overvaluation of the exchange rate implies that the prices of low labor-intensive tradable goods fall relative to the prices of high labor-intensive nontradable goods. Thus, through the Stolper-Samuelson (1941) effect, wages rise relative to capital rental values. This change in relative prices could help explain why the (pretax) share of labor income in GDP has increased significantly.[12] Similar to the tax shift noted above, this income redistribution between labor and capital could have been a driving force behind the postdisinflation cycle.

7. Tax Smoothing, Labor Supply Bulges, and Government Finances

When the government levies taxes, it not only transfers resources from private hands to public use. The tax-transfer process also entails some waste of resources. In other words, when the government raises one dollar in tax revenues, private losses amount to more than one dollar. The difference between the loss and tax revenue is called the excess burden (or the deadweight loss) of taxation. Some important studies have shown that the deadweight loss can be very substantial and, at the margin, reach as much as 50 cents per dollar of tax revenues.[13/14]

This all means that it would not be optimal to maintain a continuously balanced budget by raising tax rates whenever spending increases or output falls. Rather, if

---

12 There is a striking similarity to the German episode in the early 1920s. In the aftermath of the successful disinflation, there were negligible transitional costs since neither industrial production declined nor unemployment rose (see Garber, 1982). The German economic decline started one to two years after the sudden end to hyperinflation. In the German post-disinflation period, the relative prices of labor-intensive goods increased together with the wage-rental ratio, and there was a significant increase in the share of labor in national income.

13 See, for instance, Browning (1987). Furthermore, it is likely that the marginal excess burden rises when the average tax burden (as measured by the ratio of tax revenues to GNP) rises. Therefore, an optimal long-term tax design, which aims at minimizing the present value of the stream of excess burdens, would tend to smooth the path of tax burden over time.

14 See Barro (1979).

these changes are not persistent, it is desirable to adjust tax rates only slightly and let future taxpayers chip in by raising the deficit and, consequently, the debt. Similarly, a transitory fall in spending or increase in output should not be met by one-to-one cuts in tax revenues. Instead, surpluses should be created and the public debt reduced. An implication of this policy prescription is that the ratio of the public debt to GNP cannot by itself serve as a policy target in the short run. On the contrary, the deficit should serve as a short-run shock absorber for non-persistent shocks in spending and/or output. That is, the fluctuations followed by the public debt are a mirror image of the tax-smoothing policy prescription. It is only in the framework of multiyear averages that the ratio of public debt to GNP can serve as an important target of public policy.

Hercowitz and Strawczynski (1994) confronted the tax-smoothing policy prescription with evidence from Israel during the years 1961-89. They specified stochastic processes for the deviations of output and government spending from a common linear trend over time. Assuming a constant average tax burden (à la tax-smoothing hypothesis), they derived the implied path for the evolution of the public debt as a function of these deviations. Their method of analysis was built on the premise that the average tax burden was in fact fairly constant and the evolution of public debt was mainly determined by variations in expenditure. The derived debt evolutionis shown to fit the data relatively well, thereby seemingly supporting the tax-smoothing hypothesis. However, their methodology lumps together tax-smoothing episodes (such as a war period), with others, which are evidently inconsistent with the tax-smoothing hypothesis during the high-inflation period (such as the sharp growth of public debt).

A brief overview of the evolution of the public debt, output, and government spending can also serve to illustrate the validity of the tax-smoothing hypothesis (see Figure 9). Noteworthy is the period 1966-78 which covered two wars (the Six-Day War of 1967 and the Yom Kippur War of 1973). As seen in Figure 9b, this period was characterized by a significant growth of government spending (led by defense expenditures), well above the growth of output: the percentage of government spending out of GNP rose from 40 to 80 with two discrete jumps in 1967 and in 1973. Evidently, tax burdens were not raised accordingly, so that the ratio of public debt to GNP, as depicted in Figure 9a, rose from about 60 percent to 150 percent. In the period following the 1985 stabilization, the ratio of public spending to output fell significantly, but again tax burdens did not follow suit, and the public debt to GNP ratio fell sharply. Indeed, the prestabilization period is a striking example of significant deviations from tax smoothing. Accumulating deficits tend to shift intertemporally the bulk of the tax burden into the future, thereby reducing consumers' real wealth. Thus, by suddenly halting the process of growing public debt, as was the case with the successful stabilization policy, the government was able to restore some intertemporal balance to the burden of taxes. This is a plausible reason why the tax hike elements of the stabilization policy were initially expansionary (similar to the Giavazzi-Pagano effect).

In this context, special attention should be devoted to the recent immigration experience. During the years 1990-94, about 600,000 immigrants, mostly from the countries of the former Soviet Union, arrived in Israel (about 12 percent of the premigration population of Israel). Civilian government spending for the absorption of these immigrants (housing,training, investments in infrastructure, etc.) rose significantly. The government adopted a labor absorption policy which facilitated the job search process for the immigrants. The housing market response to immigration, aided by various government incentives, was a key element in enhancing the mobility of labor.[15]

In spite of a curb on defense spending and other public services, the budget deficit rose significantly at first. However, government finances in a broader sense did not worsen, as the ratio of public debt to GDP declined.

---

15 The government followed a "direct absorption" approach designed to minimize involvement in the absorption process. The budget provided a standard "absorption basket" of about US$ 7,000 per family of three during the first year as the main economic assistance instrument, and the immigrants themselves were left to determine the best use of their resources and location of residence and work. In addition, the budget included other immigration-related outlays for: (i) construction of housing and mortgage lending; (ii) language and professional training; (iii) wage subsidies for new employees in the manufacturing and construction sectors for a limited time; and (iv) enhanced infrastructure and education expenditures. The relatively free mobility of immigrants across jobs and geographical areas contributed significantly to the quick integration of immigrants into the labor market.

A key to the successful integration of immigrants into the labor market was that real wages in Israel, particularly in the business sector, proved more flexible than envisaged by many economists. Unit labor costs fell, and together with a housing elastic supply, stimulated a revival of output growth (see the set of labor market indicators in Figure 10). At the same time, inflation did not pick up. On the contrary, the rate of inflation in 1992 decreased to a one-digit level for the first time since the Yom Kippur War of 1973. Output growth reached an annual average rate of about 6 percent. As a result, the ratio of government spending to GNP fell from 58.7 percent in 1990 to 54.0 percent in 1994. Interestingly, tax burdens did not fall to the same extent, so that the public deficit, as a percentage of GNP, declined from 4.2 percent in 1990 to 1 percent in 1994. Similarly, as mentioned above, public debt fell from 124 percent of GNP at the end of 1989 to 92 percent at the end of 1994.

Israel thus provides a striking example of a sudden increase in the labor force that has been smoothly absorbed, generating output growth, no inflation, and a fall in the public debt to output ratio. Although German unification provides another example of tax smoothing, it is in the opposite direction to the Israeli migration experience. German unification which amounted to absorption of about 17 percent of the labor force of preunification West Germany, similarly required massive government spending, but it did not simultaneously generate output growth. As a result, the ratio of public spending to output rose sharply in Germany. The tax burdens did not immediately rise to the same extent. Large public deficits ensued, resulting in a growing public debt to output ratio. The main difference in the Israeli experience as compared to Germany is that the Israeli immigrants got jobs whereas the East German workers lost jobs. Indeed, while the East German workers priced themselves out of the market (thanks to strong trade unions and the East-West currency union at terms which were unfavorable to East German employment). Accordingly, real wages in Israel fell while East German wages increased (see Figure 10).[16]

16 When wages are rigid (due to unionism, search costs, efficiency wage elements), migration, or labor market integration of two previously separate markets, may lower the income of the established population (see Razin and Sadka, 1995b). Relatively low job search and labor mobility costs, combined with a flexible housing market, and wage flexibility, can explain why there has been little resistance to migration in Israel, whereas resistance is relatively strong in some European countries.

Figure 9a
Public Debt
(in percent of GNP)

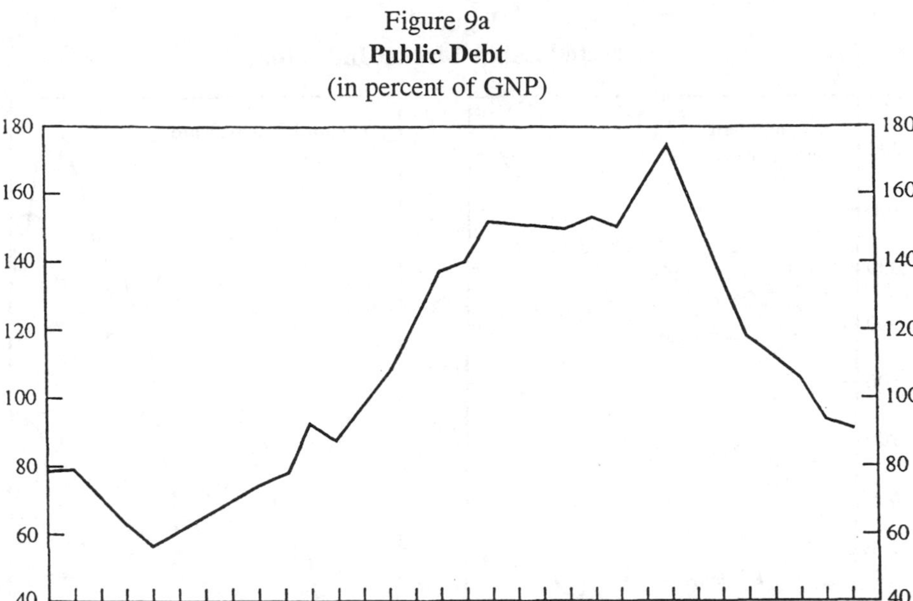

Figure 9b
Public Spending
(in percent of GNP)

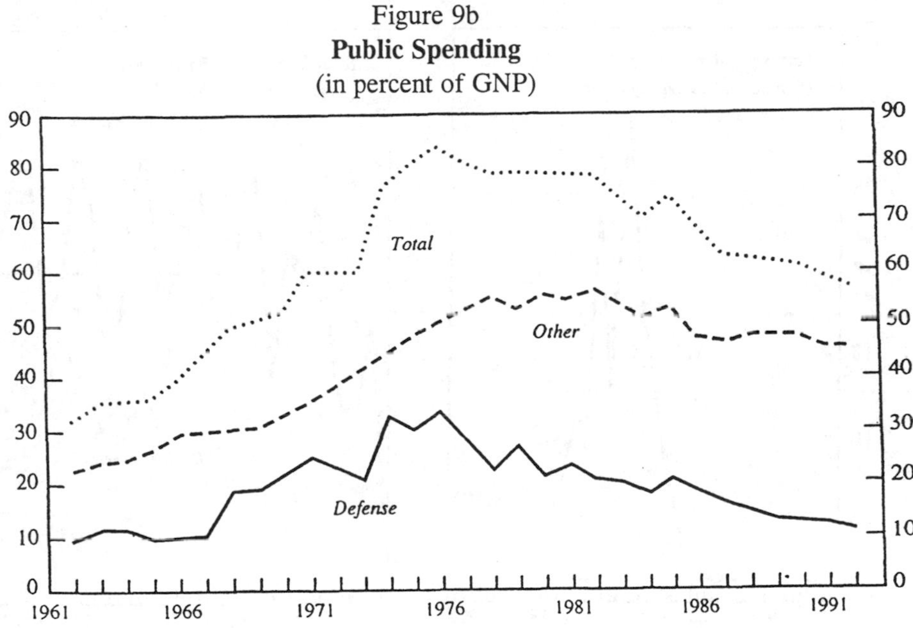

Source: Hercowitz and Strawzcynski (1994)

Figure 10
Selected Labor Market Indicators

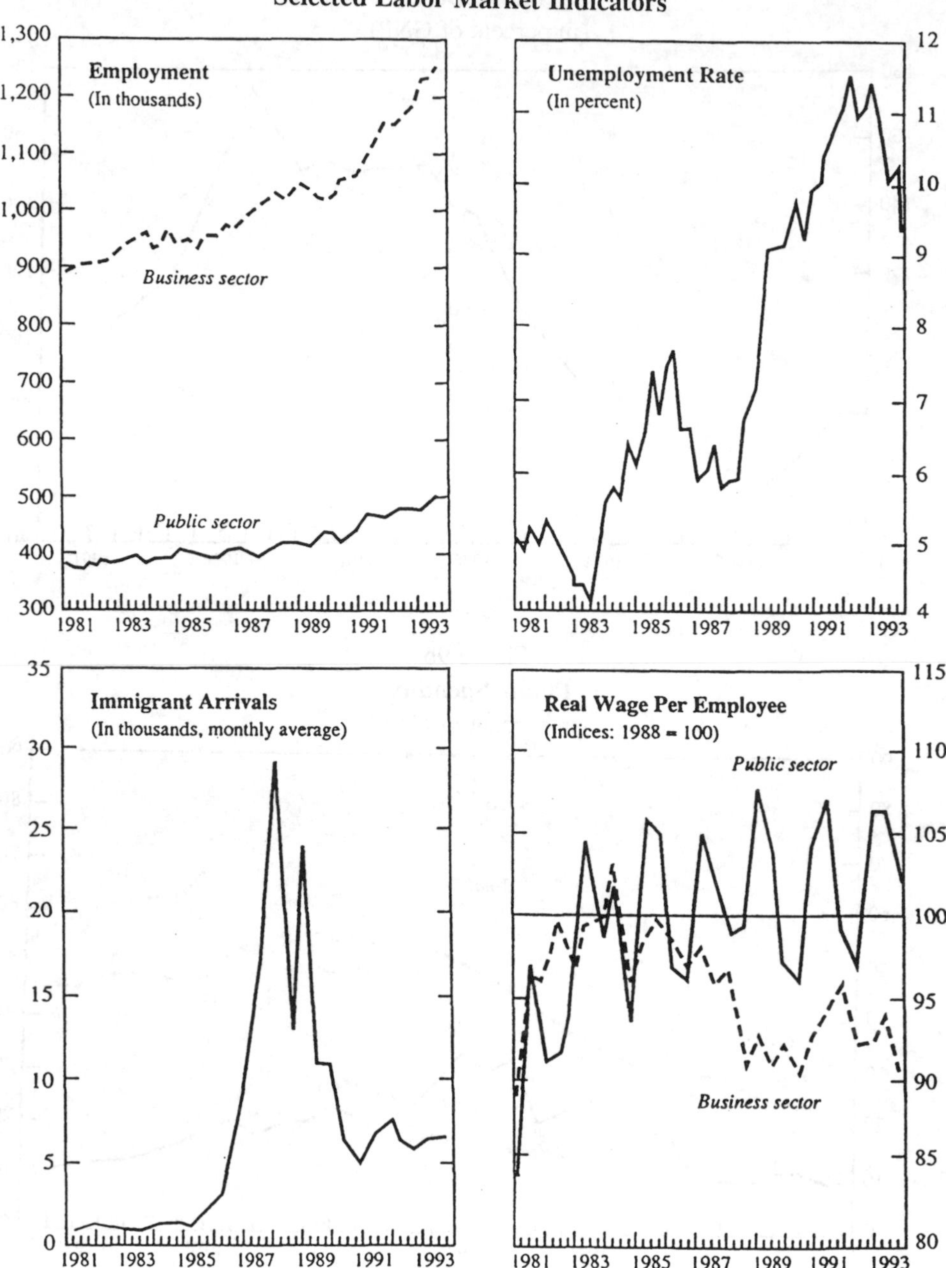

Source: Bank of Israel

8. Conclusions

The main conclusions from Israeli budgetary developments may have a general validity: (a) deficits lead to inflation and stopping inflation requires elimination of deficits; (b) a major effect of inflation is a large shift of the tax burden from capital to labor; (c) aggregate demand effects of fiscal stabilization are not large due to debt neutrality, in low-debt cases; (d) aggregate demand may rise with severe fiscal contractions in high-debt cases; (e) when the exchange rate is used as a nominal anchor, in the presence of international capital movements, the economy typically ends up with overvalued currency, which eventually leads to recession; (f) inflation-induced and disinflation-induced redistributions of the tax burden between capital and labor cause a poststabilization output/employment cycle; (g) shocks to labor supply, such as massive labor inflow through immigration, can be absorbed without worsening government finances when the labor and the housing markets are sufficiently flexible; and (h) productivity increases with a significant lag, however, in the presence of a large inflow of skilled labor. Only after jobs have been upgraded to accommodate the skills which the new workers bring with them, will there also be productivity gains. Furthermore, the learning by doing on downgraded jobs that these workers initially accept will also show up as an increase in productivity with a significant lag.

The main policy lesson that could be learned from the Israeli experience is that the absence of budget discipline, coupled with an almost inevitable monetary accommodation, will eventually fuel an inflationary process that could run out of control. The huge budgetary expansion in Israel and the associated monetary expansion were initiated by wars and severe terms-of-trade shocks (the oil crises). At the same time, there were the usual attempts in a democracy to "cater to the people" through subsidies to necessities, other transfers, cheaper public education, as well as some "supply-side economics" measures. As we have shown, the emergent inflation proved in the end to be extremely detrimental to income distribution objectives, to factor productivity and to economic growth. Inflation undermined the tax system and tilted the income distribution in favor of capital and against labor. Even worse, the inflation induced tax concessions to capital that were highly distortionary without having any positive effect on growth.

Several attempts to curb inflation without fiscal consolidation were made but proved futile. A critical element in the successful stabilization policy of 1985 was the elimination of the fiscal deficit. The restoration of the tax system, with a background of a relatively stable economy proved beneficial to labor. Interestingly, in this episode, private savings reacted to a large extent according to the debt-neutrality hypothesis "à la Ricardo."

Another interesting aspect is that the budgetary expansion associated with absorption of the massive wave of immigration from the countries of the former Soviet Union was not reflected in growth of public debt relative to output, even though the tax burden was not raised. This surprising outcome occurred because output was capable of responding swiftly to the increased aggregate demand, by utilizing excess capacity of capital (residual of the poststabilization recession) and high-labor-force participation rates among the newcomers.

References

Alesina, Alberto, and Roberto Perotti (1996), "Reducing Budget Deficits," *Swedish Economic Policy Review.*

Bank of Israel (1984), *Annual Reports.*

Barro, Robert J. (1974), "Are Government Bonds Net Wealth?", *Journal of Political Economy,* Vol. 82, pp. 1095-1117.

Barro, Robert J. (1979), "On the Determination of Public Debt," *Journal of Political Economy*, Vol. 87, No. 5, pp. 941-71.

Bruno, Michael (1993), *Crisis, Stabilization and Economic Reform: Therapy by Consensus*, Oxford University Press, Oxford.

Bruno, Michael, and Stanley Fischer (1986), "Israel's Inflationary Process: Shocks and Accommodation," in: Yoram Ben-Porath (ed.), *The Israeli Economy: Maturing Through Crises*, Harvard University Press, Cambridge, Massachusetts.

Browning, Edgar, K. (1987), "On the Marginal Welfare Cost of Taxation," *The American Economic Review,* Vol. 77, No. 1 (March 1987), pp. 11-23.

Buffman, Gil, and Leonardo Leiderman (1994), "Israel's Stabilization: Some Important Policy Lessons," in: Rudiger Dornbusch and Sebastian Edwards (eds.), *Reform, Recovery and Growth: Latin America and the Middle East*. University of Chicago Press, Chicago, Illinois, pp. 177-222.

Calvo, Guillermo, and Carlos A. Vegh (1993), "Exchange Rate-Based Stabilization Under Imperfect Credibility," in: Helmut Frisch and Andreas Wargotter (eds.), *Open Economy Macroeconomics*, MacMillan, London, pp. 3-28.

Eckstein, Zvi, and Leonardo Leiderman (1992), "Seigniorage and the Welfare Cost of Inflation," *Journal of Monetary Economics*, Vol. 29 (1992), pp. 389-410.

Frenkel, Jacob, Morris Goldstein, and Paul Masson (1991), "Characteristics of Successful Exchange Rate System," *Occasional Paper*, International Monetary Fund, Washington, No. 82 (July 1991).

Garber, Peter M., "Transition from Inflation to Price Stability," *Carnegie-Rochester Conference Series in Public Policy*, Vol. 16 (1982), pp. 11-42.

Giavazzi, Francesco, and Marco Pagano (1988), "The Advantage of Tying One's Hand: EMS Discipline and Central Bank Credibility," *European Economic Review*, (June 1988).

Giavazzi, Francesco, and Marco Pagano (1990), "Can Severe Fiscal Contractions be Expansionary? Tales of Two Small European Countries," *NBER Macroeconomics Annual*, pp. 75-116.

Helpman, Elhanan, and Assaf Razin (1987), "Exchange Rate Management: Intertemporal Tradeoffs", *American Economic Review*, Vol. 77, pp. 107-23.

Hercowitz, Zvi, and Michel Strawzcynski (1994), *"Public Debt Policy" in Israel*, Bank of Israel Discussion Paper Series No. 94.06 (April 1994) (in Hebrew).

Kiguel, Miguel, and Nissan Liviatan (1992), "The Business Cycle Associated with Exchange Rate Stabilization," *World Bank Economic Review*, Vol. 6, pp. 279-305.

Leiderman, Leonardo, and Assaf Razin (1988), "Testing Ricardian Neutrality with an Intertemporal Stochastic Mode," *Journal of Money, Credit and Banking*, Vol. 20, No. 1, pp. 1-21.

Razin, Assaf, and Efraim Sadka (1993), *The Economy of Modern Israel: Malaise and Promise*. The University of Chicago Press, Chicago, Illinois.

Razin, Assaf, and Efraim Sadka (1995a), "Israel's Disinflation: Taxation and Income Distribution," *International Journal of Finance and Economics* Vol. 1, No. 1, pp. 37-46.

Razin, Assaf, and Efraim Sadka (1995b), "Resisting Migration: Wage Rigidity and Income Distribution, *American Economic Review, Papers and Proceedings,* Vol. 85, No. 2 , pp. 312-16.

Ruge-Murcia, Francisco, J. (1995), "Credibility and Changes in Policy Regimes," *Journal of Political Economy,* Vol. 103, pp. 176-208.

Sachs, Jeffrey, Aaron Tornell and Andres Velasco (1995), "The Collapse of the Mexican Peso: What Have we Learned?", mimeo, Harvard University.

Sadka, Efraim (1991), "An Inflation-Proof Tax System? Some Lessons from Israel," *Staff Papers* International Monetary Fund, Washington, Vol. 1, No. 1, pp. 135-55.

Sargent, Thomas, and Neil Wallace (1985), "Some Unpleasant Monetarist Arithmetic," *Federal Reserve Bank of Minneapolis Quarterly Review,* Vol. 9, No. 1, pp. 15-31.

Stolper, Wolfgang, and Paul A. Samuelson (1941), "Protection and Real Wages," *Review of Economic Studies*, Vol. 9, pp. 58-73.

Tanzi, Vito (1977), "Inflation, Lags in Collection, and the Real Value of Tax Revenue," *Staff Papers*, International Monetary Fund, Washington, Vol. 24, pp. 154-67.

Tornell, Aaron, and Andres Velasco (1995), "Fiscal Discipline and the Choice of Exchange Rate Regime", *European Economic Review*, Vol. 39, pp. 759-70.

Woodford, Michael (1996), "Control of the Public Debt: A Requirement for Price Stability?" Paper presented in the International Economic Association Conference, The Debt Burden and its Consequences for Monetary Policy, Frankfurt, March 20-23, 1996.

A New Breed of Exchange Rate Bands:

Chile, Israel and Mexico*

Elhanan Helpman,
Leonardo Leiderman and
Gil Bufman**

Abstract

Following inflation stabilization programmes where a fixed exchange rate is used as an anchor, a number of countries have gradually shifted towards a regime of increased flexibility. In particular, Chile, Israel and Mexico have adopted for a few years a regime of crawling exchange rate bands. This article documents and analyzes their unique experience. Of immediate concern is the question whether the shift from fixed to crawling bands is perceived as the signal of a tilt towards policy relaxation. On the contrary, it could be seen as a way of restoring external competitiveness after a period of real appreciation. The evidence collected in this article supports the latter view. As a way of moving towards a sustainable equilibrium, the shift to crawling bands is found to have a stabilizing influence on financial markets, on inflation expectations, and on the passthrough from exchange rates to prices.

---

* The chapter was first published in *Economic Policy*, October 1994, and is reproduced here with the permission of the Centre for Economic Policy Research, London, Great Britain.

** We benefited from insightful and useful comments and suggestions by Vittorio Grilli and Charles Wyplosz on earlier drafts. In addition, we are grateful to George Alogoskoufis and Economic Policy Panel participants for their comments. For data and insightful discussions on Chile and Mexico we are grateful to Augustin Carstens, Daniel Oks, Moises Schwartz, Rodrigo Vergara and numerous individuals at the Banco de Mexico.

1. Introduction

A common feature of the aftermath of several important heterodox stabilizations was the gradual shift towards a regime of increased flexibility in nominal exchange rates. While the first phase of heterodox stabilizations typically relies on the role of a fixed exchange rate in breaking inertia and producing rapid disinflation, it is commonly followed by a loss of competitiveness as reflected in cumulative real exchange rate appreciations. Experience indicates that sooner or later policymakers begin perceiving this erosion in competitiveness as a serious risk to the ultimate success of the whole programme. When this happens, and once it has become clear that fiscal and monetary fundamentals have been adjusted and major disinflation is being achieved, countries tend to enter a second phase in which they relax the fixity of the exchange rate. It is in this spirit that Chile, Israel and Mexico adopted exchange rate bands a few years after the inception of exchange-rate-based disinflations. In doing so, these countries have not given up the role of the exchange rate as an important nominal anchor. Instead, bands are viewed as introducing enough flexibility for the nominal exchange rate to respond to external and internal shocks without reneging on the medium- and long-term signals provided by the policy embodied in the setting of the band's central parity. Furthermore, the shift from a fixed exchange rate to an exchange rate band opens room for greater autonomy of domestic monetary policy.

Adopting an exchange rate band forces the authorities to take a stand on key operational issues. First, the central parity can be fixed or it can crawl. In countries with rates of inflation above those of their trade partners (e.g. Chile, Israel and Mexico), a permanently fixed central parity is not feasible. Therefore for such countries the real choice is between infrequent realignments (as in the EMS) and a crawl. As evident in recent European developments, infrequent realignments may generate substantial uncertainty, produce interest rate volatility, and damage the sustainability of the band. On the other hand, a major difficulty with crawling bands is that the frequent realignments of the central exchange rate may elicit inflationary expectations precisely as a serious attempt at disinflation is taking place. Second, if a crawling central parity is adopted the authorities have to choose a criterion for determining the crawl's pace. It can be based on a nominal objective (e.g. an inflation target) or on a real target (e.g. the real exchange rate). Third, it is necessary to specify the width for the exchange rate band. This involves an assessment of the variance of potential shocks as well as the degree to which the authorities can commit to narrow limits of exchange rate flexibility. Fourth, the frequency and size of intramarginal interventions has to be determined. For example, the authorities may choose to react to a drop in the profitability of exports, or to a downturn in economic activity, by accelerating the rate of depreciation within the band. Similarly, they may slow down the rate of depreciation if and when the rate of inflation is expected to increase.

The exchange rate bands adopted by previously high-inflation countries are substantially different from the bands observed in Europe. In addition to their market clearing roles, nominal exchange rates are used in these countries as key anchors of inflation expectations. Typically, these bands feature a crawling central parity, a unilateral commitment by the country's authorities to intervene to support the band, and a much larger width than in Europe before the recent crisis. For example, Chile's current band features a crawling central parity and fluctuation limits of 10% around this rate. At the beginning of each month the authorities announce the rate of crawl of the central parity for that month based on the difference between the rate of inflation in the previous month and a forecast of foreign inflation. In Israel, the authorities announce their inflation target for a given year, and then pre-announce a daily nominal depreciation for that year mostly based on the difference between the inflation target and a forecast of external inflation over the same time period. At the present time, the exchange rate is allowed to fluctuate within 5% of the central parity. Mexico's band is quite unique: it features a gradual crawl of the band's upper limit while the lower limit is maintained fixed. Consequently, the band's width rises over time, and it is expected to reach 7% by the end of 1994.

This kind of exchange rate bands is appealing to countries with persistent inflation differentials. In fact, bands could be an appealing exchange rate system for other economies in Latin America and for several former centrally-planed economies in Eastern Europe. Thus Colombia has replaced in February 1994 its crawling-peg arrangement with a crawling band. Most of the available evidence about exchange rate bands has been based on the experience of Western European economies that operated their bands under a multilateral commitment to maintain and defend them. In contrast, this paper documents and analyses the experience with exchange rate bands in Chile, Israel and Mexico. In particular, it will be useful to rely on Israel's experience to assess whether a shift from fixed- to crawling-central-parity bands was associated with a stabilizing or destabilizing influence on financial markets, on inflationary expectations, and on the passthrough from exchange rates to prices.

We review in the next section the main theoretical considerations that guided our empirical work. Based on that discussion, we elaborate in Section 3 on the case of Israel. Section 4 employs various statistical indicators to compare behaviour under fixed- vs. crawling-bands. Evidence for Chile and Mexico is provided in Section 5. Last, Section 6 draws the main lessons from the comparison of the three countries and discusses some of the practical policy implications of the analysis.

2. Theoretical Considerations

2.1 Implications of target zones

Recent analyses of target zones provide a useful benchmark for the empirical analysis of exchange rate fluctuations within the announced exchange rate bands. Krugman (1991) has shown how the mere existence of set limits on exchange rate movements affect the behaviour of the rate within its band. Under a number of conditions, to be criticised shortly, Krugman found that the relation between the exchange rate and its fundamentals – assumed to be fully described by one composite indicator – exhibits an S shape, with tangency at the band's limits (Svensson, 1992, offers a useful survey of the literature). This finding has several important implications. First, the exchange rate should spend most of its time close to the edges of the band (its distribution is bimodal and U-shaped). Second, the expected rate of depreciation is highest at the band's lower bound (when the exchange rate is strongest) and declines as the exchange rate depreciates, rising towards the band's upper limit (the distribution exhibits mean reversion). Third, this means that the exchange rate is expected to depreciate in the lower part of the band: uncovered interest parity then implies that the differential between the domestic and foreign interest rate is highest when the exchange rate is at the band's lower limit and declines as the exchange rate rises toward the upper limit. Fourth, both the exchange rate and the interest rate differential are expected to exhibit more variability in the middle of the band that at its extremities where interventions are expected to stabilize the exchange rate (see Svensson, 1992, and references therein for more details on these results).

These results crucially depend on two unsatisfactory assumptions: (i) that the market fully believes that the monetary authorities can and will defend the bands so that the exchange rate will never break through its set limits; (ii) that the central banks only intervene at the margin. When more realistic forms of interventions are allowed, Krugman's results are radically modified. For example, with "leaning against the wind" interventions, the exchange rate is now expected to spend most of its time near the centre of the band (its distribution now exhibits an inverted-U shape, as shown by Lewis, 1991). Thus the behaviour of the exchange rate within the band may be strongly affected by the specific intervention method that maintains the target zone.

Regardless of the specifics of interventions, as long as the bands are credible, both the interest rate differential and expected depreciation rise as the exchange rate moves toward its higher band because of the probability that it will soon decline. This result is overturned in the presence of a realignment risk, when the exchange rate band is not fully credible. For example, consider the case when markets believe that the authorities may well devalue rather than defend the central parity when the exchange rate approaches the ceiling of the band. Bertola and Caballero (1992) have shown that the relation between the exchange rate and its fundamentals then assumes an inverted-S shape. This means that the exchange rate spends most of its time towards the middle of the band, and than the interest differential now increases when the exchange rate moves toward its ceiling because the perceived probability of a depreciation rises instead of declining when the target zone is believed to be cast in iron.

The realistic possibility that the band will not be defended leads us to express the expected rate of depreciation as the sum of two components: the expected rate of realignment – the change of the central parity – and the expected rate of currency depreciation within the band – movements within the band. Each of this component has a different implication of the relation between the interest rate differential and the position of the exchange rate within the band: a devaluation risk implies that the interest differential rises as the exchange rate depreciates (rises) within the band while credible bands means that the interest differential declines. This is why Svensson (1992) has argued that the interest rate differential alone could be a misleading indicator of realignment expectations.[1]

2.2 Imperfect capital mobility

Key aspects of the preceding analysis (and in what follows), such as the relation between the interest rate differential and the exchange rate, rely on the assumption of uncovered interest rate parity and a time-invariant foreign exchange risk premium.

---

1 As shown by Helpman, Leiderman and Bufman (1993), most of these theoretical implications are also valid for cases in which continuous preannounced realignments of the central parity are part of the existing band regime, as in Chile, Israel and Mexico. In this case, it is important to redefine variables so that now exchange rates are expressed in terms of their deviation from the central parity, and fundamentals in terms of their deviation from their underlying trend.

Although for most recent periods this assumption is a reasonably good approximation in the cases of Chile, Israel and Mexico, there have been episodes that could be interpreted as deviations from this parity relation. The reason is that capital mobility has been less-than-perfect, a consequence of the non-negligible information and transaction costs as well as of the remaining regulations that characterize financial markets in these countries. For example, it has not been uncommon to observe episodes in which, in an attempt to stimulate employment in the short-run, an expansionary monetary policy resulted in lower domestic nominal interest rates while at the same time foreign exchange market intervention was performed to avoid a depreciation of the exchange rate. The less-than-perfect degree of capital mobility in the countries under study, which increases the short-run efficacy of monetary and exchange rate policy, severs the predicted links between interest rates and exchange rates. This effect, however, is temporary because such actions typically give rise to increased capital outflows and to a reduction in the stock of international reserves at the domestic central bank. In this context an examination of the behaviour of capital flows and central bank international reserves can provide useful information on the sustainability and credibility of an existing exchange rate band. In particular, it can be argued that those configurations of interest rates and exchange rates that result in sizeable and persistent capital flows in only one direction are likely to weaken the sustainability of the band and to give rise to pressure for change in either the band's parameters or in monetary policy.

2.3 Policy trade-offs: inflation and the real exchange rate

The adoption of bands in Chile, Israel and Mexico was perceived as a way to resolve the fundamental short-run policy trade-off between the level of the real exchange rate and the level and variability of the nominal exchange rate (or rate of inflation).[2] On the one hand, the authorities in these countries have used exchange rate realignments to compensate for persistent inflation differentials, and have expressed their concern to preserve and improve the profitability of exports and the current account position by having a competitive real exchange rate. On the other hand, it has been recognised that frequent exchange rate depreciations could weaken the role of the exchange rate as a nominal anchor and could elicit inflationary expectations. In fact, other things equal, an accommodative exchange rate policy may have a destabilizing impact on the rate of inflation and other nominal variables in economies with a history of pronounced inflation inertia and with widespread indexation of nominal wages. (See, e.g., Dornbusch, 1982, Bruno, 1993 and Leiderman, 1993).

The crawling exchange rate bands regime is a simple and verifiable system for the policy-maker to make a clear commitment about a key nominal anchor such as the path of the central nominal exchange rate, while allowing for some degree of exchange rate flexibility needed to shield exports and the current account from the impact of adverse shocks. As shown by Cukierman, Kiguel and Leiderman (1994), under such a regime, other things equal, expectations of realignments increase as the exchange rate moves toward the upper limit of the band. The reason is that the policy-makers' choice is governed by the trade-off between credibility and flexibility: when the exchange rate has been for a while at its limit under the pressure of a high inflation rate, the cost of maintaining credibility with an increasing overvalued parity is bound to become excessive, an assessment well understood by the markets.

The upshot is that the behaviour of real (and not only nominal) exchange rates and of the rate of inflation can play an important role in determining the sustainability of an existing band. Thus if, for example, the parameters chosen for a given band and the

---

[2] This is borne out, for example, by the statement of the president of the Banco Central de Chile in Zahler (1992). That real exchange rate behavior is an important consideration in assessing the performance of bands in small industrial countries is transparent in the various papers collected in Argy and De Grauwe (1990).

underlying shocks result in an acceleration of inflation and an overvaluation of the domestic currency, pressures for a realignment and for a change in the band's parameters are likely to rise. These features which may well seriously damage the credibility of an existing band are not revealed in an analysis that focuses on nominal exchange and interest rates alone.

3. Israel

Israel's exchange rate policy has followed three main phases after the stabilization programme of July 1985. First, the NIS (New Israeli Shekel) was pegged to the US dollar. This fixed exchange rate policy was a major building block of the disinflation programme. In August 1986 the dollar peg was replaced by a peg to a basket of currencies. Second, following a sequence of devaluations of the NIS/Basket exchange rate in 1987, 1988 and early January 1989, the government adopted an exchange rate band on January 3, 1989. The band consisted of a fixed NIS/Basket central parity with a 3% fluctuation zone around this parity. The band's width was enlarged to 5% in March 1990. Third, in December 1991, after an upward adjustment of the central parity, the authorities relaxed the fixity of the central parity and announced an upward crawl of the exchange rate band. In addition, an official inflation target was announced for the first time. The rate of crawl (or depreciation) of the central parity rate was set at 9% per year, to reflect the difference between Israel's inflation target (14.5%) and a forecast of foreign inflation for 1992. The announced rate of crawl for the central parity was reduced to an annual rate of 8% per year starting from November 1992 and to 6% per year starting from July 1993, and the announced inflation targets for 1993 and 1994 were 10 and 8%, respectively.

We begin this section by examining the behaviour of exchange and interest rates under the various bands. In particular, we seek to determine whether the evidence conforms with the implications of the analysis presented in the previous section. We then turn to movements in foreign exchange reserves, a measure of intervention by the authorities. Lastly, we present econometric evidence on realignment expectations and a discussion of real exchange rate and inflation developments, both of which are relevant for assessing the sustainability of a given set of band policy parameters.

3.1 Exchange rates

Figure 1 shows the daily NIS/Basket exchange rate from mid-1985 to the end of 1993 and Table 1 provides basic data on the various bands. Each exchange rate band is identified in Figure 1 by three lines: its central parity and its upper and lower limits. A number of features stand out: (i) the nominal exchange rate followed an upward trend, a combination of depreciation within bands and adjustments of the central parity; (ii) the central parity was realigned no less than seven times in five years; and (iii) some upward adjustments of the central parity took place when the exchange rate was not close to its upper limit (March 1990 and 1991).

The exchange rate spent too much time around the middle of the bands and too little time at their upper parts to fit the simple target zone interpretation (this visual impression is formally confirmed by statistical tests in Helpman, Leiderman and Bufman, 1993). This suggests either that the authorities have been conducting mean-reverting interventions inside the bands and/or that the bands were not particularly credible. Furthermore, also in contrast to the predictions from the basic target zone interpretation, the exchange rate was on average more volatile near the limits of the band than near the central parity and no significant differences were found in the average rate of change of the exchange rate across the various regions of the band.

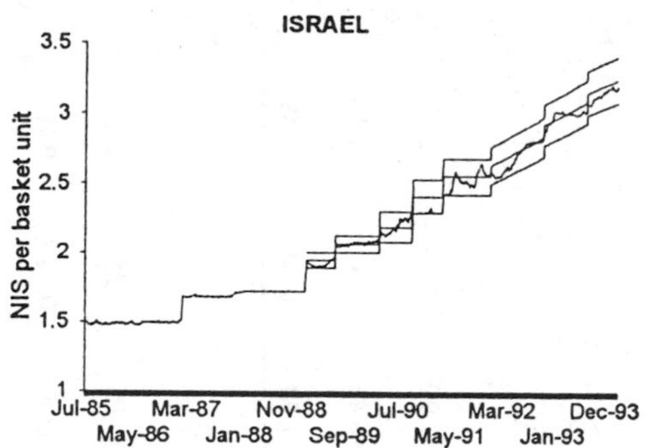

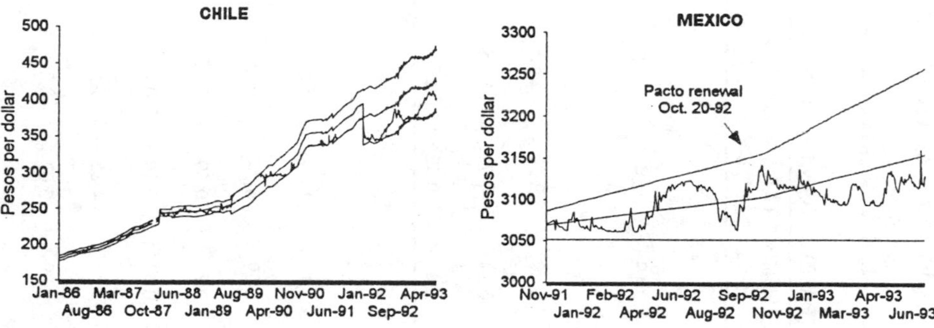

Figure 1. Exchange rate bands (daily data)

Notes: Israel: For the period July 1985-July 1986 the exchange rate shown is that of the NIS against the US dollar. From August 1986 onwards the exchange rate shown is that of the NIS against the Israeli currency basket. Chile: For the period January 1986-June 1992 the exchange rate shown is that of the Peso against the US dollar. From July 1992 onwards the exchange rate shown is that of the Peso against the Chilean currency basket. Date of last observation: Israel-28 January 1994; Chile-28 June 1993; Mexico-30 June 1993.

Table 1. Israel: Band characteristics, exchange rate, interest rates, prices and foreign currency reserves

						Crawling Bands			
	BAND 1	BAND 2	BAND 3	BAND 4	BAND 5	BAND 6	BAND 7	BAND 8	BAND 6,7,8
Period	1989.01-89.06	1989.07-90.02	1990.03-90.08	1990.09-91.02	1991.03-91.11	1991.12-92.11	1992.11-93.07	1993.07-93.12	1991.12-93.12
Band characteristics and the exchange rate, using daily data:									
Mid-band rate (NIS/basket)	1.95	2.07	2.19	2.41	2.55	-	-	-	-
Band width +/- (in %)	3	3	5	5	5	5	5	5	5
Crawl of mid-band rate, annualized (in %)	-	-	-	-	-	9	8	6	8
Average exchange rate	1.92	2.07	2.20	2.29	2.52	2.69	2.99	3.14	2.89
Average deviation of exchange rate from mid-band (in %)	-1.41	0.19	0.34	-4.79	-1.15	-1.45	-0.41	-1.79	-1.15
Standard deviation from mid-band (in%)	1.06	0.69	2.29	0.32	2.31	1,71	1.24	0.54	1.48
Interest rates, using weekly data, in percent per month terms:									
Average domestic interest rate (monetary auction rate)	1.07	1.12	1.15	1.09	1.19	0.91	0.91	0.75	0.88
Standard deviation of domestic interest rate	0.18	0.22	0.09	0.08	0.29	0.09	0.06	0.03	0.10
Average foreign interest rate (LIBID) (1)	0.71	0.71	0.71	0.69	0.58	0.50	0.40	0.35	0.43
Average interest differential (Israel-Foreign)	0.36	0.40	0.43	0.40	0.61	0.42	0.51	0.40	0.44
Annualized average interest differential	4.42	4.95	5.31	4.85	7.61	5.10	6.28	4.94	5.47
Standard deviation of interest rate differential	0.20	0.21	0.09	0.07	0.30	0.08	0.08	0.03	0.09

Inflation, using monthly data, in percent per month terms:									
Average domestic inflation rate (CPI)	1.11	1.01	1.34	0.88	1.47	0.66	0.85	0.81	0.79
Average foreign inflation rate (CPI) (1)	0.44	0.30	0.35	0.25	0.27	0.25	0.23	0.21	0.24
Average inflation differential (Israel-Foreign)	0.67	0.71	0.98	0.63	1.19	0.41	0.62	0.60	0.54
Annualized average inflation difference	8.38	8.83	12.47	7.85	15.28	5.07	7.66	7.47	6.74
Standard deviation of inflation differential	0.07	0.15	0.04	0.02	0.12	0.28	0.06	0.03	0.21
Foreign currency reserves (non-gold), using monthly data, in millions of dollars per month terms:									
Average change in reserves	203	0	-28	238	-32	-96	-8	367	43
Standard deviation of change in reserves	525	212	258	363	500	398	526	662	546
Real effective exchange rate									
Average real exchange rate (index, 86.01-88.04 avg.=100)	100.0	100.6	101.2	101.7	100.2	100.0	104.9	104.8	102.7
Standard deviation of real exchange rate change (in %)	3.10	0.89	0.84	1.09	1.74	1.10	1.24	0.41	1.04

Note: (1) Weighted average - using Israel's currency basket weights.
Sources: Bank of Israel; Central Bureau of Statistics - Israel

3.2 Interest rates

The shortest reliable free market interest rate available in Israel is determined in monetary auctions, where the Bank of Israel auctions off credit funds to financial institutions. The auctions took place once a week in the past, and were expanded to daily auctions at the end of 1990. For this reason we now work with weekly observations. Table 1 provides some basic interest rate data and Figure 2 presents a plot of the interest rate differential for the various bands.

Figure 2. Interest rate differentials (annualized terms)

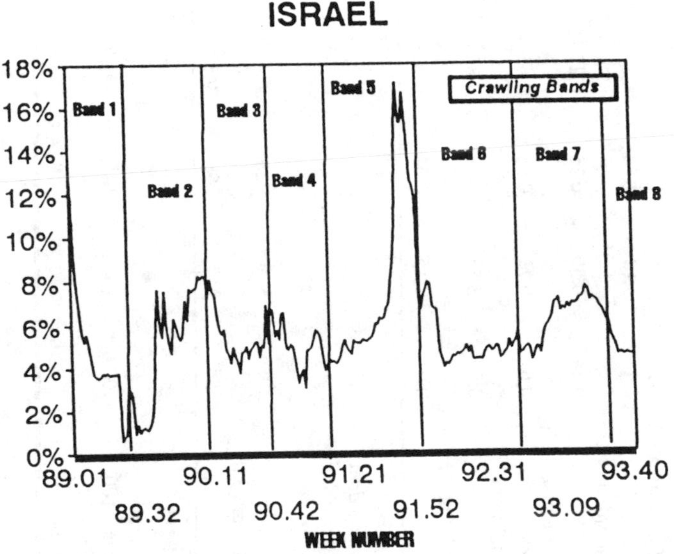

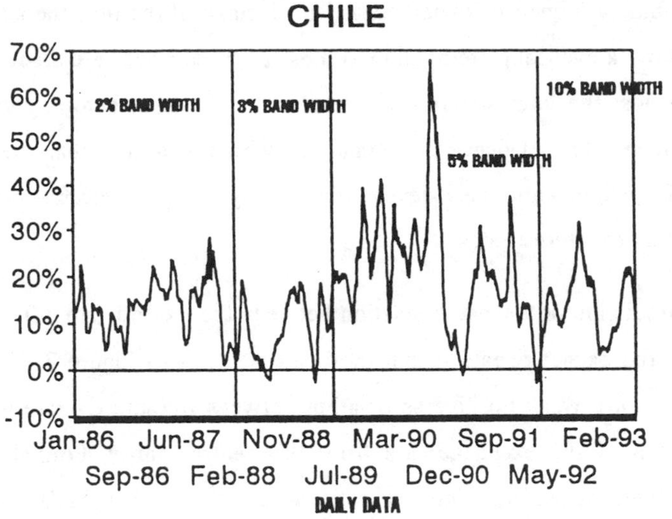

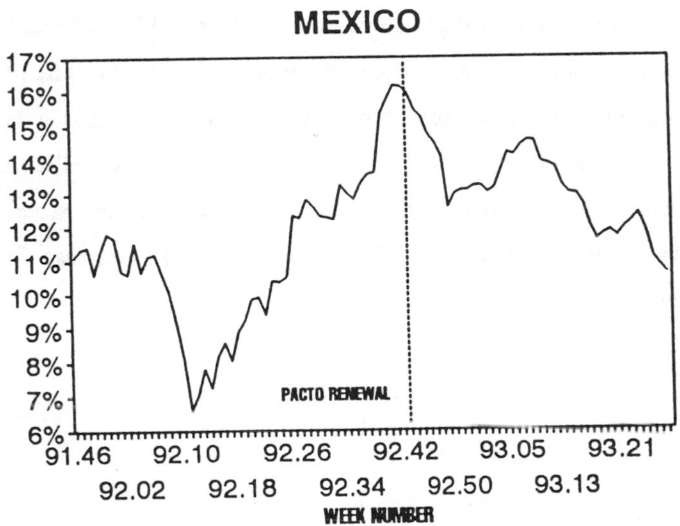

Notes: Israel: The differential shown is calculated using the Bank of Israel's monetary auction rate and a currency basket weighted composite of foreign interest rates. Chile: For the period January, 86 - June, 92 the differential is calculated using short-term Peso deposit rates and U.S. T-bill rates with similar maturity periods. From July, 92 onwards the differential shown is calculated using a currency basket weighted composite of foreign interest rates. Mexico: The differential shown is calculated using 28 day CETES rates and U.S. T-bill rates for similar maturity periods. Date of last observation: Israel-Week ending December 31, 1993; Chile-June 28, 1993; Mexico-Week ending July 17, 1993.

The figure exhibits two important characteristics: (i) most of the time the interest rate differential follows a cyclical pattern; and (ii) most of these cycles are associated with shifts across bands: the interest rate differential generally rises before, and declines after a realignment. The evidence is compatible with the notion that the market's anticipation of realignments (i.e., devaluations) played an important role in the observed volatility of interest rates.

To check the prediction of a negative relation between the interest rate differential and the position of the exchange rate within the band we turn to Figure 3. If anything, there is evidence of a weak positive association between the interest rate differential and the deviation of the exchange rate from the central parity. Formal statistical analysis of movements in the interest rate differential within bands (Helpman, Leiderman and Bufman, 1993[3]) further reveals that the distribution of the interest rate differential across various band regions does not conform with the basic target-zone pattern. This could well reflect the impact of monetary and exchange rate policy under imperfect capital mobility, along the lines of the discussion in subsection 2.2. For example, the combination of a low domestic interest rate (aimed at stimulating employment) and increased expectations of devaluation gave rise to a sizeable outflow of capital in late 1992 which was associated with a loss of more than $1 billion of official reserves.

---

[3] Most of the evidence is qualitatively similar to that discussed by Svensson (1992) for the EMS.

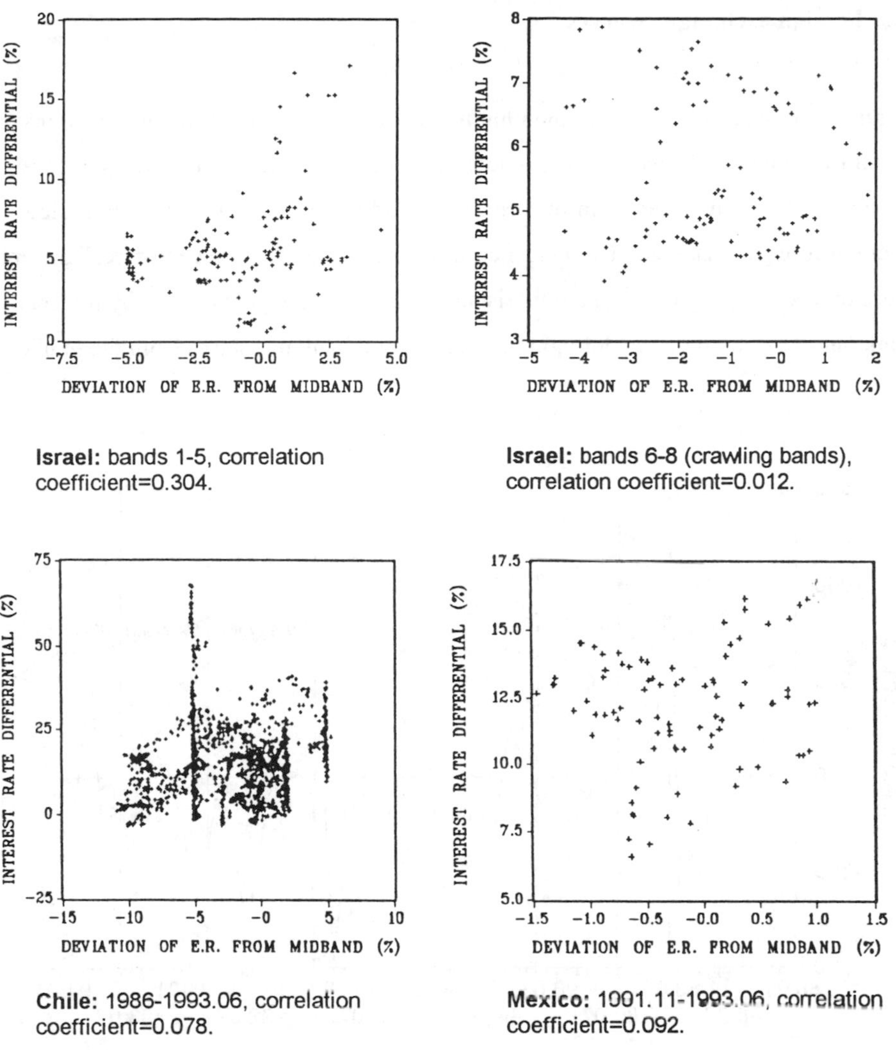

Israel: bands 1-5, correlation coefficient=0.304.

Israel: bands 6-8 (crawling bands), correlation coefficient=0.012.

Chile: 1986-1993.06, correlation coefficient=0.078.

Mexico: 1991.11-1993.06, correlation coefficient=0.092.

Figure 3. Interest rate differentials and the deviation of the exchange rate from mid-band

Notes: The interest rate differentials are shown in annualized terms. For Mexico the mid-band rate is calculated as the average of the upper and lower bounds of the band. For further information regarding the data shown here, see notes to Figures 1 and 2.

3.3 Foreign exchange reserves

Figure 4 provides a plot of the monthly net sales of foreign currency by the Bank of Israel to the public. In Israel, the public sector obtains substantial resources in foreign currency, especially in the form of foreign aid, and the central bank ends up selling on average foreign exchange. The evidence in Figure 4 indicates that most realignments were preceded by high and generally rising net sales of foreign currency by the central bank, and were followed by foreign-currency central bank purchases from the public.

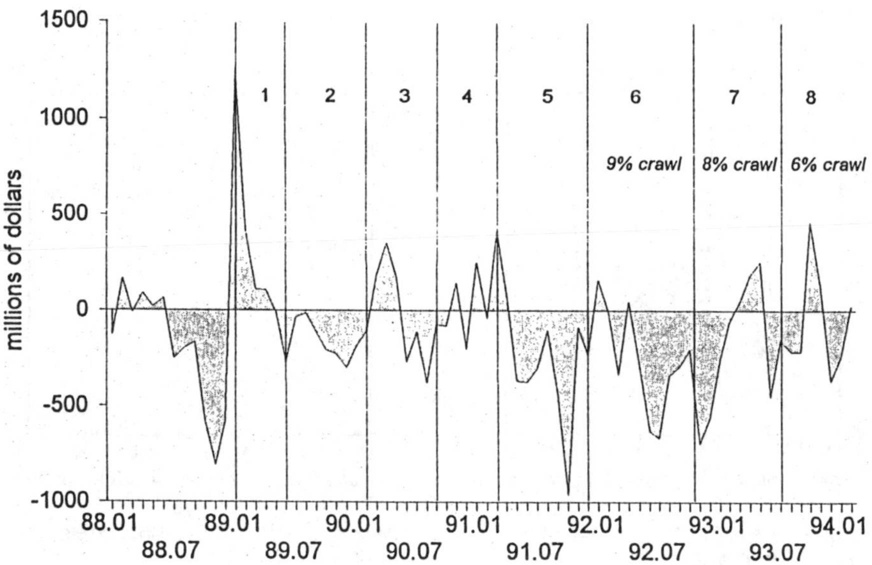

Figure 4. Purchases of foreign currency. Purchases (–) / sales (+) by the public

Note: The series shown is the net contribution of Israel's private sector to changes in Israel's foreign currency reserves.
Source: The Bank of Israel

The notion that in an economy such as Israel movements in foreign currency sales can serve as a useful indicator of a band's credibility and sustainability – beyond other indicators such as the exchange rate and interest rate differential – can be illustrated with developments in 1992. During the second half of 1992 the authorities kept a relatively low domestic interest rate with the aim of accommodating an apparent slowdown in inflation and to possibly stimulate economic activity in the short-run. At the same time, institutional measures were taken to further liberalize the capital account (for example final clarification of the status of taxation of income from mutual funds invested abroad). Together with rising expectations of a stronger US dollar these developments were associated with a net capital outflow of about $1 billion over a short time period. While these circumstances gave rise to considerable doubts about the sustainability of the band's parameters at that time, they did not affect the interest and exchange rates because of heavy intervention by the authorities.

3.4 The real exchange rate and inflation

The lack of a stable competitive real exchange rate during the second half of the 1980s, shown in Figure 5 (monthly data), was perceived as a major problem in an open economy such as Israel.[4] Being an exchange-rate based stabilization, the 1985 programme and the policies that followed its implementation did not prevent a severe real appreciation. Rising concerns by policy-makers about the loss of external competitiveness prompted the devaluations of December 1988-January 1989 and the adoption of an exchange rate band.

---

4 The real exchange rate was calculated as the product of the nominal basket exchange rate times a (basket weighted) foreign price level divided by the domestic price level.

Figure 5. Real exchange rate

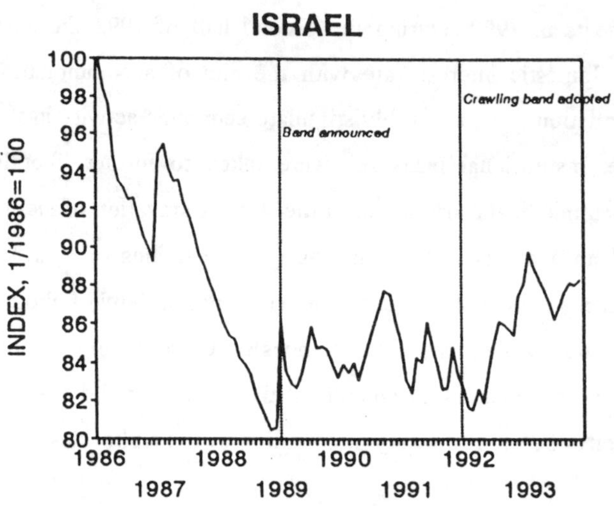

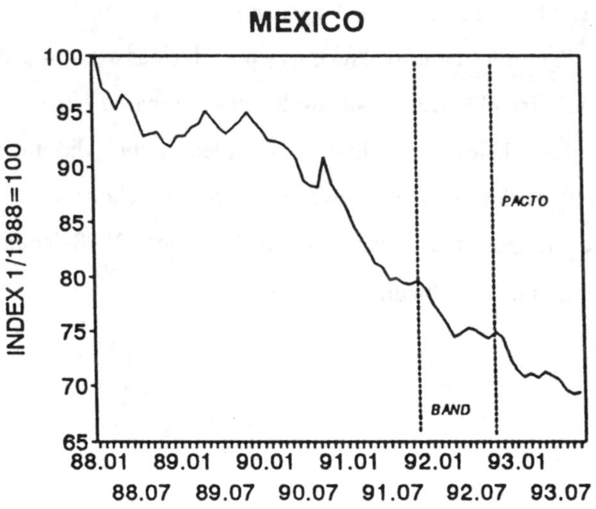

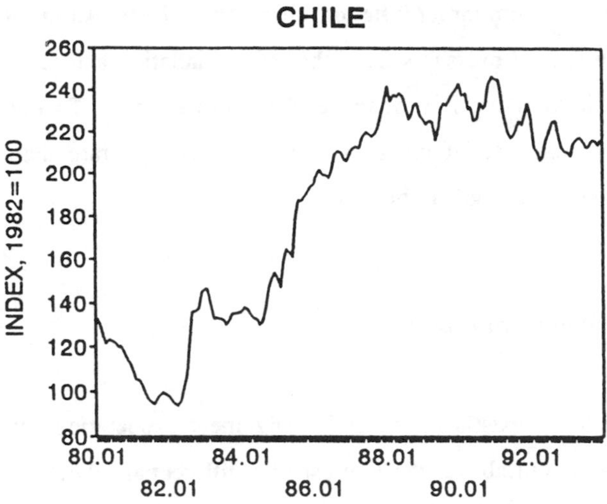

Note: Israel: The real exchange rate shown is computed using Israeli wholesale prices, a currency basket-weighted composite of foreign wholesale prices and the currency basket exchange rate. Mexico: The real exchange rate shown is computed using Mexican wholesale prices, U.S. wholesale prices and the exchange rate of the peso against the U.S. dollar. Chile: Real effective exchange rate.
Source: International Financial Statistics, IMF

Stability of the real exchange rate was attained under the first band regime (with fixed central parity), albeit at an overvalued level, without an acceleration of the rate of inflation (see Figures 3 and 5). At the end of 1990 the real exchange rate appreciation was of about 15% as compared to the start of 1986. However, a partial reversal took place under the crawling band in 1992, with a 9% real exchange rate depreciation (measured in terms of the basket, from December 1991 to December 1992). In spite of early fears that this real exchange rate depreciation, and more generally the shift to a crawling band, would be associated with a rise in the rate of inflation, the opposite occurred. The rate of inflation reached a single-digit figure in 1992 (9.4%) for the first time in more than two decades. However, this did not eliminate the concern about potential inflationary consequences of exchange rate fluctuations, especially in light of the deviation of actual from target inflation observed in 1993. All in all we conclude that there were no special pressures from the rate of inflation and real exchange rate developments on the sustainability of the exchange rate bands. To the contrary, the recent reduction in the rate of inflation and real exchange rate depreciation have probably contributed to strengthen this regime.

3.5 Estimated realignment expectations

The sustainability of an existing band and realignment expectations are not directly observable. Yet, as noted above, the interest rate differential reflects expectations of (i) expected realignments and (ii) expected movement of the exchange rate within the band. In this section we use a procedure developed by Svensson (1992) (known as the drift-adjustment method) which permits to unscramble these two components. Appendix A explains how we extend the procedure to crawling bands.

The pattern of the expected realignments thus computed shown in Figure 6 is plausible. During the first band there was a gradual decrease in devaluation expectations, only partially reversed a few weeks before the end of the band. In the second band there was a gradual upward trend until the next realignment. The third band featured an initial decrease in realignment expectations followed by a sharp rise. An upward realignment was expected throughout the fourth band. The shift to the first crawling band (i.e., the sixth band) was preceded by a sharp increase in realignment expectations. Yet, no such expectations were associated with the shift to the second and third crawling bands. Overall, Figure 6 confirms Svensson's (1992) point that movements in the interest rate differential could be misleading indicators of realignment expectations. As with European countries, fluctuations in expected realignments are much more volatile, and fit more closely realignment dates, than movements in the interest rate differential.

Figure 6. Expected realignment and the interest rate differential

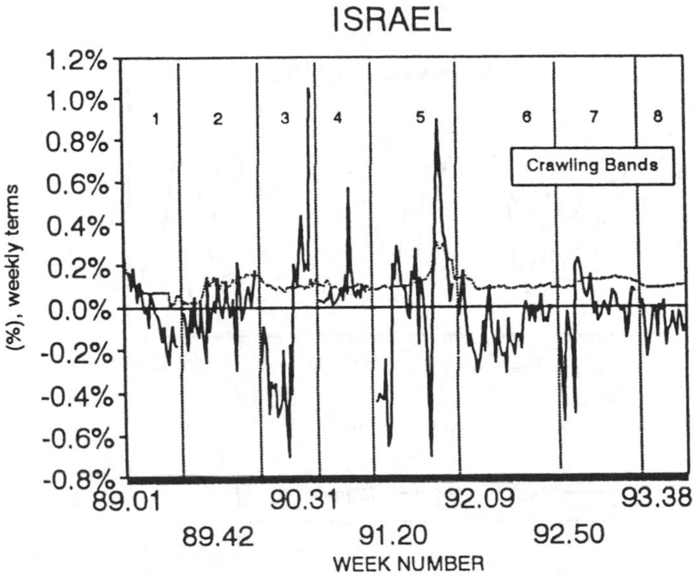

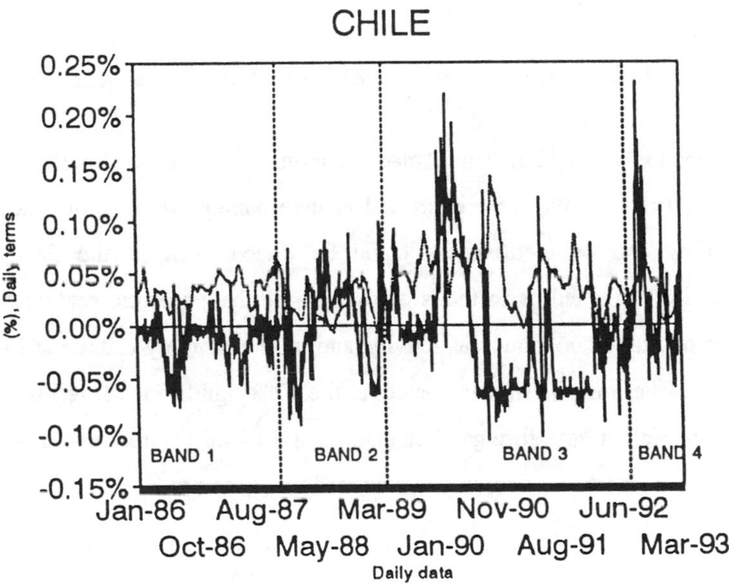

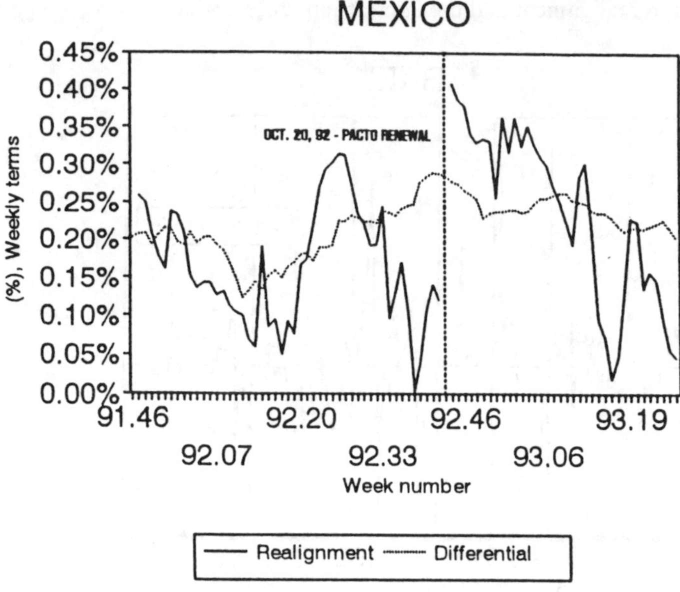

Note: The expected realignment series shown are fitted values of equation (3) in Appendix A.

We have also explored whether some macroeconomic indicators affect expected realignments. In particular, we were interested in determining whether the trade-off between credibility and competitiveness could be traced back in the data. The reasoning in Section 2 has led us to focus on the rate of change of the real exchange rate, on the rate of change in economic activity, and on the monthly change in foreign currency reserves. There is plausible evidence (at the 10% significance level) that past increases in economic activity, foreign exchange reserves, and the real exchange rate are associated with a significant decrease in expected realignments.[5]

---

5 However, it would be hard to consider the estimates as providing a strong case for using these macroeconomic variables in expected-realignment equations.

4. From Fixed to Crawling Bands: A Regime Change?

Among the three countries discussed in this study, Israel is unique in featuring an important change in the functioning of the exchange rate band, from a fixed to a crawling central exchange rate. There was, and still is, considerable controversy around the possible effects of this shift. On the one hand, by allowing the parity to change gradually over time – in a series of small preannounced daily steps – rather than in the sudden discrete changes that were characteristic of the earlier bands, the new system could have a stabilizing influence on financial markets as well as on the real exchange rate. On the other hand, these frequent realignments of the central exchange rate could weaken the role of the exchange rate as a nominal anchor and elicit inflationary expectations. Put differently, a shift toward a more accommodative exchange rate policy could, in principle, have a destabilizing impact on the rate of inflation and other nominal variables, especially in an economy with a history of pronounced inflation inertia and widespread wage – and financial – indexation. As a matter of fact, part of the aversion to exchange rate flexibility was rooted in Israel's experience with a crawling peg in the mid-1970s which was associated with a rise in the level and volatility of the rate of inflation.[6]

While it is too early now to settle (ex-post) this controversy, our purpose here is to rely on various statistical indicators to provide an empirical comparison of the bands with fixed and crawling central parity and to draw some preliminary conclusions. The section proceeds as follows. First, we discuss whether there has been a change in the volatility of nominal and real exchange rates and of interest rate differentials. Then, evidence is provided on shifts in realignment expectations, and on other indicators of band credibility such as the parallel market exchange rate premium, following the

---

[6] The acceleration in the rate of inflation was related to the accommodation policies, and indexation effects, that followed the oil shock of 1973-74 as well as the relatively high government budget deficits that prevailed at that time. For details, see Bruno (1993) and Leiderman (1993).

policy shift. Last, we examine the impacts of this shift on inflation expectations and on the passthrough from exchange rates to prices.

Figure 2, and Table 1 show that there has been a reduction in the volatility of the interest rate differential under the crawling bands. (The unconditional standard deviation of the differential was on average less than half the standard deviation before the shift to a crawl, a change that is statistically significant.) This visual impression is formally confirmed by various statistical tests presented in Appendix B.

In regards to the nominal exchange rate, Figure 1 suggests that while under the earlier bands the exchange rate remained quite often distant from the central parity, it has recently little moved away from the crawling path of the central exchange rate, thus suggesting that there has been a reduction in the volatility of deviations of actual from central exchange rates (see also Table 1). This is confirmed by formal statistical tests presented in Appendix B.

Another important aspect of the comparison across bands is the behaviour of realignment (or devaluation) expectations: the stronger these expectations, the greater is the probability of collapse in the exchange rate regime. The weekly expected realignment series previously estimated and plotted in Figure 6 suggest that the move to crawling bands has been accompanied by a significant reduction in both the level of expected realignments and their variability (measured by the conditional standard deviation). Again, the formal tests presented in Appendix B confirm these impressions. Another way of making the point is by looking at the percentage of days for which Figure 6 indicates that markets may have been expecting a devaluation. Table 2 shows that this proportion has decreased in the crawling band period relative to the earlier bands.

Table 2. Israel: band credibility index

Band number	Credibility index
1	17%
2	18%
3	38%
4	22%
5	54%
6	7%
7	19%
8	0%

Note: This index shows the percentage of days for which there were significantly positive devaluation expectations of the exchange rate from the maximal feasible rate under the current regime (0% = full credibility, 100% = full non-credibility).

Still further evidence pointing in the same direction is provided by two market-based indicators. First, the premium on the parallel (black) market exchange rate is plotted in Figure 7. Second, the Bank of Israel sells, via auctions, options on the exchange rate of the local currency against the US dollar. Figure 8 shows the premium for three-month "at the money" (i.e., European) options. The premium is shown as a percentage of the exchange rate prevailing on the day of the auction of the options. Increased premiums on these three-month options are ordinarily interpreted as signalling an increase in the expected volatility of the exchange rate. The reversal in the trend of these premiums – from positive to negative – following the shift to crawling bands shown in Figure 8 suggests a decrease in volatility.

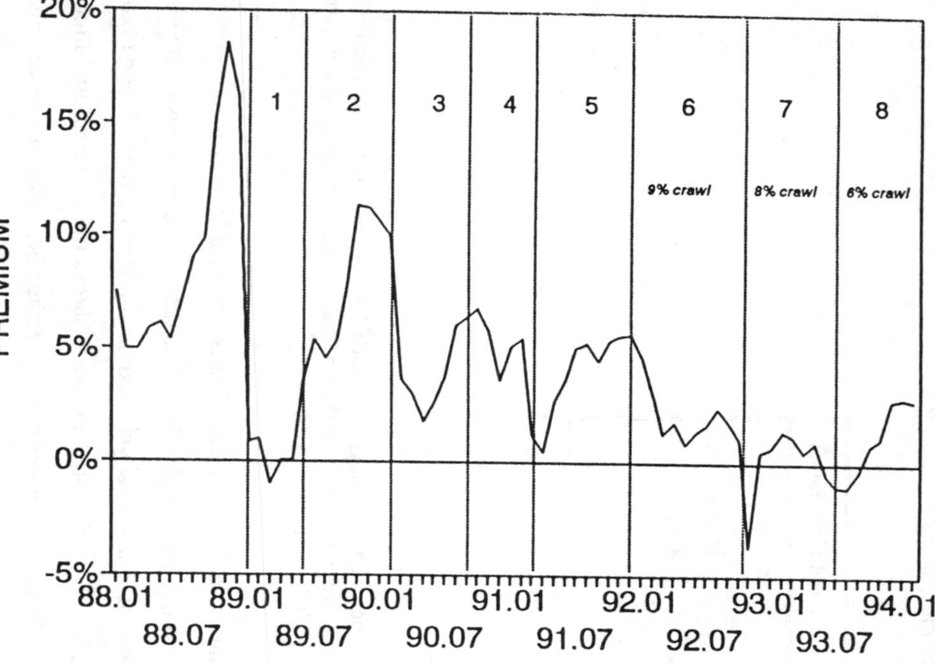

Figure 7. Black market premium on the U.S. dollar (black market rate over official rate)

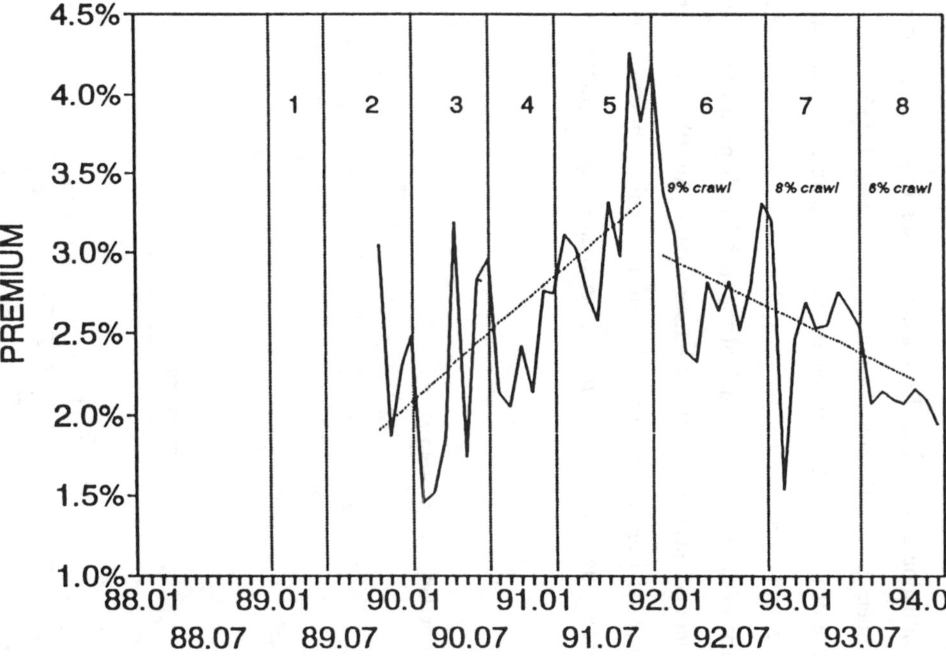

Figure 8. Currency option premium (premium as a percent of exchange rate)

Notes to Figs. 7 and 8: The black market premium is the difference between the black market exchange rate and the official exchange rate as a percent of the official exchange rate. The currency option premium is shown as a percent of the exchange rate known on the day of the option auction (the effective premium). The premium shown is that of 3-month "at the money" options written and auctioned by the Bank of Israel.

Did the shift rekindle inflationary expectations as often feared? A negative answer can be given once we derive inflation expectations from a comparison of yields on nominal and CPI-indexed government bonds of similar maturity (see Yariv, 1989). Figure 9 depicts the term structure of these inflation expectations one month before and after the announcement of the shift to a crawling band in December 1991. As indicated above, this announcement of the policy shift, and of the new band's parameters, was made jointly with the announcement of an official inflation target for 1992. It can be seen in Figure 9 that there has been a downward shift of the whole term structure of inflation expectations from about 19% prior to the announcement to about 14% afterwards.

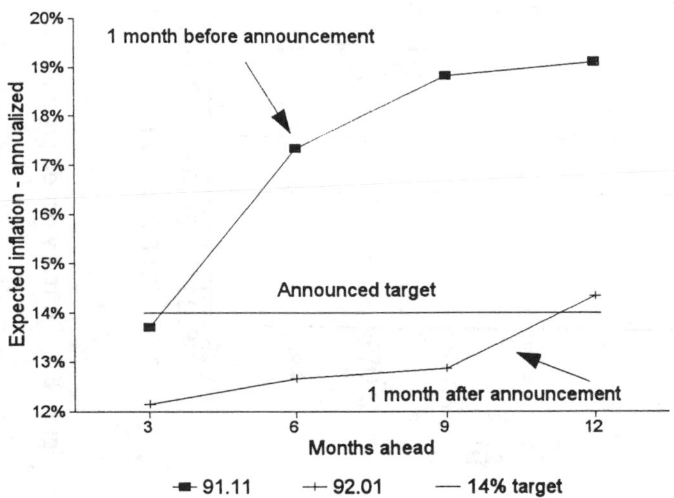

Dec. 1991: Announcement of 9% crawl and inflation target of 14% - 15%

Figure 9. Response of inflationary expectations to crawl rate and inflation target announcement

Note: Inflationary expectations are market-based and are calculated using the difference between the yield to maturity of non-indexed government T-bills and CPI indexed government bonds with similar maturity periods. For further details see Yariv (1989).
Source: The Bank of Israel

Finally, we ask whether the shift to a crawling band was associated with a marked change in the transmission of exchange rate (or foreign price) impulses into domestic prices of tradable goods. The results of our estimates are presented in Figure 10 which depicts the simulated impact of a one-time exchange rate 1% depreciation on the domestic price of traded goods. The effect is clearly much weaker in the recent crawling band period, in contradiction with the view that the shift to increased exchange rate flexibility has been followed by a rise in the inflationary impact of exchange rate depreciation.[7]

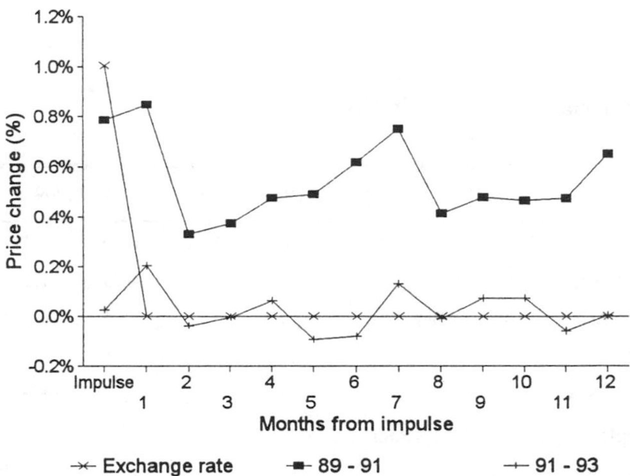

Figure 10. Impulse response of traded prices to a 1% shock to the exchange rate

Note: Simulation based on bivariate VAR of traded goods price changes and basket exchange+foreign WPI changes. The simulation shows the response of traded goods prices to a 1% shock of the exchange rate.

---

7 We conducted bivariate vector autoregressions for the periods 1989-1991 and 1991-1993. The systems included monthly data for the rate of change of traded-goods prices and for the sum of the rates of change of the exchange rate and foreign prices (measured by a trade-weighted foreign WPI). The estimated parameters and standard errors on dummy variables for the crawling bands period indicate that there has been a statistically significant reduction in the degree of passthrough in the second sub-period compared to the earlier period. Similar evidence was obtained from estimating direct passthrough equations.

To recapitulate, we find that, contrary to fears from the past, enhanced flexibility of the band's central exchange rate did not come at the cost of accelerating inflation. The shift from fixed- to crawling-central-parity bands was accompanied by a reduction in the volatility of exchange rates and interest rate differentials, a decrease in the relative size and importance of realignment expectations, and a reduction in the passthrough from exchange rates to prices of traded goods. On the other hand, it would be difficult to argue that the shift to a crawl *per-se* had beneficial effects. Table 3 suggests that the same factors that probably led to a marked reduction in the rate of inflation in 1992-93 – such as the persistent fiscal discipline, the relatively high (and persistent) rate of unemployment, and the reduction in foreign inflation – could well account for some of our findings.

Table 3. Israel: macroeconomic indicators

	1989	1990	1991	1992	1993
Domestic inflation (CPI) (%)	20.7	17.6	18.0	9.4	11.2
Foreign inflation (basket weighted WPI) (%)	3.1	3.8	-0.3	1.2	-0.7
Domestic budget deficit (as a % of GDP)	4.9	3.9	5.6	4.0	3.0
Money growth (%)	36.9	30.0	19.1	30.2	27.5
Unemployment rate (%)	8.9	9.6	10.6	11.2	10.0
Real wage per employee post - business sector (rate of change) (%)	-1.6	-1.3	-5.2	1.8	-0.1
Change in labor productivity (%)	0.5	4.0	2.2	0.4	...
Change in real wage per unit of output (%)	-2.1	-5.1	-7.3	1.4	...
Current account deficit(-), (as a % of GDP)	1.6	2.1	-0.9	0.3	...
Foreign currency reserves, end of year (billions of $)	5.3	6.3	6.3	5.1	7.4

Source: The Bank of Israel, Annual Report - 1989, 1990, 1991, 1992.

5. Additional Evidence: Chile and Mexico

5.1 Background

5.1.1 Chile

As in Israel, the evolution of Chile's exchange rate system is closely related to efforts to reduce and stabilize the rate of inflation. During Chile's macroeconomic stabilization of 1973 the government adopted a set of orthodox policy measures consisting mainly of tight fiscal and monetary policies. The next stage was exchange-rate-based stabilization. The authorities first established a *tablita*, i.e., a preannounced schedule of nominal depreciation. In 1979 they shifted to a fixed exchange rate against the US dollar which was maintained until 1982. The fixed exchange rate, along with the accompanying policies, resulted in a considerably lower rate of inflation, but it was also associated with a sharp overvaluation of the domestic currency. The fixed exchange rate was abandoned in 1982, and considerably depreciated, when new policies and reforms were adopted. The crawling band was adopted in 1985.

Chile's exchange rate is determined in an intra-bank market. It is allowed to fluctuate within a band around a reference rate set by the Banco Central (see Banco Central de Chile, 1991; and French-Davis and Vial 1990, for details and additional references). Following two steep devaluations in 1985, the authorities adopted a policy of daily adjustments in the Peso/US Dollar reference exchange rate. At the start of each month, the authorities announce the size of the daily exchange rate adjustments for that month, based on the estimated difference between domestic inflation in the previous month and a forecast of foreign inflation. The width of the band was 2% around the central parity in the initial phase, increased to 3% in January 1988, and further widened to 5% in June 1989. On January 23, 1992 there was a discrete revaluation of

5% in the central parity and the band's width was increased to 10% around the reference rate. From July 6, 1992 the band policy is defined in terms of a basket of foreign currencies (as in Israel) and not in relation to the US dollar as in the earlier periods. Accordingly, the analysis that follows divides the sample into five sub-periods.

5.1.2 Mexico

The adoption of an exchange rate band in Mexico in November 1991 is another case of a policy shift toward increased exchange rate flexibility some time after a major disinflation has been achieved. The Mexican economy was at the edge of a major crisis in the mid-eighties, with growing inflation (143% in 1987), a high and rising public sector external debt, and limited access to international capital markets. The Economic Solidarity Pact, signed in December 1987, aimed at breaking the inflationary spiral. The Pacto consisted of a social/economic accord between workers, government, and entrepreneurs and it was supported by deep fiscal and monetary adjustments, as well as major structural reforms. These changes resulted in sharp disinflation: 18.8% in 1991, 11.9% in 1992 (i.e., the lowest rate in 17 years), and 9% in 1993. The budget swung from a deficit of 16.1% of GDP in 1987 to a surplus of 0.4% in 1992. The ratio of external debt to GDP fell from 92.5% in 1987 to 24.4% in 1992. Similarly, the ratio of internal debt to GDP was reduced by about 20% of GDP during that period.

Exchange rate policy went through three main phases after stabilization. First, after an initial devaluation of 38.9%, the Pacto established a fixed Peso/US dollar rate. Second, the authorities shifted toward increased flexibility by adopting a preannounced crawling peg after January 1989: the Peso was allowed to depreciate by 1 Peso per day in 1989, 80 cents per day in 1990, and 40 cents per day in 1991. Third, an exchange rate band was adopted on November 11, 1991.

Mexico's band differs from those of Israel and Chile in three main respects. First, while the band's ceiling is subject to a daily pre-announced depreciation by a fixed amount, the band's floor remains fixed. Consequently, the width of the band has been increasing with time. Second, the rate of crawl of the band's upper limit is specified in nominal terms, a fixed number of cents per day, rather than in percents. Third, there is no official announcement of a central parity. Only the band's upper and lower limits are officially announced. The authorities also announce, every day before trading begins, their narrow band of intra-marginal intervention for that day.

The band's upper limit was depreciated at the rate of 20 cents per day in 1992. Its total width increased from 1.2% in November 1991 to 4.3% in December 1992. So far there has been one "realignment" of the band's parameters: in October 1992, upon renewal of the Pacto, the rate of crawl of the upper limit was increased to 40 cents per day in order to allow for an annual depreciation of 4.6% in 1993. The band's width reached 8.7% at the end of 1993 – a width that is not very different from the 10% in Israel. Under the October 1993 renewal of the Pacto, the floor of the exchange rate band remains fixed and the ceiling continues to be depreciated 40 cents a day. By the end of 1994 the exchange rate band width will become 14%.

5.2 Exchange rates

5.2.1 Chile

Key indicators for Chile's exchange rate bands are provided in Table 4, and Figure 1 depicts daily observations of the Peso/US Dollar rate from the inception of the crawling band until March 1993. Two salient features arise from Figure 1: (i) there is a marked upward trend in the exchange rate, which is characterised by a sizeable depreciation over the entire period; and (ii) exchange rate fluctuations make full use of

Table 4. Chile: Band characteristics, exchange rate, interest rates, prices and foreign currency reserves

	PERIOD 1	PERIOD 2	PERIOD 3	PERIOD 4	PERIOD 5
Period	Band Width = 2% 1986.01-88.04	Band Width Increased to 3% 1988.05-89.05	Band Width Increased to 5% 1989.06-91.12	Band Width Increased to 10% 1992.01-92.06	Exchange Rate Basket adopted 1992.07-93.06
Band characteristics and the exchange rate using daily data:					
Average mid-band rate (1)	204.0	249.2	323.3	381.6	409.1
Band width +/- (in %)	2	3	5	10	10
Annualized average crawl of mid-rate of the band	22.0	5.3	27.9	13.9	15.4
Average exchange rate (1)	205.4	247.4	316.2	351.8	384.5
Average deviation of exchange rate from mid-band (in %)	0.67	-0.70	-2.22	-7.82	-6.03
Standard deviation from mid-band (in %)	1.24	1.20	4.02	2.07	2.28
Interest rates using weekly data, in percent per month terms:					
Average domestic interest rate (short term deposits)	1.66	1.34	2.28	1.11	1.42
Standard deviation of domestic interest rate	0.47	0.50	0.82	0.41	0.52
Average foreign interest rate (LIBID) (2)	0.49	0.62	0.55	0.31	0.41
Average interest rate differential (2)	1.16	0.72	1.72	0.79	1.00
Annualized average interest rate differential (2)	14.8	9.0	22.7	9.9	12.7
Standard deviation interest rate differential (2)	0.43	0.49	0.80	0.46	0.56

Inflation using monthly data, in percent per month terms:					
Average domestic inflation rate (CPI)	1.35	1.07	1.72	0.52	0.94
Average foreign inflation rate (CPI) (2)	0.24	0.58	0.34	0.25	0.19
Average inflation rate differential (2)	1.10	0.49	1.37	0.27	0.75
Annualized average inflation rate differential (2)	14.1	6.0	17.8	3.3	9.4
Standard deviation of inflation differential (2)	0.54	0.74	0.89	0.72	0.62
Foreign currency reserves (non-gold) using monthly data, in millions of dollars per month terms					
Average change in reserves	6.8	54.7	119.0	211.1	143.2
Standard deviation of change in reserves	128.8	197.7	220.6	226.2	137.2
Real effective exchange rate					
Average real exchange rate (index, 86.01-88.04 avg.=100)	100.0	106.4	108.1	99.4	100.7
Standard deviation of real exchange rate change (in %)	1.6	1.7	2.2	3.2	1.8

Notes: (1) For periods 1-4 the exchange rate vis-a-vis the dollar is shown.
For period 5 the exchange rate vis-a-vis the Chilean currency basket is used.
The base of this index is such that the exchange rate of 1$ on July 1, 92 = the exchange rate of 1 currency basket unit on July 1, 92.
The rate of change of this index equals that of the Peso/$ exchange rate up to June 30, 92 and that of the Peso/basket rate from July 1, 92 onwards.
(2) For periods 1-4 these values are vis-a-vis the U.S. dollar.
For period 5 these values are basket weighted values using the Chilean currency basket weights.

Sources: Banco Central de Chile - Boletin Mensual; International Financial Statistics - IMF.

the band's width. In particular, there were several episodes in which the exchange rate persistently stayed at either the upper or lower limit of the band.

This second point can be illustrated by a particular episode. During the second half of 1989, the exchange rate stayed at the upper limit of the band when the authorities intervened in the foreign exchange market in order to weaken the Peso. The aim was to reduce the demand for imports and preserve external competitiveness that had declined in previous months. The resulting depreciation of 9% in real terms between May 1989 and the end of 1989 was reversed as high domestic real interest rates along with other factors attracted about $1 billion of short term capital inflows in the first half of 1990. The appreciation prompted the central bank to purchase about $4.5 billion of Pesos in 1990 and 1991. The outcome was that, for several years now, the exchange rate has remained very close to the lower limit of the band and yet it depreciates along with the crawling depreciation of the central parity. These persistent pressures toward appreciationhave contributed to the latest official realignment on January 23, 1992 when the reference rate was revalued by 5% while the band's width was enlarged to +/–10%.

Overall, a detailed analysis shows that the Chilean experience partly backs the simple target zone model since most of the time the exchange rate was very close to either the upper or lower limit of the band but also contradicts it since volatility has been higher near the limits (see Helpman, Leiderman and Bufman, 1993).

5.2.2 Mexico

Exchange rate behaviour under the Mexican band is plotted in Figure 1 and basic data are presented in Table 5 (the figure includes also the latest observations for the crawling peg in 1991 that preceded the band). Intervention inside the band is the rule rather than the exception and this is manifested in the daily announcement of an intra-marginal intervention band. It is not surprising, therefore, that the exchange rate has stayed most of the time near the middle of the band. Along with more volatility near the limits, the Mexican experience also contradicts the simple target zone predictions.

Table 5. Mexico: Band characteristics, exchange rate, interest rates, prices and foreign currency reserves

Period	Nov. 11, 91 - Oct. 20, 92	Oct. 21, 92 - June 30, 93
Band characteristics and the exchange rate		
Using daily data (in percents):		
Total band width at:		
Beginning of period	1.15	3.41
End of period	3.41	6.73
Annualized crawl of upper limit of band	2.40	4.70
Annualized crawl of calculated mid-band	1.20	2.35
Average exchange rate (Peso/dollar)	3.087	3.113
Average deviation of exchange rate from calculated mid-band	0.02	-0.51
Standard deviation from calculated mid-band	0.58	0.62
Average deviation from upper bound	-1.10	-2.95
Standard deviation from upper bound	0.57	1.02
Interest rates		
Using weekly data, in percent per month terms:		
Average domestic interest rate (28 day CETES T-bill)	1.19	1.29
Standard deviation of domestic interest rate	0.15	0.10
Average foreign interest rate (LIBID, U.S. dollar)	0.31	0.25
Average interest differential (Mexico-U.S.)	0.88	1.04
Annualized average interest differential	11.1	13.2
Standard deviation of interest rate differential	0.18	0.08
Inflation		
Using monthly data, in percent per month terms:		
Average domestic inflation rate	1.07	0.73
Average U.S. inflation rate (CPI)	0.24	0.20
Average inflation differential	0.83	0.53
Annualized average inflation differential	10.4	6.5
Standard deviation of inflation differential	0.69	0.37
Foreign currency reserves (non-gold); Using monthly data, in millions of dollars per month terms:		
Average change in reserves	108	176
Standard deviation of change in reserves	1.028	148
Real effective exchange rate:		
Average real exchange rate (index, 91.11-92.10 avg.=100)	100.0	94.2
Standard deviation of real exchange rate change (in %)	0.9	1.0

Source: Banco de Mexico; International Financial Statistics - IMF

5.3 Interest rate differentials

5.3.1 Chile

Differentials based on creditory nominal interest rates (on deposits for 30 to 89 days) in Chile are plotted in Figure 2. Except for the first half of 1990, these rates did not exhibit a marked trend, but rather fluctuated around a relatively constant mean with a relatively stable degree of volatility (means and standard deviations are presented in Table 4). The sharp rise in rates in the first half of 1990 was mainly due to two factors: (i) a contractionary monetary policy aimed at reducing the very rapid expansion of aggregate demand; and (ii) the sterilization of sizeable capital inflows.

5.3.2 Mexico

The interest rate differential in Figure 2 exhibits long cycles since the adoption of the band: it decreased until the first quarter of 1992, went on a strong upward trend which reached a peak with the renewal of the *Pacto* and since then has moved down. The amplitude of these fluctuations is quite large: from a low of about 6.5% in early 1992 to a high of about 16% in October 1992. This pattern confirms the important role of devaluation expectations and of anticipations of a *Pacto* renewal.

Overall, both Chile and Mexico contradict the basic model's predictions since the interest rate differential is higher at the margins and there is no systematic relation between the level of the interest rate differential and the deviation of the exchange rate from mid-band.

5.4 The real exchange rate and inflation[8]

5.4.1 Chile

The real effective exchange rate of the Chilean Peso is plotted in Figure 5. From 1985 to 1988 the crawling band regime was associated with a considerable real effective depreciation. From 1988 to 1992, in contrast, there was a weak trend of real appreciation as the consequence of large and persistent capital inflows. This pattern of capital inflows and real exchange rate appreciation is not unique to Chile as documented in Calvo, Leiderman and Reinhart (1993). In order to reduce the scope for excessive short-term capital inflows in the form of domestic borrowing abroad, the central bank imposed on June 1991 a capital import tax of 20% that applies to loans with maturity of less than one year. The tax was raised to 30% in May 1992. The real effective exchange rate returned in the first quarter of 1993 to the level that prevailed in early 1987, which was rather depreciated relative to the early 1980s. Overall, the Chilean band allowed for considerable fluctuations in the real exchange rate.

The economy's performance since the inception of the crawling band (and the adoption of other policies) has been impressive. During the seven years 1986-1992 GDP grew at more than 6% per year, inflation averaged 16% per year (see Figure 11), unemployment fell from 12% of the labour force in late 1985 to less than 6% in 1992, non-copper exports rose by about 14% per year in volume, and there was a sharp reduction in the ratio of external debt to exports. Underlying these developments was a supportive budget with near fiscal balance (the budget deficit was only about 1% of GDP between 1985 and 1992).

---

8 At variance with Israel, we do not discuss here the behaviour of foreign exchange reserves because it was primarily determined by the authorities' intervention in the face of capital inflows from abroad and not so much by considerations having to do with the band *per se*.

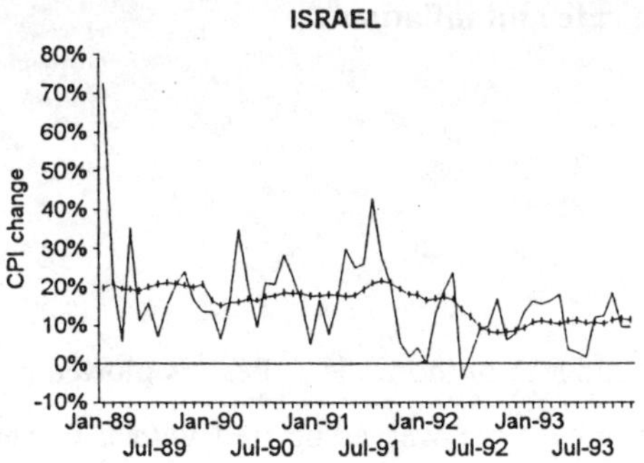

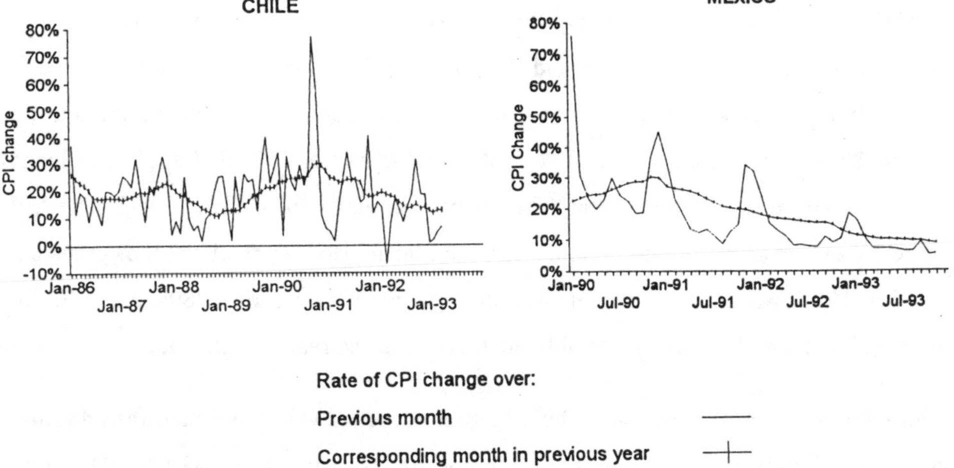

Figure 11. Rate of Inflation (annualized terms)

5.4.2 Mexico

The marked reduction in the rate of inflation in Mexico since 1990 shown in Figure 11 happened in spite of increased flexibility of the exchange rate policy and of the possibility that this flexibility would lead to a weaker role of the exchange rate as an inflation-expectations anchor. At the same time, the considerable real appreciation of the Peso of about 20% in less than two years after the implementation of the band, shown in Figure 5 and in Table 5 has given rise to mounting pressures on policy-makers to increase the rate of crawl of the exchange rate.

5.5 Devaluation expectations

As for Israel, we have estimated the expectation of devaluations for Chile and Mexico. The results are reported in Appendix A, Tables A1 and A2, and plotted in Figure 6.[9] Clearly devaluation expectations rise as the exchange rate moves toward the upper limit of the band. Again we find that interest differentials do not match expected devaluations. In Chile, there were marked expectations of revaluation for quite some time before revaluation actually took place, e.g. in January 1992, despite the fact that no major change occurred then to the interest rate differential. We also find (Table A2) that increases in economic activity, in foreign exchange reserves, and in the real exchange rate (i.e., real depreciation) are associated with reductions in expected devaluations, though these effects are imprecisely estimated.

6. A Comparison and Policy Implications

From comparison of the experience of Chile, Israel and Mexico we draw the five main conclusions.

First, crawling bands *per-se* do not eradicate expected devaluations. There always exist circumstances in which unexpected shocks or other factors lead to a policy actions that renege on the band's commitment. In all three countries under review there have been some waves of speculative foreign exchange purchases (or sales) as well as discrete realignments of the whole band (as opposed to the built-in crawl). However,

---

9 We suggest caution in interpreting Chile's estimated expected devaluation because of the low explanatory power of the underlying regression.

the case of Israel shows that the shift from a fixed- to a crawling-band may reduce realignments uncertainty and may be associated with a reduction in the volatility of the interest rate differential, at least when inflation is high. Moreover, when the realignments have a transparent objective and do not provoke sizeable capital gains, the regime's credibility is not seriously damaged.

Second, exchange rate bands are compatible with wide varieties of real exchange rate experiences. In Mexico, the crawling band was associated with a marked real exchange rate appreciation in 1992-93, Chile underwent a sharp real depreciation during the first years of its crawling band, and in Israel the real exchange rate first remained stable and then depreciated. These differences correspond to alternative methods of setting the rate of crawl. In Israel the authorities announce the daily crawl for the next year based on the difference between their inflation target and a forecast of foreign inflation. In Chile the authorities announce each month the planned daily rate of depreciation of the central parity based on the difference between inflation in the previous month and a forecast of world inflation. Thus, if inflation accelerates in month t, real appreciation will be larger in Israel than in Chile where the exchange rate is more likely to be accommodative in month $t + 1$. The counterpart is that inflation shocks are more likely to persist in Chile than in Israel. Mexico is similar to Israel in that the exchange rate target is pre-announced on an annual basis, except that this target applies only to the band's upper limit. In practice, Mexican authorities have devalued at a slower pace than the inflation differential, hence the real appreciation.

Third, despite the considerable width of the bands under study, only in Chile was the exchange rate allowed to widely fluctuate. Israel and Mexico conducted extensive intra-marginal intervention which kept the exchange rate within an inner band narrower than the official band.[10] Such interventions are often explained by the risk of destabilizing expectations of inflation and devaluation as the exchange rate approaches

---

[10] The standard deviation for Chile is about twice the size of that for Israel, which in turn is about three times the level of Mexico's (see Tables 1, 3 and 5).

its upper limit. To assess this issue, we use our earlier estimates of devaluation expectations to simulate the effects of movements of the exchange rate within the band.[11] The simulated paths are shown in Figure 12. In Israel and Mexico we observe a rapid and strong response of expected realignments to exchange rate deprecations within the band. On the other hand, in Chile such an effect is absent. Thus, it is precisely those countries where exchange rate movements appear to have strong impacts on realignment expectations that intra-marginal interventions have been actively used. However, there could be a problem of causality here. It may well be that expectations are relatively more destabilizing in Israel and Mexico than in Chile because of agents' knowledge of the authorities' preference for exchange rates near the central parity.

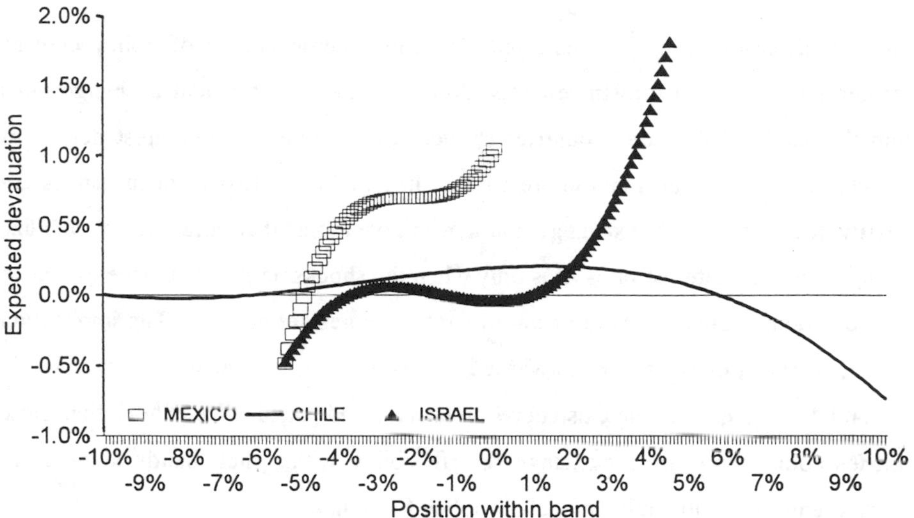

Figure 12. Expected devaluation as a function of the exchange rate's position within the band

[11] Specifically, we use the estimated coefficients on the *x*-variables in Table A1, assuming all else constant, and plot the calculated expected devaluations for hypothetically feasible values for *x* depending on each country's band characteristics.

Note: x_t is defined as the deviation of the exchange rate from central parity. Y_t is defined as the deviation of the exchange rate from the upper limit band. Based on equation (3) and parameter estimates shown in Table A1 in Appendix A.

Fourth, in the three countries the shift toward more flexible exchange rate regimes, under a relatively tight fiscal discipline, was not associated with a rise in inflation. On the contrary, the rate of inflation exhibits a downward trend in recent periods, and has reached single-digit figures in Israel and Mexico. Moreover, in Israel the shift from fixed- to crawling-bands was associated with a reduction in market-based inflation expectations and in the passthrough from exchange rates to prices of traded goods. When there is considerable uncertainty about the exact trend of disinflation, it may be useful to have a band flexible enough to accommodate for various low-inflation outcomes, such as in Mexico.

Finally, in all cases bands are sustained by various combinations of policy choices regarding movements in foreign reserves, domestic interest rates, and exchange rates within the band. Of the three countries studied, Chile exhibits the greatest degree of flexibility in exchange rates and interest rates. In Israel and Mexico, disturbances are primarily met by foreign exchange market interventions that attempt to stabilize exchange rates and interest rates. It is only when the shocks persist that large exchange rate fluctuations within the band or interest rate changes are allowed. The implication is that monetary policy has been awarded a very limited degree of independence in Israel and Mexico despite the existence of relatively wide bands. We believe that these countries could allow more exchange rate flexibility within their bands in order to provide themselves with added monetary policy flexibility.

Appendix A. Methodology Used to Estimate Realignment Expectations

At each point in time, the log of the spot exchange rate e_t can be expressed as the sum of two components: the log of the central parity c_t and the log of the deviation of the exchange rate from the central parity x_t; i.e., $e_t = x_t + c_t$. Accordingly, $\Delta e_{t+1} = \Delta x_{t+1} + \Delta c_{t+1}$. Taking expectations of both sides of this equation conditional on time t information yields an expression for the expected rate of exchange rate depreciation:

$$E_t \Delta e_{t+1} = E_t \Delta x_{t+1} + E_t \Delta c_{t+1} \tag{1}$$

That is, the expected rate of depreciation equals the expected rate of depreciation within the band $E_t \Delta x_{t+1}$ plus the expected rate of realignment $E_t \Delta c_{t+1}$. Now assume that uncovered interest parity holds and that the foreign exchange risk premium is negligible. Then the left-hand side of (1) equals the interest rate differential $(i_t - i_t^*)$. In the case that the authorities pre-announce a rate of crawl for the central parity for a given time period, this built-in expected adjustment is included in the second term on the right-hand side of (1) and it will be denoted by $E_t \Delta c_{t+1}^w$ (where 'w' stands for within the present regime). And in the presence of a fixed-central-parity band this term is equal to zero. Thus, the method is general enough to adjust comparisons across various bands for built-in differences in their rates of crawl. We can now subtract from the interest rate differential both the expected rate of depreciation within the band and the expected crawl of the central parity within the existing regime in order to obtain a measure of the expected rate of realignment:

$$E_t(z_{t+1} - z_t) = (i_t - i_t^*) - E_t \Delta e_{t+1} - E_t \Delta c_{t+1}^w \tag{2}$$

The first term on the right-hand side of (2) can be measured directly. For the last term, it is reasonable to rely on the rate of crawl announced by the authorities. This leaves the term for the expected depreciation within the band, which is unobservable.

Accordingly, in order to obtain econometric-based time series of this measure and thereby of expected realignments, we use estimates of the following projection of the left-hand side variable on a set of information variables:[12]

$$E_t(z_{t+1} - z_t) = \sum_{j=1}^{n} \beta_{0,j} d_j + \beta_1 x_t + \beta_2 x_t^2 + \beta_3 x_t^3 + \beta_4 (z_t - z_{t-1}) \tag{3}$$

where d_j is a dummy for 'regime j' defined as a period j between realignments or any other changes in the parameters of the band. These equations are estimated by least squares with the covariance matrix corrected for heteroskedasticity.

Table A1 presents the various parameter estimates of equation (3) using weekly data for Israel and Mexico, and daily data for Chile.[13] In the case of Israel; based on preliminary results, the number of dummy variables was reduced from eight to five: the first dummy is for bands 1 and 2; the next three dummy variables are for bands 3-5; and the last dummy variable is for bands 6 to 8. For Chile, the sample period includes four band sub-periods which differ in the width of the band. For Mexico, the sample period includes two regimes: from the initiation of the band in November 1991 until the renewal of the *Pacto* in October 1992, and from this date to the present.[14]

The estimated parameters indicate that there is a positive and significant role of nonlinearities in the exchange rate's deviation from mid-band in accounting for devaluation expectations. As the exchange rate rises from the mid-band toward the upper limit this has a more-than-proportional impact on devaluation expectations. In

---

[12] Svensson (1992) provides the rationale for including non-linear x-terms as explanatory variables in equation of this type.

[13] As in Svensson (1992), data corresponding to realignment dates were not included in the regressions.

[14] Because of the asymmetric nature of the Mexican band, equation (3) was slightly modified and the variable x (i.e. the percentage deviation of the exchange rate from the central parity) was replaced by the deviation of the exchange rate from the band's upper limit. This enables us, by construction, to capture expectations of devaluation due to both change in the central parity rate and in the width of the band.

addition, lagged devaluation expectations have positive and significant explanatory power for current devaluation expectations, a finding which could correspond to a 'Peso problem'.

Table A1. Expected devaluation (estimates of equation (3))

$$E_t(z_{t+1}-z_t)=\sum_{j=1}^{n}\beta_{0,j}d_j+\beta_1 x_t+\beta_2 x_t^2+\beta_3 x_t^3+\beta_4(z_t-z_{t-1})$$

	ISRAEL		CHILE		MEXICO	
	Parameter estimate	Standard error	Parameter estimate	Standard error	Parameter estimate	Standard error
β_{01}	-0.0006	0.0006	0.0001	0.0001	0.0042	0.0011
β_{02}	-0.0035	0.0011	0.0005	0.0002	0.0063	0.0013
β_{03}	0.0043	0.0019	0.0016	0.0006	-	-
β_{04}	-0.0004	0.0008	0.0030	0.0011	-	-
β_{05}	-0.0006	0.0005	-	-	-	-
β_1	0.0285	0.0278	0.0192	0.0056	0.4891	0.2514
β_2	4.3654	0.9899	-0.7310	0.2560	22.657	14.095
β_3	108.03	25.871	-6.3560	2.3114	349.32	217.68
β_4	0.3646	0.0627	-0.0280	0.1024	0.1797	0.1033
R^2	0.22		0.02		0.16	
D.W.	2.07		1.98		2.01	
N	237 (89.01-93.12)		1794 (86.01-93.03)		84 (91.11-93.06)	
σ	0.0044		0.0037		0.0024	

Note: Weekly data used for Israel and Mexico, daily data used for Chile. x_t is defined as the deviation of the exchange rate rom central parity. In the case of Mexico, x_t is replaced by y_t which is defined as the deviation of the exchange rate from the upper bound of the band.

In order to explore the role of macroeconomic indicators as explanatory variables for expected realignment, we expanded the projection in equation (3) to include the rate of change of the real exchange rate, the rate of change in economic activity, and the monthly change in foreign currency reserves. The expanded equation is given by:

$$E_t(z_{t+1}-z_t)=\sum_{j=1}^{n}\beta_{0,j}d_j+\beta_1 x_t+\beta_2 x_t^2+\beta_3 x_t^3+\beta_4(z_t-z_{t-1})$$
$$+\beta_5(Y_{t-1}-Y_{t-2})+\beta_6(R_{t-1}-R_{t-2})+\beta_7(RER_{t-1}-RER_{t-2}) \quad (4)$$

where Y is the log of an index of economic activity, R is non-gold foreign currency reserves (in millions of dollars), and RER is the log of the real effective exchange rate. Estimates of this equation based on monthly data are reported in Table A2.

Table A2. Macroeconomic variables and expected devaluation (estimates of equation (4))

	ISRAEL		CHILE	
	Parameter estimate	Standard error	Parameter estimate	Standard error
β_{01}	-0.0016	0.0035	0.0017	0.0022
β_{02}	0.0034	0.0058	0.0039	0.0039
β_{03}	0.0447	0.0175	0.0201	0.0056
β_{04}	0.0025	0.0055	0.0281	0.0114
β_{05}	0.0032	0.0034	-	-
β_1	-0.5688	0.2211	0.1520	0.0844
β_2	2.8049	6.4980	-6.2359	2.4530
β_3	672.43	211.64	-39.317	30.267
β_4	-0.6214	0.4031	0.1839	0.1548
β_5	-0.4683	0.2193	-0.0216	0.0155
β_6	-6.6E-6	3.9E-6	-6.4E-7	7.8E-6
β_7	-0.7243	0.4692	-0.1001	0.0680
R^2	0.67		0.32	
$D.W.$	1.50		2.03	
N	33 (89.01-93.06)		77 (86.01-93.03)	
σ	0.008		0.011	

Note: The expanded equation is as follows:

$$E_t(z_{t+1}-z_t)=\sum_{j=1}^{n}\beta_{0,j}d_j+\beta_1 x_t+\beta_2 x_t^2+\beta_3 x_t^3+\beta_4(z_t-z_{t-1})+\beta_5(Y_{t-1}-Y_{t-2})$$
$$+\beta_6(R_{t-1}-R_{t-2})+\beta_7(RER_t-RER_{t-1})$$

Where Y_t is the logarithm of an index of economic activity, R is non-gold foreign currency reserves (millions of dollars) and *RER* is the log of the real effective exchange rate. In the case of Israel, Y_t is the log of the Bank of Israel state of the economy index. In the case of Chile the activity variable used is the log of the industrial production index and the macroeconomic variables were lagged one period beyond that shown in equation (6). For both countries monthly data were used in the estimation of the equation.

Appendix B. Quantitative Indicators of Reduced Volatility in the Crawling Band Period

We present here the tests used in Section 4.

B1. Interest rate differential

A first series is based on the time series procedure employed by Schwert (1989), which is a generalisation of a rolling standard deviation estimator (see e.g. Fama, 1976, for a similar estimator) and is similar to the autoregressive-conditional-heteroskedasticity (ARCH) model of Engle (1982). Using this method, an eight-week long rolling conditional standard deviation was constructed. The rolling conditional standard deviation was then regressed on a constant and a dummy variable for the crawling band period (using weekly data). The regression results are:

$$IDIF_t = \underset{(26.290)}{0.005} - \underset{(5.697)}{0.002}\, DCRAWL_t$$

(figures in parenthesis are t-statistics),
$R^2 = 0.12$; $n = 245$; S.E. of regression = 0.0024

The parameter of *DCRAWL* has a significant negative sign thus indicating a significant reduction in interest rate differential volatility in the crawling band period.

B2. Exchange rate deviation from mid-band

We use Schwert's (1989) method on the basis of daily data for exchange rates. A one-month rolling conditional standard deviation was regressed on a constant and a dummy variable for the crawling band period. The regression results are:

$$x_t = 0.002 - 0.0008\, DCRAWL_t$$
$$(47.485)\ (16.553)$$

(figures in parenthesis are t-statistics),

$R^2 = 0.16$; $n = 1218$; S.E. of regression = 0.0009

The parameter of *DCRAWL* has a significant negative sign thus indicating a significant reduction in exchange rate volatility in the crawling band period.

B3. Realignment expectations

The expected realignment series that was estimated in a previous stage (see Appendix A) was regressed on a constant and a dummy variable for the crawling band period (using weekly data). The regression results are:

$$EC_t = -9.610^{-5} - 0.0006\, DCRAWL_t$$
$$(0.500)\quad (2.091)$$

$R^2 = 0.02$; $n = 245$; S.E. of regression = 0.0023

The parameter of *DCRAWL* has a significant negative sign thus indicating a significant reduction in realignment expectations in the crawling band period. Table 2 provides information as to the proportion of observations with expected realignment values significantly higher than zero. It appears that this proportion has decreased in the crawling band period in comparison to that of the previous band regime.

A rolling conditional standard deviation of expected realignment was regressed on a constant and a dummy variable for the crawling band period. The regression results are:

$$SDEC_t = 0.001 \ - \ 0.0004\, DCRAWL_t$$
$$(20.129) \quad (4.097)$$

$R^2 = 0.12$; $n = 124$; S.E. of regression = 0.0005

The parameter of *DCRAWL* has a significant negative sign thus indicating a significant reduction in realignment expectation volatility in the crawling band period.

B4. Black market exchange rate premium

The black market premium was regressed on a constant and a dummy variable for the crawling band period (using monthly average data). The regression results are:

$$BMKT_t = 0.045 \ - \ 0.034\, DCRAWL_t$$
$$(10.555) \quad (5.181)$$

$R^2 = 0.31$; $n = 62$; S.E. of regression = 0.026

The parameter of *DCRAWL* has a significant negative sign thus indicating a significant reduction in exchange market premium in the crawling band period.

B5. Kolmogorov-Smirnov tests

The Kolmogorov-Smirnov test is used to detect shifts in the distributions of the variables of interest – here: the exchange rate (measured in terms of deviation of actual from central parity rates), the interest differential and the real exchange rate – before and after the presumed regime change. The test applies to distributions whose exact form is not known and can not be parametrized. Samples from two independently distributed populations of a variable x are characterised by the (unknown) cumulative density functions $H(x)$ and $J(x)$. The functions H and J are estimated from the empirical distribution functions $H_n(x)$ and $J_m(x)$, where m and n are the numbers of observations in the samples. The Kolmogorov-Smirnov statistic for testing the null hypothesis that $H = J$ is given by $D = \max_x |H_n(x) - J_m(x)|$, and the critical value for the 0.01 significance level is approximated by $1.63[(n+m)/nm]^{0.5}$.

The results are shown in Table B1. They always reject the null that the distributions have remained unchanged.

B6. Price equations

Another approach is the estimation of a price equation with 12 monthly dummy variables and several lags of the rate of exchange rate change and of rate of foreign *WPI* change. Dummy variables for the crawling band period are included as well in the regression in order to quantify the changes in the equation during the crawling band period. The main results are as follows. First, it appears that pass-through from the exchange rate to traded prices is rapid and is completed within two months from the change in the exchange rate. The degree of pass-through for the 1989-1991 period is within the interval 0.15 to 0.39 (i.e. 15% to 39% of the changes in the exchange rate are translated to traded goods prices change), for the period 1991-1993 the interval is -0.19 to 0.22. Based on an F-test, the hypothesis that the decrease in the degree of pass-through is not significant is rejected with a high degree of confidence (97.3%). Also, the hypothesis that the contribution of wages to the explanation of traded goods price change is rejected.

Table B1. Israel: tests for changes in band characteristics - crawling band period against horizontal band period

<A>

Tests for differences in mean values, unweighted variances and distributions of the deviations of the exchange rate from central parity

Difference in bands 6-8 in comparison to bands 1-5		Statistically significant?
Means:	0.039%	No
Unweighted variance:	-3.52E-04	Yes
Distribution:	0.20	Yes
(Kolomogorov-Smirnov statistic shown)		

<B>

Tests for differences in mean values and unweighted variance changes of the interest rate differential

Difference in bands 6-8 in comparison to bands 1-5		Statistically significant?
Means:	-0.002%	No
Unweighted variance:	-2.35E-07	Yes

<C>

Tests for differences in mean values, unweighted variances and distributions of the real exchange rate

Difference in bands 6-8 in comparison to bands 1-5		Statistically significant?
Mean of real exchange rate:	2,24%	Yes
Unweighted variance of real exchange rate change:	-8.53E-05	Yes
Distribution of real exchange rate change:	0.00	Yes
(Kolomogorov-Smirnov statistic shown)		

Note: Differences are shown as bands 6-8 less bands 1-5.

Appendix C. Description of Data Used in the Econometric Applications

C1. Israel

Domestic interest rate – weekly observations of the 1-week monetary auction rate for the period between the first week of 1989 and the last week of 1993 (260 weekly observations). *Source:* Bank of Israel data base.

Foreign interest rate – daily observation of Eurocurrency 1-month rates, weighted using Israel's effective currency basket weights and compounded into weekly averages (the official weights of the basket are: 0.6 dollars, 0.4177 DMs, 0.067 UK pounds and 7.7 Yen). *Source:* DRI data base.

Exchange rate data – daily data of the exchange rate of the NIS against the currency basket and the exchange rate band limits and mid-band rate were used. *Source:* Bank of Israel data base.

Black market exchange rate data is based on daily observations. *Source:* Bank of Israel data base.

Currency option premiums or those of 3-month "at the money" options written and auctioned by the Bank of Israel. *Source:* Bank of Israel data base.

C2. Chile

Domestic interest rate – daily observation of the 30-89 day non-indexed deposit rate for the period January 2nd, 1986 to June 28th, 1993.

Foreign interest rate – daily observation of Eurocurrency 1-month rates. For the currency basket period (July, 1992 onwards) a basket weighted interest rate was constructed using the effective currency basket weights. For the period prior to the currency basket, the dollar Eurocurrency rate was used. *Source:* DRI data base.

Exchange rate data – daily data of the exchange rate of the Peso against the U.S. dollar for the period up to June 30th, 1992 and weighted basket rate for the period of July 1, 1992 onwards (the official weights of the basket are: 0.3497 dollars, 0.3182 DMs and 17.45 Yen). Daily exchange rate band limits and mid-band rate were used. *Source:* Boletin Mensual – Banco Central de Chile.

C3. Mexico

Domestic interest rate – weekly observations of the 28-day CETES non-indexed T-Bill auction rate for the period between the 46th week of 1989 and the 26th week of 1993 (86 weekly observations). *Source:* Banco de Mexico.

Foreign interest rate – daily observation of dollar Eurocurrency 1-month rates compounded into weekly averages. *Source:* DRI data base.

Exchange rate data – daily data of the exchange rate of the Peso against the dollar and the exchange rate band limits were used to compute weekly averages. *Source:* Banco de Mexico.

References

Argy, Victor, and Paul De Grauwe (eds.) (1990), *"Choosing an Exchange Rate Regime – The Challenge for Smaller Industrial Countries"*, International Monetary Fund.

Banco Central de Chile (1991), *"Evolucion de la Economia en 1991 y Perspectivas Para 1992"*.

Banco de Mexico (1993), *"The Mexican Economy 1993"*, Mexico.

Bertola, Giuseppe, and Ricardo J. Caballero (1992), "Target Zones and Realignments", *American Economic Review* 82, June, pp. 520-536.

Bruno, Michael (1993), *"Crisis, Stabilization and Economic Reform: Therapy by Consensus"*, Oxford University Press, Oxford.

Calvo, Guillermo A., Leiderman, Leonardo, and Carmen M. Reinhart (1993), "Capital Inflows and Real Exchange Rate Appreciation in Latin America", *IMF Staff Papers* 40, March, pp. 108-151.

Cukierman, Alex, Kiguel, Miguel, and Leonardo Leiderman (1994), "Choosing the Width of Exchange Rate Bands: Credibility vs. Flexibility", Discussion Paper No. 907, Centre for Economic Policy Research, London, 37 – January 1994.

Dornbusch, Rudiger (1992), "PPP Exchange Rate Rules and Macroeconomic Stability", *Journal of Political Economy* 90, pp. 158-165.

Engle, Robert F. (1982), "Autoregressive Conditional Heteroskedasticity with Estimates of the Variance of United Kingdom Inflation", *Econometrica* 50, pp. 987-1007.

Fama, Eugene F. (1976), "Inflation Uncertainty and Expected Returns on Treasury Bills", *Journal of Political Economy* 84, pp. 427-448.

Ffrench-Davis, Ricardo, and Joaquin Vial (1990), "Trade Reforms in Chile: Policy Lessons for the Nineties", Paper presented at the seminar "Latin America: Facing the Challenges of Adjustment and Growth", EDI, The World Bank, Caracas, July.

Helpman, Elhanan, Leiderman, Leonardo, and Gil Bufman (1993), "A New Breed of Exchange Rate Bands: Chile, Israel and Mexico", Discussion Paper No.6-93, The Pinhas Sapir Center for Development, Tel Aviv University, November 1993.

Krugman, Paul R. (1991), "Target Zones and Exchange Rate Dynamics", *Quarterly Journal of Economics* 106, pp. 669-682.

Leiderman, Leonardo (1993), *"Inflation and Disinflation: The Israeli Experiment"*, University of Chicago Press, Chicago.

Lewis, Karen K. (1991), "An Empirical Exploration of Exchange Rate Target Zones: A Comment", Carnegie-Rochester Conference Series on Public Policy 35, pp. 67-78.

Marom, Arie (1992), "The Premium on the Black Market Dollar in Israel", *Bank of Israel Economic Review 66*, pp. 35-50.

Schwert, G. William (1989), "Why Does Stock Market Volatility Change Over Time?", *Journal of Finance* XLIV, pp. 1115-1153.

Svensson, Lars E.O. (1992), "Target Zones and Interest Rate Variability", *Journal of International Economics* 31, pp. 27-54.

Svensson, Lars E.O. (1992), "An Interpretation of Recent Research on Exchange Rate Target Zones", *Journal of Economic Perspectives* 6, Fall, pp. 119-144.

Yariv, Dani (1989), "Estimating Inflation Expectations in Israel", *Bank of Israel Economic Review* 64, pp. 17-36.

Zahler, Roberto M. (1992), "Politica Monetaria en un Contexto de Apertura de la Cuenta de Capitales", Banco Central de Chile, *Boletin Mensual* 771, May, pp. 1169-1180.

The International Transmission of Economic Shocks in a Three-Country World under Mixed Exchange Rates*

Nikolaus K.A. Läufer and
Srinivasa Sundararajan**

Abstract

The international transmission of economic disturbances is analysed in a three-country world where two countries have no macroeconomic impact on a third country but are large enough to influence each other under a system of mixed exchange rates - a system that combines the fixed exchange rates (FERs) among two EC member countries (Germany and France) and the flexible exchange rates (FLERs) towards a third country, the rest of the world (USA). We find that a positive output demand shock originating in Germany or France has a positive effect on domestic output, but, due to a special third country effect, is likely to produce a *contractionary* impact on foreign output (negative transmission) while the total effect on the world economy is *expansionary*. Money supply shocks in either Germany or France have identical effects on the output of the two countries. The FLER component of the MER regime serves as an important tool for dampening the impact of US shocks on the output of the EC.

---

* This chapter was first published in *Journal of International Money & Finance*, Vol. 13, No. 4, 1994 and is reproduced here with the permission of Butterworth-Heinemann, Oxford, UK.

** Comments by Axel Börsch-Supan and Bernhard Eckwert are gratefully acknowledged.

1. Introduction

Modern stochastic macroeconomic theory[1] asserts that economic disturbances and policies are, in general, transmitted across countries, although the channels of transmission and the exact way in which economies respond to foreign shocks - whether the transmission is positive or negative - may depend on the type of exchange rate regime, the type of shock and the degree of capital mobility. Of particular concern has also been the extent to which an economy is insulated from foreign disturbances under a flexible exchange rate (FLER) regime. But researchers have preferred to analyse the transmission of real and monetary shocks[2] in pure exchange rate regimes, either the FER or the FLER regime.

Long before the inception of the current system of managed exchange rates, a number of studies with open economy macroeconomic models suggested that transmission effects may be smaller under FLERs than under FERs, given the greater insulation properties of the former.[3] These results suggest that the small transmission effects found in previous research for the OECD area depend largely on the existence of FLERs among the countries of this region. One is also led to suspect that the degree of interdependence and the transmission of economic shocks may be much larger among the countries forming the European Monetary System (EMS). The EMS region is, in fact, characterised by a very high degree of openness, pegged exchange rates and economic integration between the member countries. But the EMS is really a system of mixed exchange rates (MERs) - a system that combines

---

1 Financial support by the Deutsche Forschungsgemeinschaft through the Sonderforschungsbereich 178 „Internationalisierung der Wirtschaft" is gratefully acknowledged.

2 The interested readers are referred to Laursen and Metzler (1950), Branson and Rotemberg (1980), Cox (1980), Schmid (1982), Corden and Turnvosky (1983) and Argy and Salop (1983) for studies of negative transmission of foreign monetary disturbances.

3 See Friedman (1953), Meade (1950), Mundell (1963, 1968), Dornbusch (1976), Mussa (1977), Turnovsky and Kingston (1977), Turnovsky (1981), Marston (1984), Argy et al. (1989), and Läufer and Sundararajan (= LS) (1992).

FERs among EC member countries and FLERs towards the rest of the world, especially the USA - a feature that so far has not been analyzed sufficiently.

A review of the literature clearly reveals that studies of MER regimes are conspicuously rare. In particular, because of the lacuna that exists in the literature concerning the international transmission of real and monetary shocks under MERs, the purpose of the present paper is to extend LS's (1992) analysis of a three-country world in order to examine the domestic impact and the international transmission of real and monetary shocks. Each of these disturbances has potential effects that depend on several factors like the degree of wage indexation, the type of exchange rate regime etc. The model used in this paper differs from other existing three-country models in several aspects. Firstly, we replace Marston's three-country assumption of a small open economy facing two large economies on which it has no impact. Instead, we assume that two countries have no macroeconomic impact on a third country, but are large enough to influence each other. Secondly, we also remove Marston's (1984) worrisome asymmetry between the degrees of wage indexation at home and abroad, as suggested by Kenen (1984) in his comments on Marston's model.[4] Thirdly, we extend Marston's supply side specification and thus avoid the fixed price assumptions of the MER analysis of Levin (1983). Fourthly, we distinguish between real and nominal interest rates and allow for expected changes of the flexible exchange rates. Thus we avoid money illusion and static exchange rate expectations and the exogeneity of the interest rate built into the MER analyses of Feuerstein and Siebke (1990) and Feuerstein (1992).

Section II presents our model, section III derives comparative static solutions for output, producer prices, consumer prices, exchange rates, reserve stocks, and nominal and real interest rates under MERs, and sections IV, V and VI discuss the analytical results. In particular, we clarify the possibility of a *contractionary* impact

---

[4] See Kenen (1984), p. 441.

of positive domestic output demand (or fiscal) shocks on the foreign output (negative international transmission).

In our three-country world, we discover an additional channel by which a negative international transmission of real shocks may occur. The additional channel is given by the FLERs between the two small countries and the rest of the world. A positive real shock in one of the two countries raises the interest rate in both small countries and causes an appreciation of the exchange rates with respect to the large third country. In both small countries, the appreciation will reduce exports to, and increase imports from country *c*, and thus reduce the demand for their output. With the additional channel, a negative transmission from one (small) country to the other (small) country is now much more likely than in Mundell's two-country world where a relatively high interest elasticity of investment demand is required in the country to which the real shock is transmitted.

2. The Model and its Solution

Consider a world consisting of three countries (*a*, *b* and *c*). For simplicity, we assume that countries *a* and *b* are identical (symmetric). That is, the structural parameters in the output demand and supply functions, and in the financial equations are the same for both countries. We further assume that countries *a* and *b* have no macroeconomic impact on country *c* but are large enough to influence each other. Thus the behaviour of country *c* is not modelled explicitly. Following LS's (1992) structure, the model of each country consists of three basic equations: aggregate demand and supply equations for the output produced in a country, and an equation describing equilibrium in financial behaviour. Perfect substitutability is assumed for the non-money assets of all three countries.

2.1 The Model

The model is set out as follows:

Demand for Output

$$Y_t^{id}=\alpha_0+\alpha_1 Y_t^{jd}+\alpha_2 Y_t^c-\alpha_3 r_t^i+\alpha_4\left(e_t^{ij}+P_t^j-P_t^i\right)+\alpha_5\left(e_t^{ic}+P_t^c-P_t^i\right)+u_t^{di}\ , \quad (1)$$

Consumer Price Index

$$q_t^i = h_1 P_t^i + h_2\left(e_t^{ij} + P_t^j\right) + h_3\left(e_t^{ic} + P_t^c\right)\ , \quad (2)$$

Supply of Output

$$Y_t^{is} = \theta\left(P_t^i - \omega_1 E_{t-1} P_t^i\right) - \theta b\left(q_t^i - E_{t-1} q_t^i\right) - \omega_2 E_{t-1} q_t^i + \theta_0\ , \quad (3)$$

Money Markets

$$\left(P_t^i + Y_t^i\right) - \beta_1 n_t^i + \beta_0 = M_t^{fsi} + \overline{M}_t^{dsi} + u_t^{mi}\ , \quad (4)$$

Equilibrium Condition

$$Y_t^{id} = Y_t^{is} = Y_t^i\ , \quad (5)$$

Interest Rate Arbitrage Conditions and Definition of Real Interest Rates

$$n_t^i = n_t^c + \left(E_t e_{t+1}^{ic} - e_t^{ic}\right)\ , \quad (6)$$

$$r_t^i = n_t^i - \left(E_t q_{t+1}^i - q_t^i\right)\ , \quad (7)$$

Triangular Arbitrage Condition

$$e_t^{ic} = e_t^{ij} + e_t^{jc}\ , \quad (8)$$

FER Part of the MER Regime

$$e_t^{ab} = \bar{k}^{ab} \quad , \tag{9}$$

$$M_t^{fsa} + \left(e_t^{ab} + M_t^{fsb}\right) = \bar{f}^{a} \quad , \tag{10}$$

Rest of the World Sector

$$Y_t^c = \overline{Y}^c + u_t^{yc} \quad , \tag{11}$$

$$P_t^c = \overline{P}^c + u_t^{pc} \quad , \tag{12}$$

$$n_t^c = \overline{n}^c + u_t^{nc} \quad , \tag{13}$$

where $i, j \in \{a,b\}$ and $i \neq j$. Apart from interest rates, all variables are in logarithms, where superscripts *d* and *s* denote demand and supply. All coefficients are positive.

Y^k	real output in country *k*.
$q^i \left(E_{t-1} q_t^i\right)$	actual (expected) consumer price index in country *i*, defined as the weighted average of domestic and foreign producer prices.
$M^{di} \left(M^{si}\right)$	money demand (supply) in country *i*.
$M^{fsi} \left(\overline{M}^{dsi}\right)$	foreign (exogenous domestic) component of the money supply in country *i*.
$n^k \left(r^i\right)$	nominal (real) interest rate in country *k* (*i*).
$u^{di} \left(u^{mi}\right)$	output demand (money supply) disturbance in country *i*.
$e^{ik} \left(E_t e_{t+1}^{ik}\right)$	actual (expected) exchange rate of currency *i* per unit of currency *k*.
$P^k \left(E_{t-1} P_t^i\right)$	actual (expected) producer prices in country *k* (*i*).

F^A	exogenous arithmetic average of the reserve (= foreign) components of the money supplies in countries a and b expressed in currency units of country a.
$\bar{f}^a$	$2lnF^A$.
$\bar{k}^{ab}$	exogenous value of the exchange rate between countries a and b.
$\bar{Y}^c\left(\bar{P}^c, \bar{n}^c\right)$	exogenous value of output (producer prices, nominal interest rates) in country c.
$u_t^{yc}\left(u_t^{pc}, u_t^{nc}\right)$	output (price, interest rate) disturbance in country c.
$\alpha_1, \ldots, \alpha_5$	export, real interest rate, and relative price elasticities of output demand (for theoretical details see Marston (1984), pp. 434-37).
β_1	nominal interest rate elasticity of the money demand.
h_k	expenditure weight in country i for country k's good $\left(\sum h_k = 1\right)$.
b	indexation parameter.
λ	elasticity of labour supply with respect to real wages.
$1-\theta'$	exponent of labour in a Cobb-Douglas production function.
θ	$\left(1-\theta'\right)/\theta'$.
θ_0	$\left(1-\theta'\right)\lambda ln\left(1-\theta'\right)/\left(\theta'\lambda+1\right)$.
ω	$1/\left(\theta'\lambda+1\right)$.
ω_2	$\lambda\left(1-\theta'\right)/\left(\theta'\lambda+1\right)$.

Equation (1) represents the demand for output in country *i*. The demand is a function of foreign output, relative prices of foreign and domestic goods, and the real interest rate. In addition, each country is exposed to a real output demand disturbance $\left(u_t^{di}\right)$.[5]

Equation (3) explains the supply side of the economy. The supply behaviour is based on a labour contract lag of one period with partial or complete indexation of wages to current prices. Output is responsive to nominal wages relative to domestic prices, but the former is partially or fully indexed to the consumer price index, which is a weighted average of domestic and foreign producer prices. The supply function (3) is derived from a Cobb-Douglas production function, the labour market equilibrium condition determining the contract wage, and the wage indexation equation. The contract wage, reflecting expectations at t - 1, is based on labour demand and supply.[6] The actual wage rate may differ from the contract wage rate if the indexation parameter is different from zero.[7]

While only domestic prices affect output supply when there is no indexation, domestic as well as foreign producer prices influence output supply (via the consumer price index) if wages are partially or fully indexed.

Equation (4) is a conventional money market equilibrium condition. Real money demand is a positive function of real income and a negative function of the nominal interest rate. The behaviour of money supply in the MER regime is assumed to be a function of an endogenously determined reserve component and an exogenously

---

5 In equilibrium analysis a positive (negative) output demand disturbance is equivalent to a negative (positive) output supply disturbance.

6 The supply of labour is assumed to be an increasing function of real wages.

7 See Gray (1976), Fischer (1977), Sachs (1980), Flood and Marion (1982), Turnovsky (1983), Aizenman and Frenkel (1985, 1986) and Devereux (1988) for studies of wage indexation behaviour.

given domestic component of the money supply. Each country is also exposed to a money supply disturbance $\left(u_t^{mi}\right)$.[8]

Equation (5) describes the goods market equilibrium condition. According to equation (6), the domestic interest rate is equal to the foreign interest rate plus the expected rate of depreciation of the domestic currency. The real interest rates in equation (7) is defined as the nominal interest rate minus the expected rate of inflation.

Equation (8) defines the exchange rate between i and c as a residual cross rate. Equations (9) and (10) describe the exogenous values of the exchange rate and reserve components of the money supply in the MER regime.[9]

Equations (11) to (13) explain that all the variables referring to country c are exogenously determined. They are expressed as a sum of a constant and a disturbance term.

---

8 In equilibrium analysis a positive (negative) money supply disturbance is equivalent to a negative (positive) money demand disturbance.

9 The specification of equation (10) needs some explanation. By definition

$$F^A \overset{def}{=} \frac{\widetilde{M}_t^{fsa} + \widetilde{e}_t^{ab}\,\widetilde{M}_t^{fsb}}{2},$$

where $\widetilde{M}$ and $\widetilde{e}$ are non-logarithmic equivalents of M and e. If $\widetilde{M}_t^{fsa} = \widetilde{e}_t^{ab}\,\widetilde{M}_t^{fsb}$, which we assume to be the case in initial equilibrium, the arithmetic mean is equal to the geometric mean. Taking logarithms of the latter, we obtain:

$$\frac{1}{2}\ln\widetilde{M}^{fsa} + \frac{1}{2}\left(\ln\widetilde{e}_t^{ab} + \ln\widetilde{M}_t^{fsb}\right) = \ln F^A,$$

which is equivalent to equation (10).

2.2 Solving the Model

Assuming that expectations follow long-run equilibrium values, we solve the equation system by using Aoki's (1981) method[10] to obtain comparative static solutions for seven endogenous variables: Y^i, P^i, q^i, e^{ic}, M^{fsi}, n^i and r^i. Aoki's method permits us (i) to decompose the system into averages and differences of the relevant variables[11] and (ii) to calculate the impact of a shock on a particular variable. It makes the model analytically tractable. The 13 equations set out above allow us to solve for all of the endogenous variables contained in our three-country world. After several substitutions and totally differentiating the resulting expressions, we can write the system more compactly both for averages and differences as follows:

Averages:

$$\begin{bmatrix} (1-\alpha_1) & \alpha_5 & \alpha_3 & -\alpha_5 \\ 1 & -\theta & \theta b & \theta b \\ 1 & 1 & 0 & \beta_1 \\ 0 & -h & 1 & h \end{bmatrix} \begin{bmatrix} dY^A \\ dP^A \\ dr^A \\ de^{ic,A} \end{bmatrix} = \begin{bmatrix} 1 & 0 & \alpha_2 & \alpha_5 & 0 \\ 0 & 0 & 0 & 0 & \theta_b \\ 0 & 1 & 0 & 0 & \beta_1 \\ 0 & 0 & 0 & (1-h) & 1 \end{bmatrix} \begin{bmatrix} du^{d,A} \\ du^{m,A} \\ du^{yc,A} \\ du^{pc,A} \\ du^{nc,A} \end{bmatrix}, \qquad (14)$$

where $h = h_1 + h_2$.

---

[10] See Turnovsky (1986) as a useful example for the application of this method.

[11] The averages and differences for any variable, say Z, are defined as follows:

$$Z^A = \frac{1}{2}\left(Z^a + Z^b\right),$$

$$Z^D = \frac{1}{2}\left(Z^a - Z^b\right).$$

The determinant of the average system is denoted by D_1 where

$$D_1 = (1-\alpha_1)\,\theta\,[b(1-h)+\beta_1(1-bh)] + (\alpha_3 h+\alpha_5)[1+\beta_1+\theta\,(1-b)] > 0\,. \qquad (15)$$

Differences:

$$\begin{bmatrix} (1+\alpha_1) & (2\alpha_4+\alpha_5) & \alpha_3 & 0 \\ 1 & -\theta & \theta b & 0 \\ 0 & -\delta & 1 & 0 \\ 1 & 1 & 0 & -1 \end{bmatrix} \begin{bmatrix} dY^D \\ dP^D \\ dr^D \\ dM^{fs,D} \end{bmatrix} = \begin{bmatrix} 1 & 0 \\ 0 & 0 \\ 0 & 0 \\ 0 & 1 \end{bmatrix} \begin{bmatrix} du^{d,D} \\ du^{m,D} \end{bmatrix}, \qquad (16)$$

where $\delta = h_1 - h_2 > 0$.[12] The determinant of the difference system, D_2, is:

$$D_2 = (1+\alpha_1)\,\theta\,(1-b\delta) + \alpha_3\delta + 2\alpha_4 + \alpha_5 > 0\ . \qquad (17)$$

3. Comparative Statics: Goods and Money Market Disturbances

Combining the average and difference systems, we obtain a set of partial derivatives which are listed in the appendix. The qualitative results are summarized in a table.

---

[12] This sign is consistent with the high values chosen for domestic expenditure shares by McKibbin and Sachs (1986), Ishii et al. (1985) and Argy et al. (1989).

Table 1: Impact of Shocks in Country *i* on Country *j*

Effects on	Degree of Indexation	Disturbance								
		u^{di}		u^{mi}	u^{yc}		u^{pc}		u^{nc}	
		$\beta_1 > 0$	$\beta_1 = 0$	$\beta_1 \geq 0$	$\beta_1 > 0$	$\beta_1 = 0$	$\beta_1 > 0$	$\beta_1 = 0$	$\beta_1 > 0$	$\beta_1 = 0$
Y^j	0	+ (?)	+ (-)	+	+	0	?	0	?	0
	$1 > b > 0$	+ (?)	+ (?)	+	+	+	?	-	?	-
	1	+ (?)	+ (?)	0	+	+	-	-	-	-
P^j	0	+ (?)	+ (?)	+	+	0	?	0	?	0
	$1 \geq b > 0$	? (?)	? (-)	+	?	-	?	+	?	+
$Y^j + P^j$	$1 \geq b \geq 0$	+ (?)	+ (-)	+	+	0	?	0	?	0
Y^w	0	+	0	+	+	0	?	0	?	0
	$1 > b > 0$	+	+	+	+	+	?	-	?	-
	1	+	+	0	+	+	-	-	-	-
q^j	$1 \geq b \geq 0$	? (?)	? (-)	+	?	-	+	+	+	+
e^{jc}	$1 \geq b \geq 0$	- (-)	- (-)	+	-	-	?	?	+	+
n^j	$1 \geq b \geq 0$	+ (+)	+ (+)	-	+	+	?	?	?	?
r^j	$1 > b \geq 0$	+ (+)	+ (+)	-	+	+	+	+	+	+
	1	+ (+)	+ (+)	0	+	+	+	+	+	+
M^{fsj}	$1 \geq b \geq 0$	+ (-)	+ (-)	- (+)	0	0	0	0	0	0

$i, j \in \{a,b\}$. Where the results may differ for $i = j$ and $i \neq j$ those in round brackets hold for $i \neq j$.

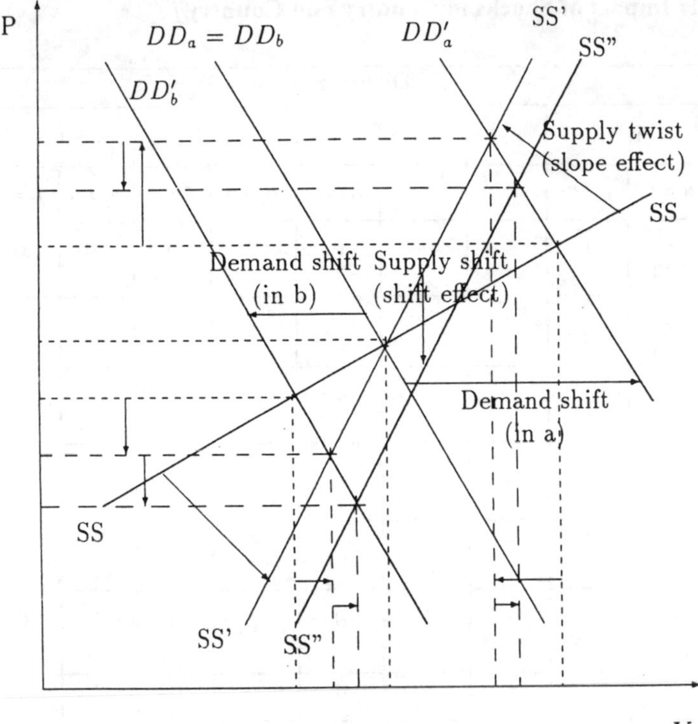

Figure 1: Goods Markets in Countries *a* and *b*

4. Goods Market Disturbances

In this section, we analyse the effects of output demand shocks originating in countries *i* and *j* $(i \neq j)$ on the output of country *i* as well as on the world[13] output.

4.1 Own-country Effects

A positive demand shock in country *i* increases its real and nominal output (see A.1) and (A.3)).[14] If $b > 0$, producer prices may fall. But even then nominal output will rise. The rise in nominal output causes an increase in the nominal and real interest rates at all degrees of indexation (see (A.6) and (A.7)). As a consequence, the dollar exchange rate $\left(e^{ic}\right)$ falls (see (A.5)), while the mark-franc exchange rate $\left(e^{as}\right)$ stays put at the initial level due to interventions in the foreign exchange market. The depreciation of the dollar, the rise in interest rates and the (relative) price changes reduce the original increase in the demand for output in country *i* without reversing its effect. The impact of the demand shock on the consumer price index $\left(q^{i}\right)$ (see (A.4)), which is also equal to the sum of the impacts on r^{i} and e^{ic} (see (A.37)), is ambiguous, irrespective of the degree of indexation.

Indexation $(b > 0)$ affects the supply of output in two opposing ways (see Figure 1). Firstly, the higher the degree of indexation, the steeper the slope of the supply curve (slope effect). Secondly, the fall of the dollar exchange rate (induced by the rise in interest rates) tends to lower the consumer price index. It therefore shifts the supply curve downwards (shift effect). A comparison of the results for our MER regime with the results of LS (1992) for the pure FER and FLER regimes suggests various patterns. Firstly, for $b = 0$, while output in country *i* increases more in the pure FER

---

[13] world = country *a* + country *b*

[14] Numbers preceded by *A* refer to equations in the appendix.

regime than in the MER regime, the increase is lower with pure FLERs than with MERs. Secondly, for partial indexation ($0 < b < 1$), FLERs are still effective in reducing the variability of output but the difference in output variability between the regimes becomes lower as the degree of indexation increases. Finally, for full indexation ($b = 1$), the increase in output in country a is identical in both the pure FER and the MER regime, while a difference remains between the output change in these and the pure FLER regimes.[15]

4.2 The Cross-Country Effect

One would expect the increased level of country i's output and prices to stimulate the demand for country j's commodities and thus to increase output and prices in country j as well. However, we observe from the formulae,

$$\frac{\partial Y^j}{\partial u^{di}} = \frac{\theta}{D_1 D_2} \left\{ \begin{aligned} & 2\alpha_1 [\beta_1(1-bh) + b\,(1-h)]\,(1-b\delta)\,\theta \\ & \quad -\alpha_3 [\beta_1(h-\delta) + \theta h\,(1-b)\,(1-b\delta) + (h-b\delta)] \\ & \quad +2\alpha_4 [b\,(1-h) + \beta_1(1-bh)] \\ & \quad -\alpha_5 [(1+\theta-\theta b\delta)\,(1-b) + b\,(h-\delta)(1+\beta_1)] \end{aligned} \right\} ?, \tag{18}$$

$$\frac{\partial P^j}{\partial u^{di}} = \frac{1}{D_1 D_2} \left\{ \begin{aligned} & \alpha_1 \theta \{\beta_1 [(1-b\delta) + (1-bh)] + b(1-h)[1-\theta\,(1-b\delta)]\} \\ & \quad -\alpha_3 \{\beta_1(h-\delta) + h[1+\theta(1-b)] + \theta b\delta(1-h)\} \\ & \quad +2\alpha_4 [\beta_1 - \theta b(1-h)] - \alpha_5 [1+\theta(1-bh)] \\ & \quad +\theta b \{\beta_1(h-\delta) - (1-h)[1+\theta(1-b\delta)]\} \end{aligned} \right\} ?, \tag{19}$$

$$\frac{\partial Y^j}{\partial u^{di}} + \frac{\partial P^j}{\partial u^{di}} = \frac{1}{2D_1}\beta_1[1+\theta(1-bh)] - \frac{1}{2D_2}[1+\theta(1-b\delta)] \;?, \tag{20}$$

---

15 In LS (1992), these differences in effectiveness with full indexation are explained by a modelling asymmetry: full indexation both in countries a and b but not in c.

that the impact of a positive demand shock in country i on the output of country j $(i \neq j)$ is ambiguous. We identify four forces affecting the output in country j: a positive income effect (see α_1 in (18)), a negative real interest rate effect (see α_3 in (18)), a positive relative price (substitution) effect (see α_4 in (18)) and a negative exchange rate effect (see α_5 in (18)). Since the negative real interest rate and exchange rate effects may be stronger than the positive income and substitution effects, a positive demand disturbance in country i may cause both output and prices in country j $(i \neq j)$ to decrease in the MER regime.

How is it possible that an output demand shock coming from country i, which has an expansionary effect on that country's output and prices, may produce a contractionary impact on country j's output and prices? A positive output demand shock in country i increases not only its output, but also prices (if $b = 0$) and real and nominal interest rates. Due to (perfect) capital mobility, the latter are also transmitted to country j and cause the dollar exchange rate, both in country i and j, to fall. The dollar depreciation causes a decline in exports from country j to the third country (rest of the world = US). This adds to the contractive effect of the rise in real interest rates on the interest sensitive output demand in country j.

While Mundell (1968) has drawn attention to the contractionary impact of interest rates on aggregate demand, our exchange rate effect is due to our three-country framework.[16] Exchange rate changes with a *third* country cannot arise in two-country models. Since the interest rate factor *may* be sufficient to cause a negative transmission from country i to j, the exchange rate factor is not necessary. But the working of the exchange rate factor increases the likelihood and the extent of a negative transmission. If country j's output demand is not sensitive to interest rates, then, in Mundell's two-country framework, a negative transmission is not possible, while it is still possible in the present three-country framework since the negative

[16] Our positive substitution effect is also absent from Mundell's framework due to his fixed price assumptions.

exchange rate effect alone may dominate the positive income and substitution effects.

Lowering the interest rate elasticity of money demand, β_1, increases the likelihood of a negative transmission. More specifically, for zero indexation ($b = 0$), if $\beta_1 = 0$, the transmission cannot be positive and the demand shock in country *i* produces definitely a contractionary effect on the output of country *j*. Consistent with the negative transmission, producer and consumer prices will then definitely fall in country *j*. The fall of the exchange rate, and the increase in real and nominal interest rates will be higher than in the case of $\beta_1 \neq 0$. The exchange rate appreciation tends to lower the rise in consumer prices in country *i* caused by the increase in producer prices in the same country without reverting it and reinforces the fall in consumer prices in country *j* caused by the decrease in producer prices there. Of course, lowering the coefficients of the positive income and substitution effects also increases the likelihood of a negative transmission.

4.3 Effects on the World Economy

Now, we turn to the impact of country *i*'s demand shock on world real output $\left(Y^w\right)$, producer prices $\left(P^w\right)$ [17] and nominal output $\left(y^w\right)$ [18]

$$\frac{\partial Y^w}{\partial u^{dj}} = 2\left\{\frac{\theta}{2D_1}\left[b(1-h)+\beta_1(1-bh)\right]\right\} > 0, \tag{21}$$

$$\frac{\partial P^w}{\partial u^{dj}} = \left\{\frac{1}{2D_1}\left[\beta_1 - \theta b\,(1-h)\right]\right\} \;?, \tag{22}$$

---

[17] World prices are averages of prices in country *a* and *b*.

[18] For reasons of symmetry, this effect does not depend on the country (*a* or *b*) in which the shock originates.

$$\frac{\partial y^w}{\partial u^{dj}} = \frac{\partial Y^w}{\partial u^{dj}} + 2 * \frac{\partial P^w}{\partial u^{dj}} \tag{23}$$

$$= \frac{\beta_1}{D_1}\left[1 + \theta\,(1 - bh)\right] > 0\ . \tag{24}$$

For any degree of indexation, a positive demand shock in country i produces an *expansionary* effect on nominal and real output of the world economy even if there is a negative transmission on country j. Average producer prices in the world may rise or fall as is the case in individual countries.

Increasing the degree of indexation will, on the one hand, steepen the supply curves (slope effect) which tends to reduce changes in equilibrium output and will, on the other hand, increase the downward shifts of the supply curves caused by a fall of the dollar exchange rate (shift effect) which tends to increase output changes. World real output reactions will therefore either increase or decrease with the degree of indexation.

5. Money Market Disturbances

5.1 Effects on Individual Countries

Due to perfect capital mobility, the effects of money supply shocks on output and other endogenous variables in either country (a or b) do not depend on the country of origin of the monetary shocks. Foreign reserves are an exception. Both countries a and b cannot increase their foreign reserves at the same time. The country in which an expansionary money supply shock occurs will lose reserves and the other country will gain them.[19]

---

19 This is an equalising difference.

An increase in the supply of money in country i puts pressure on the mark-franc exchange rate, and the intervention in the exchange market, which keeps the exchange rate fixed, results in an offsetting reserve outflow to country j $(i \neq j)$. Irrespective of the degree of indexation, a one per cent increase in the money stock of country i results in an offsetting reserve outflow to country j equal to 0.5 per cent of j's money stock (see (A.16)). The monetary shock lowers interest rates in both countries (a and b) (see (A.14) and (A.15)) and causes a depreciation with respect to country c (see (A.12)). Both effects stimulate the demand for output and lead to an increase of real and nominal output (see (A.9) and (A.11)), as well as of producer and consumer prices (see (A.10) and (A.13)) in the two countries.

The output supply curve exhibits again shift and slope effects. An increase in the indexation parameter b steepens the supply curve (slope effect). The depreciation with respect to country c causes an upward shift in the supply curve (if indexation is not zero), a shift which increases with the degree of indexation. An upward shift in the supply curve of country i may also be caused by an increase of producer prices in country j $(i \neq j)$. These slope and shift effects of the supply curve reduce the output expansion more and more as the degree of indexation increases. With full indexation, real output and real interest rates do not respond anymore to the monetary shock.[20]

While the slope and shift effects of the output supply curve lower the real output reaction to a monetary shock as the degree of indexation rises, they, at the same time, increase the producer price reaction. The reaction of nominal output may therefore rise or fall with the degree of indexation.

---

[20] Prices in a and b and the exchange rate with respect to c rise to the same extent. The movements of the supply curve produce results as if the supply curve were fixed but perpendicular.

The interest rate and exchange rate reactions may be explained by the nominal output reaction. If nominal output reactions rise with the degree of indexation, then the changes in the demand for money rise with the degree of indexation. This would cause the interest rates to fall less and the exchange rate to depreciate less as the degree of indexation increases.

A comparison of our results for MERs with LS' (1992) results for pure FERs and pure FLERs suggests that while the FER regime offers complete insulation of output from monetary shocks in country *a* or *b* for all degrees of indexation, the MER regime is more effective than the FLER regime in reducing the variability of output. The difference in output reaction between the pure FER and the MER regime becomes smaller as the degree of indexation rises and disappears for full indexation, while a difference in output reaction still remains between the MER and the pure FLER regime even if indexation is full.[21]

5.2 Effects on the World Economy

We now consider the effect of monetary shocks in country *i* on the world economy. Firstly, for no or less than full indexation $(0 \leq b < 1)$, the monetary shock in country *i* increases world real and nominal outputs, and producer prices. Secondly, the higher the degree of indexation, the lower the increase in world equilibrium real output, and the higher the increase in world producer prices. Finally, world real output and real interest rates are completely insulated from monetary shocks if wages are fully indexed to the consumer price index ($b = 1$).

---

21 As in the case of demand shocks, these differences in effectiveness with full indexation may be explained by a modelling asymmetry: full indexation both in countries *a* and *b* but not in *c* (see LS (1992)).

6. Disturbances from Country *c*

Since the behaviour of country *c* is not modelled explicitly here, its shocks are grouped as output, price and interest rate shocks rather than as what we have so far called real and monetary shocks.

6.1 Output Demand Disturbances

With no indexation ($b = 0$), a rise in country *c*'s *output* increases real output and producer prices in countries *a* and *b* (see A.17) and (A.18)). The reaction of the consumer prices is ambiguous (see (A.20)). With indexation ($b > 0$), real output still expands, but now both consumer and producer prices react ambiguously.

These results may be explained with the help of changes in the demand and supply of output. The shift in the demand curve due to the shock from country *c* causes interest rates to rise and the dollar exchange rate to fall. With $b > 0$, the depreciation of the dollar shifts the supply curve in countries *a* and *b* to the right, a shift which tends to lower producer prices while it further increases real output. This shift increases with the degree of indexation. Thus, while the output shock of country *c* tends to increase producer and consumer prices in countries *a* and *b*, the ensuing fall of the dollar exchange rate tends to reduce consumer prices and, under indexation, also producer prices.

Setting $\beta_1 = 0$ results in a complete insulation of *nominal* output in countries *a* and *b* from an output shock in country *c*, irrespective of the degree of indexation (see (A.19)). With no indexation ($b = 0$), the fall of the dollar exchange rates and the rise in interest rates completely offset the original increase in output demand such that *real* output (see (A.17)) and producer prices (see (A.18)) do not change as well. With indexation ($b > 0$), the dollar depreciation shifts the supply curves to the right and causes both an increase in real outputs[22] and a decrease in producer prices such that nominal outputs remain unchanged.

6.2 Price and Interest Rate Disturbances

Higher *prices* in country *c* have two conflicting influences on the demand for output in countries *a* and *b*. Firstly, they tend to raise the demand for output (rightward shift of the output demand curve) through the international relative price mechanism (see α_5 in (A.25)). Secondly, the price shock directly increases current consumer prices in countries *a* and *b* and thus creates deflationary expectations, which shift the real interest rates up and reduce the demand for output (leftward shift of the output demand curve), through the real interest rate mechanism (see α_3 in (A.25)).

With indexation, the price shock from country *c* will move the supply curve to the left (shift effect) and this tends to decrease the equilibrium output (or lower its increase) and to increase equilibrium producer prices (or lower their decrease). Introducing or increasing indexation will also steepen the supply curve (slope effect) and this reduces the change in equilibrium real output and increases the change in equilibrium producer prices caused by an output demand shift. As a net result, the reactions of producer prices, exchange rates and nominal interest rates may be positive or negative at all degrees of indexation (see (A.26), (A.29), and (A.33)). This is different for real output. With full indexation ($b = 1$) output will definitely decline.[23] Obviously, there exists a critical degree of indexation smaller than 1 ($b < 1$), where real output is completely insulated from the price shock. While the relative price effect on output demand (see α_5 in (A.25)) dominates the output reaction below the critical value, the real interest rate effect on output demand (α_3 in (A.25)) dominates the output reaction above the critical value.

---

22 The slope effect of increasing the parameter *b* is overruled by the shift effect.

23 The supply curve is perpendicular and any output change is determined by the leftward shift of the output supply curve.

A positive shock in country c's *nominal* interest rate has effects which are largely identical to those of a positive price shock. Only the reaction for exchange rates are different (see (A.29), (A.30), and (A.32)). Given perfect capital mobility, the positive shock in the nominal interest rate of country c implies a *primary* depreciation of the exchange rates in countries a and b with respect to country c and therefore a primary rise in the real interest rate of countries a and b. These initial changes either stimulate or reduce the output demand and shift the output supply curve upwards to the same extent as a country c price shocks would do if it were equal in size to the primary change in exchange rates. Thus, the effects of the price and the nominal interest rate disturbances in country c on output, prices, nominal and real interest rates in countries a and b are equivalent. The critical difference between the two cases arises in the reaction of the exchange rates. But this is an equalising difference which establishes the equivalence in all other respects.[24] Given the equivalence between the price and interest rate shocks, all explanations carry over from one case to the other.

Setting $\beta_1 = 0$ produces results that partially vary with the degree of indexation. With zero indexation ($b = 0$), we obtain a complete insulation of the real and nominal outputs, and of the producer prices of countries a and b from both interest rate and price shocks in country c. Introducing or increasing indexation ($b > 0$) shifts the output supply curve to the left and makes it steeper and leads to negative reactions of the real outputs and to positive reactions of the producer prices while leaving the nominal outputs unchanged. Consumer price and real interest rate reactions remain positive, while nominal interest rate reactions remain ambiguous. For the price shock the exchange rate reaction also remains ambiguous. These ambiguities do not depend on the degree of indexation.

---

[24] The total (primary and secondary) exchange rate reaction for an interest rate shock in country c is equal to the exchange rate reaction for a price shock in country c plus 1 (see (A.32)). The 1 represents the primary depreciation mentioned above.

7. Concluding Remarks

We have examined the international transmission of economic shocks in a three-country world in which two countries (*a* and *b* or Germany and France) have no macroeconomic impact on a third country (*c* or the US) but are large enough to influence each other in a MER regime. Solving the model with Aoki's (1981) method, we obtain the following results. Firstly, an increase in output demand in country *i* increases the output of that country, while it may produce a *contractionary* effect on country *j*'s $(i \neq j)$ real and nominal output and prices.[25] With an interest inelastic money demand $(\beta_1 = 0)$, the transmission is definitely negative if indexation is zero ($b = 0$), while the likelihood of a negative transmission is increased for all other degrees of indexation $(0 < b \leq 1)$. Secondly, a positive demand shock in country *i* produces an *expansionary* effect on world real and nominal output, even when it produces a *contractionary* effect on country *j*'s output. Thirdly, positive money supply shocks from countries *a* and *b* increase their real and nominal outputs but lesser and lesser as the degree of indexation increases. Full indexation *completely* insulates real outputs and real interest rates of countries *a* and *b*, and of the world, from monetary shocks. Fourthly, while a positive output demand shock from country *c* produces a positive effect on the real and nominal outputs of countries *a* and *b*, the output effects of price and interest rate shocks from country *c* are ambiguous as long as the indexation is not full. With full indexation, positive price and interest rate shocks produce a *contractionary* impact on the real outputs of countries *a* and *b*. Fifthly, with an interest inelastic money demand $(\beta_1 = 0)$ and no indexation ($b = 0$), real and nominal outputs and producer prices of countries *a* and *b* are *completely* insulated from the price and interest rate shocks of country *c*.

---

[25] $i, j \in \{a, b\}$.

Still with an interest inelastic money demand $(\beta_1 = 0)$ but with positive indexation $(b > 0)$, the positive price and interest rate shocks of country c are *negatively* transmitted to real output in countries a and b while nominal output still remains insulated. Sixthly, there exists a critical degree of indexation $(b < 1)$ where the real outputs of countries a and b are *completely* insulated from the interest rate and price shocks of country c. Seventhly, as an important contributing factor to the possibility of a negative transmission of real shocks from country i to j $(i \neq j)$, we have identified the exchange rates with respect to country c. This is a determinant which cannot occur in two-country models. Finally, while Mundell observed a negative transmission for a sufficiently high interest elasticity of output demand, the exchange rate factor may be sufficient to produce a negative transmission even if the interest elasticity of the demand for output is zero.

APPENDIX

In the following list of partial derivatives, $i, j \in \{a,b\}$. Where the results may depend on whether $i = j$ or $i \neq j$ the signs for $i \neq j$ are stated in brackets. A question mark is given for indetermined signs. The qualitative part of the results is further summarized in the table of the text.

Output Demand Disturbances:

$$\frac{\partial Y^i}{\partial u^{dj}} = \frac{\theta}{2D_1}\left[\beta_1(1-bh)+b(1-h)\right] + \underset{(-)}{\frac{\theta}{2D_2}(1-b\delta)} \qquad \underset{(?)}{>0} \qquad \text{(A.1)}$$

$$\frac{\partial P^i}{\partial u^{dj}} = \frac{1}{2D_1}\left[\beta_1-\theta b\,(1-h)\right] + \underset{(-)}{\frac{1}{2D_2}} \qquad \underset{(?)}{?} \qquad \text{(A.2)}$$

$$\frac{\partial Y^i}{u^{dj}} + \frac{\partial P^i}{\partial u^{dj}} = \frac{1}{2D_1}\beta_1\left[1+\theta(1-bh)\right] + \underset{(-)}{\frac{1}{2D_2}\left[1+\theta\,(1-b\delta)\right]} \qquad \underset{(?)}{>0} \qquad \text{(A.3)}$$

$$\frac{\partial q^i}{\partial u^{dj}} = \frac{1}{2D_1}\left[h\left(1+\beta_1+\theta\right)-(1+\theta)\right] + \underset{(-)}{\frac{\delta}{2D_2}} \qquad \underset{(?)}{?} \qquad \text{(A.4)}$$

$$\frac{\partial e^{ic}}{\partial u^{dj}} = -\frac{1}{2D_1}\left[1+\theta\,(1-bh)\right] \qquad <0 \qquad \text{(A.5)}$$

$$\frac{\partial n^i}{\partial u^{dj}} = -\frac{\partial e^{ic}}{\partial u^{dj}} \qquad >0 \qquad \text{(A.6)}$$

$$\frac{\partial r^i}{\partial u^{dj}} = \frac{h}{2D_1}\left[1+\beta_1+\theta\,(1-b)\right] + \frac{\delta}{2D_2} \qquad > 0 \qquad \text{(A.7)}$$

$$\qquad\qquad\qquad (\text{-}) \qquad\qquad (>0)$$

$$\frac{\partial M^{fsi}}{\partial u^{dj}} = + \frac{1}{2D_1}\left[1+\theta\,(1-b\delta)\right] \qquad > 0 \qquad \text{(A.8)}$$

$$(\text{-}) \qquad\qquad\qquad (<0)$$

Monetary Disturbances:

$$\frac{\partial Y^i}{\partial u^{mj}} = \frac{1}{2D_1}(1-b)\,\theta\left(\alpha_3 h+\alpha_5\right) \qquad \geq 0 \qquad \text{(A.9)}$$

$$\frac{\partial P^i}{\partial u^{mj}} = \frac{1}{2D_1}\left[\left(\alpha_{3h}+\alpha_5\right)+\theta b\left(1-\alpha_1\right)(1-h)\right] \qquad > 0 \qquad \text{(A.10)}$$

$$\frac{\partial Y^i}{\partial u^{mj}} + \frac{\partial P^i}{\partial u^{mj}} = \frac{1}{2D_1}\left\{\left(\alpha_{3h}+\alpha_5\right)\left[1+\theta\left(1-b\right)\right]+\theta b\left(1-\alpha_1\right)\left(1-h\right)\right\} > 0 \qquad \text{(A.11)}$$

$$\frac{\partial e^{ic}}{\partial u^{mj}} = \frac{1}{2D_1}\left[\left(\alpha_3 h+\alpha_5\right)+\theta\left(1-\alpha_1\right)(1-bh)\right] \qquad > 0 \qquad \text{(A.12)}$$

$$\frac{\partial q^i}{\partial u^{mj}} = \frac{1}{2D_1}\left[\left(\alpha_3 h+\alpha_5\right)+\theta\left(1-\alpha_1\right)(1-h)\right] \qquad > 0 \qquad \text{(A.13)}$$

$$\frac{\partial n^i}{\partial u^{mj}} = - \frac{\partial e^{ic}}{\partial u^{mj}} \qquad < 0 \qquad \text{(A.14)}$$

$$\frac{\partial r^i}{\partial u^{mj}} = - \frac{\theta h}{2D_1}\left(1-\alpha_1\right)(1-b) \qquad \leq 0 \qquad \text{(A.15)}$$

$$\frac{\partial M^{fsi}}{\partial u^{mj}} = -\frac{1}{2} \qquad < 0 \qquad \text{(A.16)}$$

$$(+) \qquad (> 0)$$

Output Demand Disturbance from Country c:

$$\frac{\partial Y^i}{\partial u^{yc}} = \frac{\alpha_2 \theta}{2D_1}\left[\beta_1 (1-bh) + b(1-h)\right] \qquad > 0 \qquad \text{(A.17)}$$

$$\frac{\partial P^i}{\partial u^{yc}} = \frac{\alpha_2}{2D_1}\left[\beta_1 - \theta b (1-h)\right] \qquad ? \qquad \text{(A.18)}$$

$$\frac{\partial Y^i}{\partial u^{yc}} + \frac{\partial P^i}{\partial u^{yc}} = \frac{\alpha_2 \beta_1}{2D_1}\left[1 + \theta(1-bh)\right] \qquad > 0 \qquad \text{(A.19)}$$

$$\frac{\partial q^i}{\partial u^{yc}} = \frac{\alpha_2}{2D_1}\left[h\left(1+\beta_1+\theta\right) - (1+\theta)\right] \qquad ? \qquad \text{(A.20)}$$

$$\frac{\partial e^{ic}}{\partial u^{yc}} = -\frac{\alpha_2}{2D_1}\left[1+\theta(1-bh)\right] \qquad < 0 \qquad \text{(A.21)}$$

$$\frac{\partial n^i}{\partial u^{yc}} = -\frac{\partial e^{ic}}{\partial u^{yc}} \qquad > 0 \qquad \text{(A.22)}$$

$$\frac{\partial r^i}{\partial u^{yc}} = \frac{\alpha_2 h}{2D_1}\left[1+\beta+\theta(1-b)\right] \qquad > 0 \qquad \text{(A.23)}$$

$$\frac{\partial M^{fsi}}{\partial u^{yc}} = 0 \tag{A.24}$$

Price and Nominal Interest Rate Shocks from Country c:

$$\frac{\partial Y^i}{\partial u^{pc}} = \frac{\partial Y^i}{\partial u^{nc}} = \frac{\theta}{2D_1}\left\{\beta_1\left[\alpha_5 - \alpha_3(1-h)\right] - b\left[\alpha_3(1-h) + \alpha_5\beta_1\right]\right\} \quad ? \tag{A.25}$$

$$\frac{\partial P^i}{\partial u^{pc}} = \frac{\partial P^i}{\partial u^{nc}} = \frac{1}{2D_1}\left\{\beta_1\left[\alpha_5 - \alpha_3(1-h)\right] + \theta b\,(1-h)\left[\alpha_3 + \beta_1(1-\alpha_1)\right]\right\} ? \tag{A.26}$$

$$\begin{aligned} \frac{\partial Y^i}{\partial u^{pc}} + \frac{\partial P^i}{\partial u^{pc}} &= \frac{\partial Y^i}{\partial u^{nc}} + \frac{\partial P^i}{\partial u^{nc}} \\ &= \frac{\beta_1}{2D_1}\left\{\left[1+\theta\,(1-b)\right]\alpha_5 + (1-h)\left[\theta b(1-\alpha_1) - (1+\theta)\alpha_3\right]\right\} ? \end{aligned} \tag{A.27}$$

$$\frac{\partial q^i}{\partial u^{pc}} = \frac{\partial q^i}{\partial u^{nc}} = \frac{1}{2D_1}\left\{\alpha_3(1+\theta)(1-h) + \beta_1\left[\alpha_5 + \theta(1-\alpha_1)(1-h)\right]\right\} \quad > 0 \tag{A.28}$$

$$\frac{\partial e^{ic}}{\partial u^{pc}} = \frac{1}{2D_1}\left\{\alpha_3(1+\theta)(1-h) - \alpha_5\left[1+\theta\,(1-b)\right] - \theta b\,(1-h)\,(1-\alpha_1)\right\} \quad ? \tag{A.29}$$

$$\frac{\partial e^{ic}}{\partial u^{nc}} = \frac{1}{2D_1}\left\{\alpha_3\left[1+\theta\,(1-bh)\right] + \beta_1\left[h\alpha_3 + \alpha_5 + \theta\,(1-\alpha_1)\,(1-bh)\right]\right\} \quad > 0 \tag{A.30}$$

$$\frac{\partial r^i}{\partial u^{pc}} = \frac{\partial r^i}{\partial u^{nc}} = \frac{1}{2D_1}\left\{\alpha_5\left[1+\beta_1+\theta(1-b)\right] + \theta(b+\beta_1)\,(1-\alpha_1)(1-h)\right\} \quad > 0 \tag{A.31}$$

$$\frac{\partial e^{ic}}{\partial u^{nc}} = 1 + \frac{\partial e^{ic}}{\partial u^{pc}} \qquad > 0 \tag{A.32}$$

$$\frac{\partial n^{i}}{\partial u^{pc}} = - \frac{\partial e^{ic}}{\partial u^{pc}} \qquad ? \tag{A.33}$$

$$\frac{\partial n^{i}}{\partial u^{nc}} = 1 - \frac{\partial e^{ic}}{\partial u^{nc}} \qquad ? \tag{A.34}$$

$$\frac{\partial n^{i}}{\partial u^{pc}} = \frac{\partial n^{i}}{\partial u^{nc}} \qquad ? \tag{A.35}$$

$$\frac{\partial M^{fsi}}{\partial u^{pc}} = \frac{\partial M^{fsi}}{\partial u^{nc}} \qquad = 0 \tag{A.36}$$

$$\frac{\partial q^{i}}{\partial x} = \frac{\partial r^{i}}{\partial x} + \frac{\partial e^{ic}}{\partial x} \tag{A.37}$$

$$\text{for} \quad x \in \left\{ u^{dj}, u^{mj}, u^{yc}, u^{pc} \right\},$$

$$\frac{\partial q^{i}}{\partial u^{nc}} = \frac{\partial r^{i}}{\partial u^{nc}} + \frac{\partial e^{ic}}{\partial u^{nc}} - 1 . \tag{A.38}$$

References

Aizenmann, J. and J.A. Frenkel (June 1985), „Optimal Wage Indexation: Foreign Exchange Rate Intervention, and Monetary Policy", *American Economic Review*, 75, pp. 402-423.

Aizenmann, J. and J.A. Frenkel (August 1986), „Supply Shocks, Wage Indexation, and Monetary Accommodation", *Journal of Money, Credit and Banking*, 18, pp. 304-22.

Aoki, M. (1981), *Dynamic Analysis of Open Economies*, Academic Press, New York.

Argy, V. and J. Salop (July 1983), „Price and Output Effects of Monetary and Fiscal Expansion in a Two-Country World under Flexible Exchange Rates", *Oxford Economic Papers*, 35, pp. 228-246.

Argy, V., W. McKibbin and E. Siegloff (December 1989), „Exchange Rate Regimes for a Small Economy in a Multi-Country World", *Princeton Studies in International Finance*, 67, Princeton University Press, Princeton.

Branson, W.H. and J.J. Rotenberg (May 1980), „International Adjustment with Wage Rigidity", *European Economic Review*, 13, pp. 309-332.

Corden, W.M. and S.J. Turnovsky (January 1983), „Negative International Transmission of Economic Expansion", *European Economic Review*, 20, pp. 289-310.

Cox, W.M. (July 1980), „Unanticipated Money, Output and Prices in the Small Economy", *Journal of Monetary Economics,* 6, pp. 359-384.

Devereux, M.(August 1988), „The Optimal Mix of Wage Indexation and Foreign Exchange Market Intervention", *Journal of Money, Credit and Banking*, 20, pp. 381-392.

Dornbusch, R. (May 1976), „The Theory of Flexible Exchange Rate Regimes and Macroeconomic Policy", *The Scandinavian Journal of Economics*, 78, pp. 255-275.

Feuerstein, S. (1992), *Studien zur Wechselkursunion*, Physica Verlag, Heidelberg.

Feuerstein, S. and J. Siebke (1990), „Wechselkursunion und Stabilitätspolitik", *Zeitschrift für Wirtschafts- und Sozialwissenschaften,* pp. 359-380.

Fischer, S. (1977), „Wage Indexation and Macroeconomic Stability", in: K. Brunner and A. Metzler (eds.), *Stabilization of the Domestic and International Economy,* Vol. 5 of the Carnegie-Rochester Conference Series on Public Policy, North-Holland, Amsterdam.

Flood, R.P. and N.P. Marion (February 1982), „The Transmission of Disturbances under Alternative Exchange-Rate Regimes with Optimal Indexing", *Quarterly Journal of Economics*, 97, pp. 43-66.

Friedman, M. (1953), „The Case for Flexible Exchange Rates", in: M. Friedman (ed.), *Essays in Positive Economics,* University of Chicago Press, Chicago.

Gray, J.A. (April 1976), „Wage Indexation: A Macroeconomic Approach", *Journal of Monetary Economics*, 2, pp. 221-235.

Ishii, N., W. McKibbin, J. Sachs (1985), „The Economic Policy Mix, Policy Cooperation, and Protectionism: Some Aspects of Macroeconomic Interdependence Among the United States, Japan, and Other OECD Countries", *Journal of Policy Modeling*, 7, pp. 553-72.

Kenen, P. B. (1984), „Comment on Exchange Rate Unions as an Alternative to Flexible Rates: The Effects of Real and Monetary Disturbances by R.C. Marston", in: J.F.O. Bilson and R.C. Marston (eds.), *Exchange Rate Theory and Practice*, The University of Chicago Press, Chicago.

Läufer, N.K.A. and S. Sundararajan (LS) (1992), „Stabilization Policy in Multi-Country Models", in: H.-J. Vosgerau (ed.), *European Integration in the World Economy,* Springer-Verlag, Heidelberg.

Laursen, S. and L.A. Metzler (November 1950), „Flexible Exchange Rates and the Theory of Employment", *Review of Economics and Statistics*, 32, pp. 281-299.

Levin, J. (1983), „A Model of Stabilization Policy in a Jointly Floating Currency Area", in: J.S. Bhandari, B.H. Putnam (eds.), *Economic Interdependence and Flexible Exchange Rates*, MIT Press Cambridge MA and London, pp. 329-349.

Marston, R.C.(February 1982), „Wages, Relative Prices and Choice Between Fixed and Flexible Rates", *Canadian Journal of Economics*, 15, pp. 87-103.

Marston, R.C.(1984), „Exchange Rate Unions as an Alternative to Flexible Rates: The Effects of Real and Monetary Disturbances", in: J.F.O. Bilson and R.C. Marston (eds.), *Exchange Rate Theory and Practice,* The University of Chicago Press, Chicago.

McKibbin, W. and J. Sachs (September 1986), „Comparing the Global Performance of Alternative Exchange Arrangements", *N.B.E.R. Working Paper*, No. 2024, National Bureau of Economic Research,Cambridge, MA.

Meade, J.E (1950), *The Theory of International Economic Policy*, Vol. I: The Balance of Payments, Oxford Economic Press, London.

Mundell, R.A.(November 1963), „Capital Mobility and Stabilization Policy under Fixed and Flexible Exchange Rates", *Canadian Journal of Economics and Political Science,* 29, pp. 475-485.

Mundell, R.A. (1968), *International Economics*, MacMillan, New York.

Mussa, M.(1979), „Macroeconomic Interdependence and the Exchange Rate Regime", in: R. Dornbusch and J. Frenkel (eds.), *International Economic Policy*, Johns Hopkins University Press, Baltimore.

Sachs, J. (June 1980), „Wages, Flexible Exchange Rates, and Macroeconomic Policy", *Quarterly Journal of Economics*, 94, pp. 731-747.

Schmid, M. (January 1982), „Devaluation: Keynesian and Trade Models and the Monetary Approach: The Role of Nominal and Real Wage Rigidity", *European Economic Review*, 17, pp. 27-50.

Turnovsky, S.J. (May 1981), „Monetary Policy and Foreign Price Disturbances under Flexible Exchange Rates: A Stochastic Approach", *Journal of Money, Credit and Banking*, 13, pp. 156-176.

Turnovsky, S.J. (November 1983), „Wage Indexation and Exchange Market Intervention in a Small Open Economy", *Quarterly Journal of Economics,* 14, pp. 574-592.

Turnovsky, S.J. (1986), „Monetary and Fiscal Policy under Perfect Foresight:. A Symmetric Two-Country Model", *Economica,* 53, pp. 139-157.

Turnovsky, S.J. and G.H. Kingston (December 1977), „Monetary and Fiscal Policies under Flexible Exchange Rates and Perfect Myopic Foresight in an Inflationary World", *The Scandinavian Journal of Economics*, 79, pp. 424-41.

B. TRADE AND TAX POLICIES IN THE GLOBAL ECONOMY

Trade Wars and Trade Talks *

Gene M. Grossman and

Elhanan Helpman **

Abstract

When governments meet in the international arena, their actions reflect the political situations at home. Previous studies of trade relations have focused on governments that are immune from political pressures and that act as benevolent servants of the public interest. Here we introduce domestic politics into the analysis of international economic relations. We study the interactions between national leaders who are concerned both with providing a high standard of living to the general electorate and collecting campaign contributions from special interest groups. Our analysis sheds light on the determinants of the structure of protection in non-cooperative and cooperative policy equilibria.

* First published in "Journal of Political Economy", 1995, and reprinted here with the permission of University of Chicago Press, Chicago, IL (grant no. 33955).

** Wc thank the National Science Foundation and the U.S.–Israel Binational Science Foundation for financial support. Grossman also thanks the John S. Guggenheim Memorial Foundation, the Sumitomo Bank Fund, the Daiwa Bank Fund, and the Center of International Studies at Princeton University. A comment by Ernst Mohr is gratefully acknowledged.

1. Introduction

Recent events have highlighted the extent to which domestic politics condition international economic relations. Special interest groups were visible and vocal in the weeks and years leading up to the Uruguay Round trade pact and the North American Free Trade Agreement. Similarly, industry representatives have been active participants in the ongoing trade conflict between the United States and Japan. There can be little doubt that interest groups have influenced these and other policy outcomes.

In the political science literature, "statist" theories have dominated recent analysis of foreign economic policy [see Cowhey (1990)]. Such theories cast an elite group of Executive Branch institutions and officials as relatively independent players in the international arena, setting policies to serve national objectives (such as balance-of-power diplomacy) while making only occasional and minimal concessions to domestic political groups. This approach has its counterpart in the economics literature on trade relations, which too has focused on the actions and interactions of autonomous governments. In his seminal paper on "Optimal Tariffs and Retaliations", Harry Johnson showed how policy interdependence between governments could be modeled as a non-cooperative equilibrium of a two-country tariff game [see also Kuga (1973), Riezman (1982), and Kennan and Riezman (1984)]. Mayer (1981) and Riezman (1982) took a similar approach to negotiated trade agreements, viewing them as equilibrium outcomes to two-government bargaining games. While these authors surely are to be commended for emphasizing the international interactions that feature prominently in foreign policy determination, one cannot help but wonder whether their analyses capture the "true" objectives of real world governments. In every case, the author has cast the government as a benevolent servant of the national interest.

It is now commonplace to view trade policy as an outgrowth of a political process that does not necessarily give rise to aggregate welfare maximization. A growing literature on endogenous policy formation treats interest groups (and sometimes voters) as participants in a competition for political favors, which are meted out by politicians serving their own selfish interests. However, this literature has focused exclusively on the case of a small or isolated country, one that sets trade policy without regard to the extant policies and possible reactions of its trade partners.

In this paper we develop a formal framework capable of capturing both strategic interaction between interest groups and politicians in the domestic arena and strategic interaction between governments in the international arena. In so doing, we follow the path suggested by Putnam (1988), who argued that international relations are best seen as just such a "two-level game". We study both non-cooperative and cooperative tariff-setting games in a context where domestic politics determine international objectives. Our goal is to understand how the political climate in one country conditions policy outcomes in another, and how domestic political pressures on politicians condition their relations with foreign counterparts.[1]

In the next section we outline our model and discuss its relation to the existing literature. Section 3 spells out the formal assumptions of the model and the nature of a political equilibrium. In Sections 4 and 5 we study two-country policy games, first assuming that governments set their policies non-cooperatively and then that they engage in international negotiations. The final section compares the predictions of our model with some of the findings in the empirical literature.

---

[1] Hillman and Moser (1995) also view trade policies as the outgrowth of interactions between politically-motivated governments. Their analysis differs from ours inasmuch as they use reduced-form political support functions to describe the objectives of each government (see discussion below). Our analysis goes further in explicitly modeling the behavior of special interest groups that determine a specific relationship between policy choices and political support. Also, they study a single sector whereas we consider the structure of protection in non-cooperative and cooperative equilibria with many goods.

2. Model Outline and Relation to the Literature

In democracies, trade policies are set by elected representatives. Because the public typically is less than fully informed about trade issues and because most elections cover many issues, these representatives need not always select policies that maximize the welfare of the median voter. Other policies may better serve the politicians' goal of being re-elected and any further objectives they may have. The literature on trade policy formation studies the choices made by elected representatives who may receive financial and other inducements from special interest lobby groups.

One strand of literature began with Brock and Magee (1978) and is most fully articulated in Magee, Brock and Young (1989). They consider an election between two parties representing protectionist and free-trade interests. Prior to the election, each party commits to a platform specifying the trade policy it would carry out if elected. Then, seeing these platforms, lobby groups representing capital (which would benefit from free trade) and labor (which would benefit from high tariffs) make campaign contributions to the respective parties championing their causes. The contributions finance campaign expenditures which in turn affect the parties' probabilities of winning the election. Magee, Brock and Young (henceforth MBY) study the Nash equilibrium platforms that emerge when the parties act as Stackelberg leaders vis-à-vis the lobbies.[2]

A second strand emanates from the writings of Stigler (1971) and Pelzman (1976) on domestic regulatory policy. Hillman (1982) applied these ideas to trade policy formation, with further elaboration by Long and Vousden (1990). Their approach sees an incumbent government that is in a position to choose trade policy, but is constrained by the prospect of the next election. The government recognizes that favors granted to special interest groups may elicit financial and other support, but also may cause dissatisfaction among elements of the general electorate. While

---

[2] Findlay and Wellisz (1982) developed a reduced form of the Brock and Magee approach. In their formulation, a *tariff formation function* summarizes the relationship between the contributions (or other spending) of the two lobbies and the policies that emerge from the political process. They study Nash equilibrium contributions by the lobbies, taking the policy function as given.

avoiding the details of motives and actions, the authors summarize the relevant trade-off in a *political support function:* the government's "support" depends directly on its policies (because these affect voter well-being) and indirectly on policy through its effect on the rents accruing to certain interests. The government selects a policy to maximize its political support.

Our own approach, first developed in Grossman and Helpman (1994), combines elements of these two. Like the political-support approach, we focus on an incumbent government that is in a position to set its nation's trade policies. We go beyond that approach, however, by modeling the actions available to the organized special interests and the incentives they face in deciding their political involvement. In other words, rather than specifying a support function exogenously, we derive one from the equilibrium actions of profit-maximizing lobby groups. The lobbies in our formulation, like those in the electoral competition models of MBY, decide on what size of campaign contributions to offer to political representatives. But whereas MBY see lobbies as setting their contributions after policy positions have been taken and with the sole objective of influencing the election outcome, we see the lobbies as offering contributions with the aim of influencing the policy announcements themselves. In other words, our lobbies seek to curry favor with politicians who covet their financial support.[3]

The outline of our model is as follows. Lobby groups represent factor owners with stakes in certain industries. Each lobby confronts its national government with a campaign *contribution schedule;* that is, a schedule relating its promised gift to the action taken by the government.[4] These schedules will not, of course, be formal contracts, nor will they often be explicitly announced. Still, the government will know that an implicit relationship exists between the way it treats each organized

---

[3] In Grossman and Helpman (1994) we discuss the empirical evidence on campaign giving by Political Action Committees in the United States. This evidence strongly suggests that "PAC money is interested money" with "more than electoral objective in mind" (quoted from Magelby and Nelson, 1990, p. 55).

[4] An issue arises as to whether the industry lobbies can also offer contributions to politicians in the other country's government. Interest groups do sometimes try to influence a foreign government's policy choices. But politicians often view gifts from foreign sources as tainted money. We choose to focus in the main text on the case where lobbies contribute only to their own national governments, while treating the case with foreign contributions in a series of footnotes.

lobby and the contributions it can expect to receive from that group. We assume that the contribution schedules are set to maximize the aggregate welfare of the lobby group's members, taking the schedules offered by the other organized groups as given.

Faced with the contribution schedules of the various lobbies, the incumbents choose a vector of trade taxes and subsidies on the various import and export goods. Their objective in this is to maximize their own political welfare. We allow the politicians' utility to depend on the welfare of the average voter and the total amount of political contributions. Average welfare is included in the government's objective to reflect the likelihood that prospects for re-election depend on the well-being of the general electorate. Contributions enter the government's utility function, because campaign funds can be used for political advertising, and because the contributions sometimes augment the candidates' personal fortunes or provide them with other political benefits [see Grossman and Helpman (1994) for more on this point].

In our earlier paper, we followed the political-economy literature in assuming that the government could take world prices as given. Accordingly, there was no scope for interaction between the governments, and no possibility for the interest groups in one country to influence policy outcomes elsewhere. Here, in contrast, we focus on the interactions between countries. First we characterize the Nash equilibrium of a non-cooperative game between the two politically-motivated governments. Then we consider a bargaining situation, where policies are set in an international negotiation.

3. The Formal Model

We consider the trade relations between two countries, "home" and "foreign". The countries have similar political and economic systems, although their tastes, endowments, and political conditions may differ. We describe in detail the political and economic structure of the home country.

Residents of the home country share identical additively separable preferences. Each individual maximizes a utility function of the form

$$u = c_Z + \sum_{i=1}^{n} u_i(c_{Xi}) \ , \tag{1}$$

where c_Z is consumption of good Z and c_{Xi} is consumption of good X_i, $i = 1, 2, \dots, n$. The functions $u_i(\cdot)$ are differentiable, increasing, and strictly concave. Good Z serves as numeraire, with a world and domestic price equal to one. We denote by p_i the domestic price of good X_i in the home country, while π_i represents its offshore price.[5] With these preferences, each resident of the home country demands $d_i(p_i)$ units of good X_i, $i = 1, 2, \dots, n$, where $d_i(\cdot)$ is the inverse of $u_i'(\cdot)$. The consumer devotes the remainder of his total spending of E to the numeraire good, thereby attaining the utility level

$$v(p, E) = E + S(p) \ , \tag{2}$$

where $p = (p_1, p_2, \dots, p_n)$ is the vector of home prices of the non-numeraire goods and $S(p) \equiv \Sigma_i u_i[d_i(p_i)] - \Sigma_i p_i d_i(p_i)$ is the consumer surplus enjoyed on these goods.

The numeraire good Z can be produced from labor alone, with constant returns to scale. We assume that the aggregate labor supply, ℓ, is sufficiently large to ensure a positive output of this good. Then we can choose units so that the competitive wage rate equals one. Each of the other goods is manufactured from labor and a sector-specific input, also with constant returns to scale. The various specific inputs are available in inelastic supply. We denote by $\Pi_i(p_i)$ the aggregate rent accruing to the specific factor used in producing good X_i, and note that the slope of this function gives the industry supply curve, i.e.,

$$X_i(p_i) = \Pi_i'(p_i) \ . \tag{3}$$

The government has a limited set of policy instruments at its disposal. We allow it to tax or subsidize trade in any of the non-numeraire goods and to collect revenues or

---

[5] The offshore price need not be the same as the price prevailing in the foreign country, because the foreign country may impose trade taxes or subsidies of its own. We use p_i^* to denote the internal price in the foreign country.

distribute tax receipts using a (neutral) head tax or subsidy. In other words, the government must use trade policies to effect any income redistribution between groups in the economy. In reality governments appear to have difficulty in using direct and transparent instruments to transfer income, so they resort to less direct means instead. Our model highlights the role of trade policy as a potential tool of income redistribution.

The ad-valorem trade taxes or subsidies drive a wedge between domestic and offshore prices. We represent these policies by the parameters τ_i such that $p_i = \tau_i \pi_i$. Then $\tau_i > 1$ represents one plus the rate of tariff on an import good or one plus the rate of export subsidy on an export good. Similarly, $\tau_i < 1$ represents an import subsidy or an export tax. The vector of trade policies $\tau = (\tau_1, \tau_2, \ldots, \tau_n)$ generates per capita government revenue of

$$r(\tau, \pi) = \Sigma_i (\tau_i - 1)\pi_i \left[d_i(\tau_i \pi_i) - \frac{1}{N} X_i(\tau_i \pi_i) \right] , \tag{4}$$

where $\pi = (\pi_1, \pi_2, \ldots, \pi_n)$ and N measures the total population, which we henceforth normalize to one. The government redistributes the tariff revenue evenly to the public.

Individuals collect income from several sources. Most earn wages as workers and all receive the same transfer (possibly negative) from the government. In addition, some individuals own claims to one of the specific inputs. These assets are indivisible and nontradable (as, for example, with claims to sector-specific human capital), so individuals cannot hold more than one type. Clearly, those who own some of the specific factor used in industry i will see their income tied to the domestic price of good X_i. These individuals have a direct stake in the trade policy τ_i, in addition to their general interest as consumers in all policies that affect domestic prices.

The owners of the specific input used in sector i, with their common desire for protection (or export subsidies) for their industry, may choose to join forces to express their policy wishes to the incumbent government. We assume that the various owners of some (or perhaps all) of the specific inputs form political action groups, while the owners of the remaining specific inputs (if any) fail to organize politically. The set of organized industries is taken as exogenous here. The organized groups enjoy a political advantage relative to individual factor owners inasmuch as the groups control substantially greater resources than most individuals. With these vast resources at their disposal, the lobbyists can gain access to politicians to communicate their political demands. We assume that the lobbies express their demands in the form of *contribution schedules;* that is, they offer to contribute to the campaign funds of the incumbent politicians an amount that depends upon the particular policies implemented by the government, as well as perhaps the concessions that the politicians manage to extract from the foreign government in the course of any trade negotiation. While the unorganized individuals (including those individuals who own none of the specific inputs) might also wish to "bid" for trade policies in this way, we assume that politicians will not take the time to hear their offers, which are likely to be small in view of the limited income of an individual factor owner and the limited stake that any one person has in the policy outcome. In short, we assume that politically unorganized individuals have no means to influence policy with their campaign contributions; they enter the political process only as voters.

The organized input owners coordinate their political activities so as to maximize their joint welfare. The lobby representing industry i submits the contribution schedule $C_i(\tau,\cdot)$ that maximizes

$$v^i = \tilde{W}_i(\tau,\pi) - C_i(\tau,\cdot) \ , \tag{5}$$

where

$$\tilde{W}_i(\tau,\pi) \equiv \ell_i + \Pi_i(\tau_i\pi_i) + \alpha_i\left[r(\tau,\pi) + S(\tau\pi)\right] \ , \tag{6}$$

α_i is the fraction of the population that owns the specific input used in sector i (also their measure, given that $N = 1$), and ℓ_i is the joint labor endowment of these factor owners.[6] Equation (6) gives the total gross-of-contributions welfare of the α_i members of lobby group i, which they derive from wages, quasi-rents, transfers from the government, and surplus from consuming the non-numeraire goods [see (2)]. Notice that we have omitted all but one argument of the contribution schedule. This allows us to distinguish the case of a trade war, where the contribution schedule depends only on the actions of the home government, from that of trade talks, where the contributions may also depend upon actions taken by the foreign government under any agreement.

Facing the contribution schedules offered by the various lobbies, the incumbents set trade policy – either unilaterally or through a process of international bargaining – so as to maximize their political welfare. We assume that the politicians care about he accumulation of campaign contributions and perhaps also about the welfare of the average voter. As we discussed in Section II, the politicians may value contributions as a source of funding for campaign advertisements and possibly for other reasons. A concern for average welfare will arise if the prospects for re-election depend upon the average voter's prosperity. We posit a linear form for the government's objective function, namely

$$G = \Sigma_{i \varepsilon L} C_i(\tau, \cdot) + a\tilde{W}(\tau, \pi) , \qquad a \geq 0 \ , \tag{7}$$

where L is the set of organized industries and

$$\tilde{W}(\tau, \pi) \equiv \ell + \Sigma_i \Pi_i(\tau_i \pi_i) + r(\tau\pi) \tag{8}$$

measures average (gross) welfare. The parameter a in (7) represents the government's weighting of a dollar of social welfare compared to a dollar of campaign contributions, considering both the perceived political value of the funding and the indirect cost associated with the contributor's loss of welfare.

---

6 In (6) we have used the notation $\tau\pi$ in the argument of $S(\cdot)$ to represent the vector $(\tau_1\pi_1, \tau_2\pi_2, \ldots, \tau_n\pi_n)$. Thus, $\tau\pi = p$ is the vector of home country prices.

As we mentioned before, the foreign country has a similar political and economic structure, although the subutility functions $u_i^*(\cdot)$, the profit functions $\Pi_i^*(\cdot)$, the set of organized industries L^*, the number α_i^* of voters with claims to the specific input used in sector i, and the weight a^* that the government places on aggregate welfare relative to contributions may differ from those in the home country (where the analogous functions and parameters have no asterisks). Equations analogous to (1) through (8) apply to the foreign country, where trade policies are $\tau^* = (\tau_1^*, \tau_2^*, \ldots \tau_n^*)$, internal prices are $p^* = (p_1^*, p_2^*, \ldots, p_n^*)$, output in sector i is X_i^*, etc.

Having specified the production and demand sides of each economy we turn now to the international equilibrium. Net imports of good i in the home country are $M_i\,(p_i) = d_i(p_i) - X_i(p_i)$, while those in the foreign country equal $M_i^*(p_i^*) = d_i^*(p_i^*) - X_i^*(p_i^*)$. Recall that $p_i = \tau_i \pi_i$ and $p_i^* = \tau_i^* \pi_i$. Then world product markets clear when

$$M_i(\tau_i \pi_i) + M_i^*(\tau_i^* \pi_i) = 0 \ , \qquad i = 1, 2, \ldots, n . \tag{9}$$

This equation allows us to solve for the market clearing price of good X_i as a function of the industry trade taxes or subsidies imposed by the two countries. We denote this functional relationship by $\pi_i(\tau_i, \tau_i^*)$. It follows from (9) that the functions $\pi_i(\cdot)$ are homogeneous of degree minus one; i.e., if the home country were to increase its tariff on imports of some good while the foreign country increased its export subsidy by the same percentage amount, then the world price would fall so as to leave the domestic prices in each country unchanged.

Using (9) it is possible to express the (gross-of-contributions) welfare levels of the organized interest groups and of the average voter in each country as functions of the trade-policy vectors τ and τ^*. For example, the expression (6) for the gross welfare of owners of the specific factor used in home industry i becomes

$W_i(\tau,\tau^*) \equiv \tilde{W}_i\left[\tau, \pi(\tau,\tau^*)\right]$, while the average welfare of home voters can be written as $W(\tau,\tau^*) \equiv \tilde{W}\left[\tau, \pi(\tau,\tau^*)\right]$. Inserting these functions into (5) and (7) and their foreign analogs gives the objectives of the lobbies and politicians as functions of the trade policy vectors in each country.

We describe finally the sequence of actions by the various agents in our two-country model. The lobbies in each country move first, setting contribution schedules that link their gifts to the various possible policy outcomes. The lobbies act simultaneously and non-cooperatively, each taking the schedules of all other lobbies in the same and the other country as given. Then the governments set their national trade policies. In Section 4, where we study trade wars, these policies are set in a non-cooperative, simultaneous-move game. In Section 5, which deals with international negotiations, the policies emerge from the specified bargaining process. In both cases we assume that the implicit contracts between the politicians and interest groups in one country (i.e., the contribution schedules that have been communicated by the lobbyists to the government) are not observable to the government in the other. The importance of this assumption will become clear as we go along.

4. Trade Wars

We begin our analysis of the international economic relations between politically-motivated governments with the case of a trade war. Here, the governments behave unilaterally, ignoring the impacts of their actions on political and economic agents in the opposite country. While purely non-cooperative outcomes are unlikely to emerge in a world with repeated interactions and many forums for trade discussions, the extreme case of non-cooperation sheds light on the political forces that shape trade policies during the frequent departures from harmony and cooperation in the trading realm.

Let us define an *equilibrium response* by each country to an arbitrary policy choice of the other. We use the home country to illustrate, although a similar definition applies to the foreign country.

Definition 1: Let τ^* be an arbitrary trade policy vector of the foreign country. Then a set of feasible contribution functions $\left\{C_i^o\right\}_{i\varepsilon L}$ and a trade policy vector τ^o are an equilibrium response to τ^* if:

(a) $\tau^o = \arg\max_\tau \Sigma_{i\varepsilon L} C_i^o(\tau,\tau^*) + aW(\tau,\tau^*)$; and

(b) for every organized interest group $i\varepsilon L$ there does not exist a feasible contribution function $C_i(\tau,\tau^*)$ and a trade policy vector τ^i such that:

(i) $\tau^i = \arg\max_\tau C_i(\tau,\tau^*) + \Sigma_{j\neq i, j\varepsilon L} C_j^o(\tau,\tau^*) + aW(\tau,\tau^*)$; and

(ii) $W_i(\tau^i,\tau^*) - C_i(\tau^i;\tau^*) > W_i(\tau^o,\tau^*) - C_i^o(\tau^o;\tau^*)$.

An equilibrium response comprises a set of feasible contribution schedules and a policy vector. Each contribution schedule prescribes a political donation for each trade policy vector τ that the home government might select. Feasible schedules are those that promise only non-negative offers that do not exceed the aggregate income of the group's members. Condition (a) for the definition stipulates that the politicians select the policy vector that best serves their own interest, given the policy of the foreign government and the contribution schedules offered by the domestic lobbies. Condition (b) states that, given the set of contributions offered by all lobbies other than itself, no individual lobby i can improve its lot by setting a contribution schedule $C_i(\cdot)$ different from $C_i^o(\cdot)$, thereby inducing the home government to choose the policy vector τ^i.

Several aspects of this definition bear further discussion. First, our definition supposes that the lobbies do not cooperate with one another. While it is occasionally the case that several lobbies in a country will coordinate their activities to pursue a common goal, and even that lobbies in different countries will join forces, the norm is certainly for the various industry representatives to take independent political action. One explanation for this observation might be that pressure groups cannot write binding contracts specifying their contributions to politicians and other political activities. In the absence of such contracts, it would be difficult for the different lobby groups to enforce any cooperative agreement among themselves. Also, in our model, the scope for cooperation between lobbies in any one country is limited, because the interests of different producers are mostly in opposition to one another. Lobbies representing the same industry in different countries also have opposing views about desirable policy interventions, as we shall see.

Our definition also presumes that the lobbies condition their promised contributions on the expected policy choices of the other country's government. In other words, the lobbies take the other country's policy as given, even though these lobbies make their decisions before the governments make theirs. The lobbies certainly would wish to influence the choices of the other government if it were possible to do so. But here is where our assumption that a lobby's offers to its own government cannot be observed by the other government comes into play. If the home lobbies could make their promises observable to foreign politicians and if they could commit to their contribution schedules immutably, then the lobbies would set their schedules strategically in order to induce a favorable policy response by the foreign government. The situation would be similar to that analyzed by Fershtman and Judd (1987), who showed that the owners of a firm generally will want to set a compensation schedule that gives the firm's managers an incentive to act aggressively in oligopolistic competition against other firms. But, as Katz (1991) later argued, a strategic design of an agent's compensation schedule can only bear fruit in a delegation game (i.e., a game in which agents play on behalf of principals) if the contracts between principal and agent are observable to the opposing players. Otherwise, the opposing players will not be influenced by (unobserved) manipulation of the principal–agent contract, and so there can be no gain to the principals (in our case, the home lobbies) from such manipulation.

It is natural for us to assume that contribution schedules cannot be observed abroad, for at least two reasons. First, it might be problematic for special interest groups to be open and explicit about their willingness to pay the government for favorable treatment. Second, even if the interest groups were to announce their intention to vary their support according to the positions taken by the politicians, these promises would not be legally binding and policy makers abroad would not know whether there were further details or subsequent agreements besides those that had been made public. In cases where multiple agreements or renegotiation are possible, a lobby's announcement of its contribution schedule carries little commitment value [see Katz (1991)]. Accordingly, we feel justified in studying an equilibrium in which the industry groups condition their lobbying strategies on what they expect will be the other government's policy choice, but do not see themselves as able to influence those policies by their own choice of contribution schedule.

To find the equilibrium responses for each country we proceed as in Grossman and Helpman (1994). There we characterized equilibrium trade policies for a small country that takes external prices as given. We noted the applicability of the theory of common agency developed by Bernheim and Whinston (1986), wherein a single actor acts simultaneously as the agent for several different principals. In the present context, once we take the foreign policy vector as given, we have a situation where the home government acts as an agent for the various special interest groups in the home country. We have already derived the payoffs to the principals and the agent for every action open to the latter, so we can proceed to apply the Bernheim-Whinston results to characterize the equilibrium responses.

We know from Lemma 2 in Bernheim and Whinston (1986) [or Proposition 1 in Grossman and Helpman (1994)] that the equilibrium policy response to τ^* satisfies, in addition to condition (a) of Definition 1, the following requirement that is implied by condition (b):[7]

$$\tau^o = \arg\max_\tau W_i(\tau, \tau^*) - C_i^o(\tau, \tau^*) + \sum_{j \varepsilon L} C_j^o(\tau, \tau^*) + aW(\tau, \tau^*) \quad \text{for every } i \varepsilon L. \tag{10}$$

This condition has a simple interpretation: The equilibrium trade policy vector must maximize the joint welfare of each lobby i and the government, when the contribution schedules of all lobbies other than i are taken as given. If this were not the case, lobby i could reformulate its schedule to induce the government to choose the jointly optimal policy vector instead of the alternative, and it could do so in such a way as to share in the surplus from the switch in policy. In equilibrium there can exist no such

---

[7] This is a necessary condition for an equilibrium. The complete set of necessary and sufficient conditions is given in Proposition 1 of Grossman and Helpman (1994).

possibilities for a lobby to improve its lot. Of course, the same holds true for the foreign lobbies, so that an equation analogous to (10) applies to τ^{*o}.

Let us assume now that the lobbies set contribution schedules that are *differentiable,* at least around the equilibrium point.[8] We have argued in Grossman and Helpman (1994) that there are compelling reasons for focusing on contribution schedules that have this property. For example, differentiable schedules may be robust to small calculation errors. With differentiability, a trade policy vector that satisfies (10) also satisfies the first-order condition

$$\nabla_\tau W_i(\tau^o;\tau^*) - \nabla_\tau C_i^o(\tau^o,\tau^*) + \Sigma_{j\varepsilon L} \nabla_\tau C_j^o(\tau^o;\tau^*) + a\nabla_\tau W(\tau^o,\tau^*) = 0\,,$$

$$\text{for all } i\varepsilon L\,. \tag{11}$$

The home politicians' utility maximization ensures, by part (a) of Definition 1, that

$$\Sigma_{j\varepsilon L} \nabla_\tau C_j^o(\tau^o;\tau^*) + a\nabla_\tau W(\tau^o,\tau^*) = 0. \tag{12}$$

Taken together, (11) and (12) imply

$$\nabla_\tau C_i^o(\tau^o;\tau^*) = \nabla_\tau W_i\;(\tau^o,\tau^*) \qquad \text{for all } i\varepsilon L; \tag{13}$$

i.e., the contribution schedules are set so that the marginal change in the donation for a small change in home policy (taking the foreign policy as given) matches the effect of the policy change on the lobby's gross welfare. In Grossman and Helpman (1994) we referred to this property of the equilibrium contribution schedules as *local truthfulness.*

---

[8] Typically, the contribution schedules would not be differentiable where the constraint that payments must be non-negative becomes binding; i.e. where $C_i(\cdot) = 0$. However, this is not a problem for our arguments, as we will assume differentiability only around equilibria where $C_i^o(\tau^o;\tau^{*o}) > 0$ for all i .

We sum equation (13) over all i and substitute the result into (12) to derive

$$\Sigma_{i\varepsilon L}\overline{V}_{\tau}W_i(\tau^o,\tau^*)+a\overline{V}_{\tau}W(\tau^o,\tau^*)=0\ . \tag{14}$$

This equation allows us to compute the equilibrium home policy response to an arbitrary foreign policy vector τ^*.

Similarly, we have

$$\Sigma_{i\varepsilon L^*}\overline{V}_{\tau^*}W_i^*(\tau^{*o},\tau)+a^*\overline{V}_{\tau^*}W^*(\tau^{*o},\tau)=0\ , \tag{14*}$$

which gives the foreign equilibrium response to an arbitrary home policy vector.

At last we are ready to define a full equilibrium in the trade war. When the policies are set, each government makes an equilibrium response to what it expects the other's policy will be. We can invoke the concept of a Nash equilibrium as follows:

Definition 2: A non-cooperative trade policy equilibrium consists of sets of political contribution functions $\left\{C_i^o\right\}_{i\varepsilon L}$ and $\left\{C_i^{*o}\right\}_{i\varepsilon L^*}$ and a pair of trade policy vectors τ^o and τ^{*o} such that $\left[\left\{C_i^o\right\}_{i\varepsilon L},\ \tau^o\right]$ is an equilibrium response to τ^{*o} and $\left[\left\{C_i^*\right\}_{i\varepsilon L^*},\tau^{*o}\right]$ is an equilibrium response to τ^o.

We proceed now to characterize the equilibrium policy vectors by substituting τ^{*o} for τ^* in (14), and τ^o for τ in (14*) and then treating these as a system of simultaneous equations. We calculate the derivatives in (14) using (4), (6), (8), and the definitions of the import functions $M_i(\cdot)$ and the gross benefit functions $W_i(\cdot)$ and $W(\cdot)$. This gives

$$(I_{iL}-\alpha_L)\left(\pi_i+\tau_i^o\pi_{i1}\right)X_i+(a+\alpha_L)\left[(\tau_i-1)\pi_i\left(\pi_i+\tau_i^o\pi_{i1}\right)M_i^{'}-\pi_{i1}M_i\right]=0\ , \tag{15}$$

where I_{iL} is an indicator variable that equals one if industry i is politically organized and zero otherwise, and $\alpha_L \equiv \Sigma_{j\varepsilon L}\alpha_j$ is the fraction of voters that is represented by a lobby. From (9) we find the partials of the world price functions, $\pi_i(\cdot)$. [9] Substituting these into (15) yields an expression for the home country's equilibrium policy, namely

$$\tau_i^o - 1 = -\frac{I_{iL} - \alpha_L}{a + \alpha_L}\frac{X_i}{\pi_i M_i^{'}} + \frac{1}{e_i^*}, \quad \text{for } i = 1, 2, \ldots, n, \tag{16}$$

where $e_i^* \equiv \tau_i^* \pi_i M_i^{*'} / M_i^*$ is the elasticity of foreign import demand or export supply (depending upon whether M_i^* is positive or negative). An analogous equation describes the equilibrium foreign trade policy; that is,

$$\tau_i^{*o} - 1 = -\frac{I_{iL}^* - \alpha_L^*}{a^* + \alpha_L^*}\frac{X_i^*}{\pi_i M_i^{*'}} + \frac{1}{e_i}, \quad \text{for } i = 1, 2, \ldots, n, \tag{16*}$$

where $e_i \equiv \tau_i \pi_i M_i^{'} / M_i$ is the home country's import demand or export supply elasticity.

Equations (16) and (16*) express the ad valorem trade tax and subsidy rates in each country as sums of two components. These components represent, respectively, the *political support* and *terms-of-trade* motives for trade intervention. The first component has exactly the same form as the expression in Grossman and Helpman (1994) for the equilibrium policy in a small country facing fixed world prices. It reflects a balancing of the deadweight loss associated with trade policies (given the terms of trade) and the income gains that special interest groups can capture via such

---

[9] We have $\pi_{i1} / \pi_i = -M_i^{'} / \left(\tau_i M_i^{'} + \tau^* M_i^{*'}\right)$

and $\pi_{i2} / \pi_i = -M_i^{*'} / \left(\tau_i M_i^{'} + \tau_i^* M_i^{*'}\right)$.

policies. The second component represents the familiar "optimum tariff" (or export tax) that applies in a large country with a benevolent dictator. Given the balancing of special and general interests implicit in the first term, this second term enters the political calculus as an added reason why non-cooperating governments will wish to tax international trade.

It is apparent from (16) and (16*) that an organized import-competing industry emerges from a trade war with a protective tariff (since $e_i^* > 0$ when the foreign country exports good *i*), while an unorganized home export industry suffers an export tax (since $e_i^* < 0$ when the foreign country imports good *i*). In the former case, the terms-of-trade considerations reinforce the industry's lobbying efforts. In the latter case, the government's desire to drive up the world price with an export tax finds support from all organized groups, whose members are consumers of the exportable good. Only in cases of organized export sectors and unorganized import sectors do the special and general interests come into conflict – at least as far as the sign, as opposed to the size, of the desired trade policy is concerned.

Consider, for example, an organized export industry (so that $e_i^* < 0$ and $I_{iL} = 1$). The industry's prospects for securing an export subsidy are the better the greater industry output, the smaller the price sensitivities of domestic supply and demand, and the smaller the weight a that home politicians place on average welfare. A large domestic output raises the stakes for owners of the specific input and makes them willing to bid more for support. Such bids have greater influence on the politicians when they are less concerned with the public interest and when the deadweight loss associated with a given departure from free trade is small (i.e., $|M_i'|$ is small). On the other hand, for a given value of a and given conditions in the domestic market, the more inelastic the foreign import demand curve, the more inclined will the home government be to choose an export tax as its equilibrium policy. This accords with intuition, since the home country's market power in trade varies with the inverse of the foreign elasticity, so the potential social gains from trade taxes become larger as $|e_i^*|$ declines. We note that the second term can outweigh the first even if the government pays no attention whatsoever to national welfare (i.e., $a = 0$). This is because the members of the various interest groups themselves share in the terms of trade gains from trade taxes, and they may collectively bid for an export tax for industry i even though the lobby that represents the industry presses for a subsidy.[10]

It is interesting to compare the policy outcomes in our model with those derived by Johnson (1953/54) under the assumption that governments maximize social welfare. This comparison allows us to isolate the role that domestic politics play in determining the outcome of a trade war. We note that our model reproduces the Johnson equilibrium as a limiting case, when the governments care overwhelmingly

---

[10] In the case where lobbies can contribute to foreign politicians as well as to their own national government, the lobbies still find it optimal to be locally truthful in their contribution offers *to each government*. The implication is that the left-hand side of (15) has some additional terms representing the effect of a marginal change in the home tariff on the aggregate welfare of foreign interest group members. To calculate the domestic tariff response functions we would need to add to the left-hand side of (15) the following expression:

$$\left(I_{iL}^{*} - \alpha_{L}^{*}\right)\tau_{i}^{*}\pi_{i1}X_{i}^{*} + \alpha_{L}^{*}\left[\left(\tau_{i}^{*} - 1\right)\pi_{i}\tau_{i}^{*}M_{i}^{*'} - M_{i}^{*}\right]\pi_{i1} \quad .$$

The resulting analog to the tariff formula (16) is somewhat complicated, but is easily interpreted for the case where the lobby groups are a negligible fraction of the voting population in each country; i.e., $\alpha_L = \alpha_L^{*} = 0$. In this special case, the home country's equilibrium tariff is given by

$$\tau_{i}^{o} - 1 = -\frac{I_{iL}}{a}\,\frac{X_{i}}{\pi_{i}M_{i}^{'}} + \frac{I_{iL}^{*}}{a}\,\frac{X_{i}^{*}}{\pi_{i}M_{i}^{*'}} + \frac{1}{e^{*}} \tag{16'}$$

when there are contributions by both national *and foreign* lobbies. Comparing (16) and (16'), we see that influence-seeking by foreign lobbies serves to reduce the size of the home tariff response to any given foreign tariff, the more so the greater is the foreign industry's output and the less price responsive is the foreign country's export supply.

The foreign output X_i^{*} measures the size and hence political clout of the foreign industry, while the slope of the foreign export supply measures the home government's willingness to accede to its wishes for a smaller tariff, in view of the induced effect on the international price.

about voters' welfare (so that a and a^* approach infinity).[11] Then the governments apply the familiar inverse elasticity rules in setting trade taxes.

In making the comparison, we focus on a special case where both countries have constant trade elasticities. We may limit our attention to the outcome in a single industry, because the equilibrium policy responses depend only on the characteristics of industry i and aggregate variables [see (16) and (16*)]. For concreteness, we make the home country the importer of good X_i. Then its import demand curve is given by $M = m(\tau\pi)^{-\varepsilon}$, with $m > 0$ and $\varepsilon = -e_i > 1$.[12] The foreign country's export supply function has the form $-M^* = m^*\left(\tau^*\pi\right)^{\varepsilon^*}$, with $m^* > 0$ and $\varepsilon^* = e_i^* > 0$.

Figure 1 shows the Johnson equilibrium at point J. This point lies at the intersection of two best-response functions, BB for the home country and B^*B^* for the foreign country, where "B" refers to the benevolent dictators that rule each country. The curves are vertical and horizontal, respectively, in the constant elasticity case. The inverse elasticity rule gives the equilibrium policies in the Johnson equilibrium, $\tau_J = 1 + 1/\varepsilon^*$ and $\tau_J^* = 1 - 1/\varepsilon$. These are, of course, a tariff at home $\left(\tau_J > 1\right)$ and an export tax abroad $\left(\tau_J^* < 1\right)$.

In the trade war between politically-motivated governments, the market clearing world price for good i can be found using (9) and the expressions that define the constant elasticity import demand and export supply functions. We find

$$\pi\left(\tau, \tau^*\right) = \left(\frac{m}{m^*}\right)^{\frac{1}{\varepsilon+\varepsilon^*}} \left(\frac{1}{\tau}\right)^{\frac{\varepsilon}{\varepsilon+\varepsilon^*}} \left(\frac{1}{\tau^*}\right)^{\frac{\varepsilon^*}{\varepsilon+\varepsilon^*}} \tag{17}$$

---

[11] The Johnson equilibrium also obtains when all voters belong to a lobby group and all industries are politically organized. In this case, all individuals are able to express their political demands to the politicians, and so all are equally represented in the political process. The opposing interest groups neutralize one another in their attempts to transfer income to themselves, and what remains is only the terms-of-trade motive for trade policy that potentially benefits them all. Becker (1983) derives a similar neutrality result in a somewhat different model of the political process.

[12] We omit the industry subscript for the time being, since all parameters and variables refer to industry i.

Figure 1

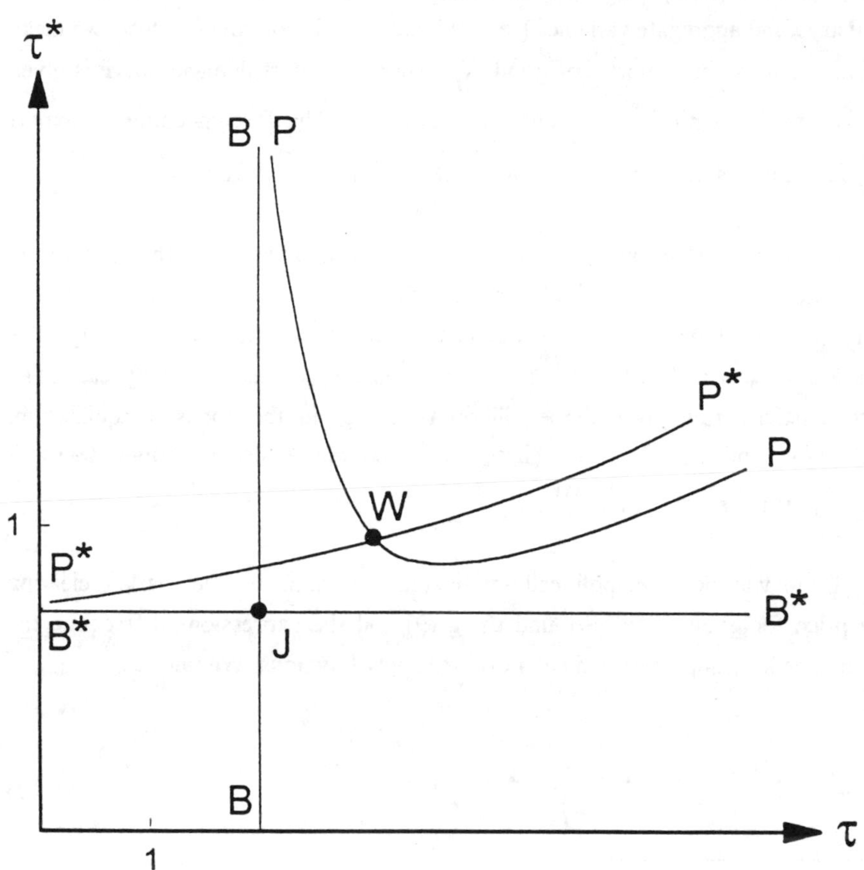

Also, (16) and (16*) give the equilibrium policy responses, which in the constant elasticity case can be written as

$$\tau = \left(1 + \frac{1}{\varepsilon^*}\right)\left[1 - \frac{I_L - \alpha_L}{a + \alpha_L}\,\frac{X(\tau\pi)}{\varepsilon m(\tau\pi)^{-\varepsilon}}\right]^{-1}, \tag{18}$$

$$\tau^* = \left(1 - \frac{1}{\varepsilon}\right)\left[1 - \frac{I_L^* - \alpha_L^*}{a^* + \alpha_L^*}\,\frac{X^*(\tau^*\pi)}{\varepsilon^* m^*(\tau^*\pi)^{\varepsilon^*}}\right]^{-1}, \tag{18*}$$

where the π in (18) and (18*) represents the equilibrium $\pi(\tau, \tau^*)$ given in (17).

Figure 1 shows the equilibrium responses for an industry with active lobby groups in both countries (i.e., $I_L = I_L^* = 1$). The home country's equilibrium response function (18) is represented by *PP* ("*P*" for political), the foreign country's (18*) by P^*P^*. The *PP* curve lies everywhere to the right of *BB* and has a u-shape: it asymptotes to *BB* at $\tau = 1 + 1/\varepsilon^*$ and to a ray from the origin as τ grows large.[13] The P^*P^* curve lies everywhere above B^*B^* and always slopes upward.[14]

Point *W* depicts the political equilibrium in the trade war.[15] This point lies to the north-east of the Johnson equilibrium at point *J*. Evidently, the politically motivated

---

13 From (18) we see that $\tau \to \infty$ if and only if the term in the second parenthesis on the right-hand side approaches zero. Since $X(\tau\pi)/(\tau\pi)^{-\varepsilon}$ is an increasing function of $\tau\pi$, this gives a unique value for $\tau\pi$ and therefore τ/τ^* [see (17) as τ grows large.]

14 The right-hand side of (18*) declines in the foreign price $p^* = \tau^*\pi$, because foreign exports ($m^* p^{*\varepsilon^*}$), which are the difference between foreign output and demand, are more sensitive to p^* than foreign supply (X^*). But, from (17), we see that the foreign price $\tau^*\pi$ increases in τ^*/τ. It follows that P^*P^* must slope upward. We note that the slope would be ambiguous if the sector's input owners were unorganized (i.e., if $I_L^* = 0$).

15 The diagram shows a unique equilibrium, as exists when the P^*P^* curve is steeper than the *PP* curve for τ and τ^* large. If the *PP* curve becomes steeper as τ and τ^* grow large, then the curves have either zero or two intersections. In the event that there are two, our remarks apply only to the equilibrium associated with the first crossing.

governments tilt trade policies in favor of their organized special interests; the home tariff is higher in the political equilibrium than in the Johnson equilibrium, while the foreign export tax is lower or possibly even a subsidy.[16]

Next we examine how the policy outcome changes when the political climate does. Suppose the home politicians were to become less sensitive to the public interest and more concerned with their campaign finances; that is, consider a decrease in a. For the case of a home import good with active lobbies in each country, Figure 1 describes the initial equilibrium. A decline in a causes the PP curve to shift up, moving the equilibrium up and to the right along the fixed P^*P^* schedule.[17] The new equilibrium entails a higher home tariff and a lower foreign export tax (or higher export subsidy). The new equilibrium entails a higher home tariff and a lower foreign export tax (or higher export subsidy). The increase in the tariff comes about in the first instance because the lobby perceives a smaller marginal cost of "buying" protection from the government. Since the foreign lobbies and the foreign government expect a more protectionist stance from the home government, the political calculus changes there as well. In particular, a higher domestic tariff means, ceteris paribus, a lower world price for the good. This decreases both the private benefit and social cost of an export subsidy, but the latter falls by proportionately more. Thus, the industry's willingness to pay for a subsidy (or to resist a tax) declines by less than the cost to the government of providing the favor. The new foreign policy is more favorable to the foreign industry.

[16] The trade war generates both higher import tariffs and higher export taxes than the Johnson equilibrium for industries in which the import-competing interests are organized while the export interests are not. Where the export interests are organized and the import-competing interests are not, the trade taxes are lower in both countries than at J, and may even turn to subsidies in one or both countries. Finally, import tariffs are lower and export taxes higher than at J in industries that have organized lobbies in neither country; then the organized groups representing other industries bid unopposed for lower consumer prices, at the expense of the unrepresented specific factor owners.

[17] Given τ, equation (18) requires an increase in τ^* in response to a decline in a, so that π rises and X/M falls.

We note that the rise in the import tariff and the fall in the export tax have offsetting implications for internal prices in each country. The increase in the home tariff raises the home price despite the resultant improvement in the terms of trade, but the fall in the foreign export tax pushes the home price down via its effect on π. Similarly, the increase in τ^* puts upward pressure on p^*, but the terms of trade movement associated with the rise in τ works in the opposite direction. The figure shows, however, that τ/τ^* must rise.[18] Since $\tau\pi$ is an increasing function of τ/τ^* and $\tau^*\pi$ is a decreasing function of this same ratio, the decline in a causes the internal price of a home import good to rise at home and to fall abroad.

The change in the political environment affects organized export industries in much the same way. Figure 2 shows the policy outcome for such a sector. Since our labeling convention makes the foreign country the exporter of the good in question, we represent a reduction in the government's concern about aggregate welfare by a cut in a^*. This shifts the P^*P^* curve to the left. The export tax (or subsidy) may rise or fall, while the import tariff always falls. But no matter which way the exporting country's policy changes, τ/τ^* must fall, so again the internal price rises in the country that experiences the change in its political environment and falls in the other. In both the export and import cases, an increased government sensitivity to the concerns of special interests in one country raises the profits of the organized factor owners in that country at the expense of their counterparts abroad.

The analysis shows how the domestic political environments color the strategic interactions between countries. We have seen that a decline in the home parameter a induces a change in the foreign country's policy that improves the home country's terms of trade. This raises the potential for a political paradox: *a government that is unresponsive to the public interest might actually serve the general voter well, because the self-interested government can credibly commit to a policy of aggressive support for the domestic industry.*

---

[18] At each point along P^*P^* the curve is flatter than a ray to that point from the origin. This implies that τ/τ^* falls as we move out and to the right along the curve.

Figure 2

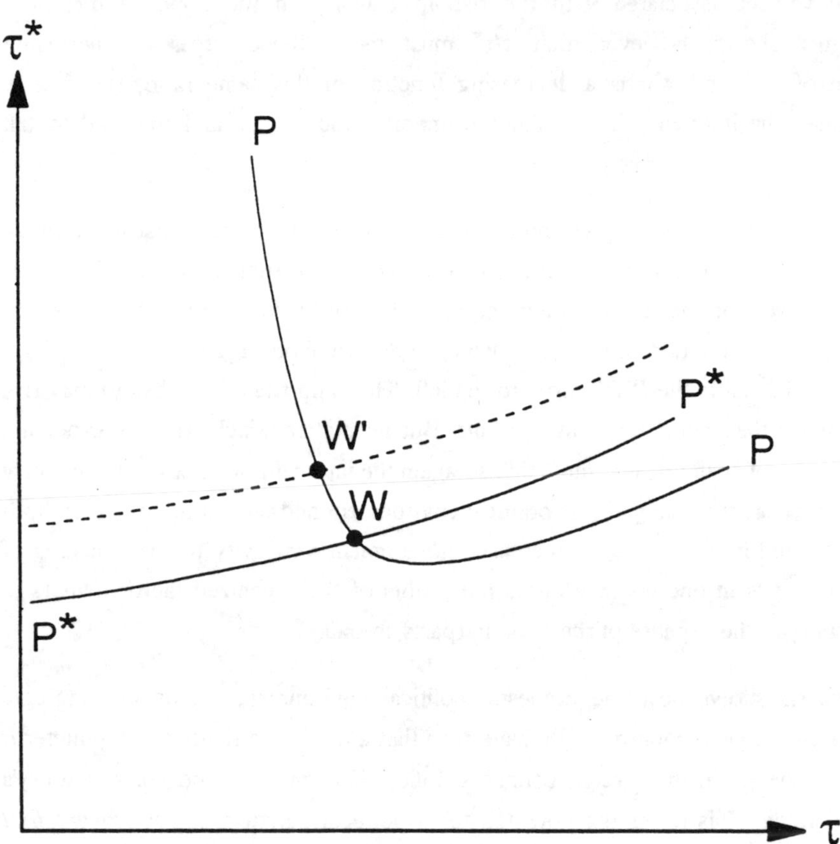

5. Trade Talks

We have portrayed the interactions between government officials in different countries who pursue their selfish interests while setting their nations' trade policies. These officials are willing to impose deadweight losses on their constituencies as a means of amassing campaign contributions. Thus, the economic inefficiency of the political equilibrium will not be a matter of overriding concern to them. However, there is another sort of inefficiency inherent in the equilibrium of Section 4 that may be of greater concern. By choosing their national policies non-cooperatively, the incumbent politicians impose avoidable political costs on one another. If the politicians recognize this, they may be willing and indeed anxious to enter into a multilateral trade negotiation. In this section we study equilibria that emerge from trade talks between politically-motivated governments.

We allow the two governments to bargain over the trade policy schedules τ and τ^*. For the moment, we also allow them to negotiate a transfer payment R (positive or negative) that the foreign country pays to the home country as part of the negotiated agreement.[19] Some trade pacts such as the European Community's common agricultural policy actually call for such inter-country transfers. However, as we will see below, the bargaining game has essentially the same equilibrium when R is constrained to zero. Thus, our results apply also when transfers are infeasible.

It proves convenient for the exposition to begin with a case where organized owners of specific factors comprise a negligible fraction of the voters in each country. With $\alpha_L = \alpha_L^* = 0$, the members of lobby groups enjoy a negligible share of the surplus from consuming non-numeraire goods and they pay a negligible fraction of the head taxes levied by the governments. Thus, the interest groups worry only about their factor incomes and the amounts of their contributions to the policies that emerge from the international talks; i.e., contributions are functions of τ and τ^*. In general the lobbies might also condition their contributions on the size of the international

[19] While we allow official, government-to-government transfers, we do not allow side-payments (i.e., "kickbacks") from one set of politicians to the other.

transfer. But they need not do so here, because their members are so few in number that they receive or contribute only a negligible fraction of any payment that is made.

Confronted with the set of contribution schedules $\{C_i(\tau, \tau^*)\}$, the home government comes to the bargaining table with the goal of maximizing

$$G = \Sigma_{i \varepsilon L} C_i\left(\tau, \tau^*\right) + a\left[W(\tau, \tau^*) + R\right] \tag{19}$$

The first term in (19) is the total amount of campaign contributions. The second term represents per capita welfare weighted by the parameter a reflecting the government's concern for the public interest. Notice that the transfer R has been added to the previously defined measure of average gross welfare. This reflects our assumption that transfer payments are combined with any net revenue from trade taxes and subsidies, and that the government redistributes the surplus (or collects the shortfall) on an equal per capita basis. The same is true of the foreign government, so its objective becomes

$$G^* = \Sigma_{i \varepsilon L^*} C_i^*\left(\tau^*, \tau\right) + a^*\left[W^*(\tau^*, \tau) - R\right] \tag{19*}$$

For now, we do not commit ourselves to any particular bargaining procedure. Rather we assume only that the politicians settle on an outcome that is efficient from their own selfish perspectives. In other words, we assume that the trade policies that emerge from the negotiation are such that G could not be raised without lowering G^*. The Nash bargaining solution and Rubinstein's (1982) non-cooperative bargaining equilibrium, among others, have this efficiency property. Efficiency requires the governments to choose the trade policy vectors to maximize the weighted sum

$$a^* G + aG^* = a^* \Sigma_{i \varepsilon L} C_i\left(\tau, \tau^*\right) + a \Sigma_{i \varepsilon L^*} C_i^*(\tau^*, \tau) + a^* a\left[W\left(\tau, \tau^*\right) + W^*(\tau^*, \tau)\right] \tag{20}$$

Once this sum has been maximized, the governments can use the international transfer to select (almost) any utility pair (G, G^*) on the straight line defined by (20).[20]

We are now in a position to define an equilibrium in the two-stage game where lobbies set contribution schedules non-cooperatively in the first stage and the governments bargain over trade policies in the second.

<u>Definition 3:</u> An equilibrium trade agreement consists of sets of political contribution functions $\left\{C_i^o\right\}_{i\varepsilon L}$ and $\left\{C_i^{*o}\right\}_{i\varepsilon L^*}$, and a pair of trade policy vectors τ^o and τ^{*o} such that:

(a)

$$\left(\tau^o, \tau^{*o}\right) = \arg\max_{(\tau, \tau^*)} a^* \Sigma_{i\varepsilon L} C_i^o\left(\tau, \tau^*\right) + a \Sigma_{i\varepsilon L^*} C_i^{*o}\left(\tau^*, \tau\right) + a^* a\left[W\left(\tau, \tau^*\right) + W^*(\tau^*, \tau)\right];$$

(b) for every organized lobby $i\varepsilon L$ there does not exist a feasible contribution function $C_i(\tau, \tau^*)$ and a pair of trade policy vectors (τ^i, τ^{*i}) such that:

(i)
$$\left(\tau^i, \tau^{*i}\right) = \arg\max_{(\tau, \tau^*)} a^*\left[C_i(\tau, \tau^*) + \Sigma_{j \neq i, j\varepsilon L} C_j^o(\tau, \tau^*)\right] + a \Sigma_{j\varepsilon L^*} C_j^{*o}(\tau^*, \tau) + a^* a\left[W(\tau, \tau^*) + W^*(\tau^*, \tau)\right]$$

and

(ii) $\quad W_i(\tau^i, \tau^{*i}) - C_i(\tau^i, \tau^{*i}) > W_i(\tau^o, \tau^{*o}) - C_i^o(\tau^o, \tau^{*o});$

---

[20] Equation (20) is derived as a weighted sum of (19) and (19*), after canceling R. The only restriction on feasible (G, G^*) is that neither government can promise to transfer to the other country more than the entirety of the national product.

(c) for every organized lobby $i \varepsilon L*$ there does not exist a feasible contribution function $C_i^*(\tau^*, \tau^*)$ and a pair of trade policy vectors (τ^j, τ^{*i}) such that:

(i) $$(\tau^j, \tau^{*i}) = \arg\max_{(\tau,\tau^*)} a^* \Sigma_{j\varepsilon L} C_j^o(\tau, \tau^*) +$$

$$a\left[C_i^*(\tau, \tau^*) + \Sigma_{j \neq i, j\varepsilon L^*} C_j^{*o}(\tau^*, \tau)\right] + a^* a\left[W(\tau, \tau^*) + W^*(\tau, \tau^*)\right]$$

and

(ii) $W_i^*(\tau^{*i}, \tau^j) - C_i^*(\tau^{*i}, \tau^j) > W_i^*(\tau^{*o}, \tau^o) - C_i^{*o}(\tau^{*o}, \tau^o)$.

Condition (a) of the definition stipulates that the settlement is efficient from the point of view of the two negotiating governments. Note that efficiency here means maximization of the joint welfare of the two sets of politicians, not Pareto efficiency for voters. Condition (b), analogous to the similarly labeled condition of Definition 1, requires that it be impossible for any organized lobby group in the home country to gain by restructuring its contribution schedule, considering that the two governments will settle on a different agreement when one of them faces an altered set of political incentives. The same must be true for organized interest groups in the foreign country, which is the meaning of (c). The equilibrium trade agreement also entails a certain transfer, R^o, the size of which will depend upon the details of the bargaining process.

This two-country game has a structure almost identical to the one that characterizes policy setting in a small country [see Grossman and Helpman (1994)]. In the case of a small country, the organized lobbies set contribution schedules that induce their common agent (the government) to take a policy action in light of the perceived costs to the agent. The various schedules are set simultaneously and each constitutes a best response to the others. Here there are two sets of organized lobbies, but still they set their schedules simultaneously and non-cooperatively. While there is no identifiable common agent, the objective function in (20) can be interpreted as being that of an "as if" mediator or a surrogate world government. In other words, the equilibrium trade agreement is the same as would arise if a single decision maker had the preferences given on the right-hand side of (20) and a large set of interest groups comprising the organized lobbies of both countries bid to influence this agent's decisions. Once again, the equilibrium policies can be found by application of Lemma 2 in Bernheim and Whinston (1986). That is, we replace conditions (b) and (c) of Definition 3 by the requirement - analogous to (10) – that the negotiated policy outcome must maximize the joint welfare of each organized lobby and the hypothetical mediator, when the contribution schedules of all other lobbies are taken as given. This requirement can be written as

$$(\tau^o, \tau^{*o}) = \arg\max_{(\tau,\tau^*)} a^*\left[W_j(\tau,\tau^*) - C_j^o(\tau,\tau^*)\right] + a^*\Sigma_{i\varepsilon L} C_i^o(\tau,\tau^*) + a\Sigma_{i\varepsilon L^*} C_i^{*o}(\tau^*,\tau) + a^* a\left[W(\tau,\tau^*) + W^*(\tau^*,\tau)\right] \quad \text{for all } j\varepsilon L, \qquad (21)$$

and

$$(\tau^o, \tau^{*o}) = \arg\max_{(\tau,\tau^*)} a\left[W_j^*(\tau^*,\tau) - C_j^{*o}(\tau^*,\tau)\right] + a\Sigma_{i\varepsilon L} C_i^o(\tau,\tau^*) + a\Sigma_{i\varepsilon L^*} C_i^{*o}(\tau^*,\tau) + a^* a\left[W(\tau^*,\tau) + W^*(\tau^*,\tau)\right] \quad \text{for all } j\varepsilon L^*. \qquad (21^*)$$

Now we introduce the assumption, as we did before, that all contribution schedules are differentiable around the equilibrium point. Then we can make use of the first-order conditions that characterize the solutions to the maximization in condition (a) of Definition 3 and the maximizations in (21) and (21*). Combining these, we find that the equilibrium contribution schedules again are locally truthful and that the agreed-upon policies must satisfy

$$a^*\Sigma_{i\varepsilon L}\nabla_\tau W_i(\tau^o,\tau^{*o}) + a\Sigma_{i\varepsilon L^*}\nabla_\tau W_i^*(\tau^{*o},\tau^o) + a^* a\left[\nabla_\tau W(\tau^o,\tau^{*o}) + \nabla_\tau W^*(\tau^{*o},\tau^o)\right] = 0\,; \qquad (22)$$

$$a^* \Sigma_{i\varepsilon L} \overline{V}_{\tau*} W_i(\tau^o, \tau^{*o}) + a \Sigma_{i\varepsilon L^*} \overline{V}_{\tau*} W_i^*(\tau^{*o}, \tau^o) +$$

$$a^* a\left[\overline{V}_{\tau*} W(\tau^o, \tau^{*o}) + \overline{V}_{\tau*} W^*(\tau^{*o}, \tau^o)\right] = 0 . \qquad (22^*)$$

It is straightforward to calculate the partial derivatives in (22) and (22*).

Substituting these expressions, we obtain

$$a^*\left[I_{jL} X_j + a(\tau_j^o - 1)\pi_j M_j'\right](\pi_j + \tau_j^o \pi_{j1}) +$$

$$a\left[I_{jL}^* X_j^* + a^*(\tau_j^{*o} - 1)\pi_j M_j^{*'}\right]\tau_j^{*o}\pi_{j1} = 0 \quad \text{for } j\varepsilon L; \qquad (23)$$

$$a\left[I_{jL}^* X_j^* + a^*(\tau_j^{*o} - 1)\pi_j M_j^{*'}\right](\pi_j + \tau_j^{*o}\pi_{j2}) +$$

$$a^*\left[I_{jL} X_j + a(\tau_j^o - 1)\pi_j M_j'\right]\tau_j^o \pi_{j2} = 0 \quad \text{for } j\varepsilon L^* . \qquad (23^*)$$

Equations (23) and (23*) are two sets of equations that, if independent, might be used to solve for τ^o and τ^{*o}. However, these equations are linearly dependent.[21] In other words, the equilibrium requirements that we have stated so far determine only the ratios τ_1^o / τ_1^{*o}, τ_2^o / τ_2^{*o}, . . . , τ_n^o / τ_n^{*o}, but not τ^o and τ^{*o} separately. We will explain the meaning of this finding presently; but first we derive from (23) and (23*) the following equation that implicitly gives the equilibrium policy ratio in industry *i*:

$$\tau_i^o - \tau_i^{*o} = \left[-\frac{I_{iL}}{a}\frac{X_i}{\pi_i M_i'}\right] - \left[-\frac{I_{iL}^*}{a^*}\frac{X_i^*}{\pi_i M_i^{*'}}\right] \quad \text{for } i = 1, 2, \ldots, n . \qquad (24)$$

---

[21] To establish this, use the properties of the price functions $\pi_j(\cdot)$ started in footnote 9.

Notice that when both sides of (24) are divided by τ_i^{*o}, the trade policies enter this equation only in ratio form.[22]

Upon reflection, it is clear why Definition 3 – which we have used to characterize an equilibrium trade pact – pins down only the ratio of the two countries' trade policies and not the levels of those policies. The definition stipulates that the equilibrium must be efficient for the two governments without specifying how the surplus will be divided between them. But the ratio τ_i / τ_i^* determines the internal prices p_i and p_i^*, which in turn determine industry outputs, demands, trade flows, and factor prices in each country. In short, the allocation of resources does not depend separately on τ_i and τ_i^*, and neither does the joint welfare available to the two sets of politicians.[23]

This brings us to an important point: *Equation (24) must characterize the equilibrium trade agreement even if inter-country transfer payments are constrained to be zero.* Since allocations do not depend separately on the sizes of the policy wedges in the two countries, the governments can mimic any international transfer payment by increasing (or decreasing) some τ_i and τ_i^* while holding their ratio constant. Consider what this would do to trade tax revenue in each country. The revenues that the home country derives from the tax or subsidy in industry i total $r_i = (\tau_i - 1)\pi_i M_i$, while those that the foreign country collects amount to $r_i^* = (\tau_i^* - 1)\pi_i M_i^*$. An equiproportionate increase in τ_i and τ_i^* leaves $\tau_i \pi_i$, $\tau_i^* \pi_i$, M_i, and M_i^* unchanged. Therefore tax receipts must rise in the country that imports good X_i and fall in the country that exports this good. Moreover, the offsetting changes in government revenue are of exactly the same size. Thus, an

[22] That is, X_i and M_i' are functions of $p_i = \tau_i \pi_i$, which is homogeneous of degree zero in τ_i and τ_i^*. Similarly, X_i^* and $M^{*'}$ are functions of $p_i^* = \tau_i^* \pi_i$, which also is homogeneous of degree zero in τ_i and τ_i^*. Finally, the term $\tau_i^* \pi_i$ appears directly in the denominator of both bracketed expressions, once the equation has been divided through τ_i^*. Thus, all of these can be expressed as functions of the ratio, τ_i / τ_i^*.

[23] Mayer (1981) noted this point in his discussion of efficient bargaining between two aggregate-welfare-maximizing governments.

equiproportionate increase in τ_i and τ_i^* is in every way equivalent to a direct transfer from the exporting country to the importing country. It follows that a bargain that is efficient when transfers are feasible remains so when they are not.[24]

Recall that we have so far restricted attention to the case in which lobby group members constitute a negligible fraction of the total voting population. We can now extend the analysis to the more general case. When $\alpha_L \geq \alpha_L^* \geq 0$, the following formula applies in place of (24):

$$\tau_i^o - \tau_i^{*o} = \left[-\frac{I_{iL} - \alpha_L}{a + \alpha_L} \frac{X_i}{\pi_i M_i'} \right] - \left[-\frac{I_{iL}^* - \alpha_L^*}{a^* + \alpha_L^*} \frac{X_i^*}{\pi_i M_i^{*\prime}} \right] \quad \text{for } i = 1, 2, \ldots, n . \quad (25)$$

This can be derived in one of two ways. First, we can impose $R = 0$ and solve the common agency problem involving lobbies with objectives $v^i = W_i(\tau, \tau^*) - C_i(\tau, \tau^*)$ and $v^{*i} = W_i^*(\tau^*, \tau) - C_i(\tau^*, \tau)$, and a hypothetical mediator who maximized the right-hand side of (20). The derivation proceeds as before. Alternatively, we can allow $R \neq 0$,but then we must permit the lobbies to condition their contributions on the sizes of the transfers obtained by the governments as part of the trade agreement. If we allow for this dependence and

---

[24] In the event that lobbies can offer contributions to politicians in either country, all campaign giving will be concentrated on the single government that is more easily swayed by such gifts. That is, each industry, no matter where it is located, will offer nothing to the government that places the greater weight on its average voter's welfare and will devote all of its efforts to influencing the negotiating position of the government that more readily trades off voter well-being for campaign funds. The upshot is that, instead of (24), the negotiated tariff schedule will satisfy

$$\tau_i^o - \tau_i^{*o} = \left[-\frac{I_{iL}}{\tilde{a}} \frac{X_i}{\pi_i M_i'} \right] - \left[-\frac{I_{iL}^*}{\tilde{a}} \frac{X_i^*}{\pi_i M_i^{*\prime}} \right] \quad \text{for } i=1, 2, , \ldots, n , \quad (24')$$

where $\tilde{a} = \min(a, a^*)$.

write $C_i(\cdot)=\tilde{C}_i(\tau,\tau^*)+\lambda_i R$, and similarly for the foreign lobbies, then we can once again derive (25) as the outcome of the common agency problem.[25]

Equation (25) reveals that, relative to free trade, the negotiated trade agreement favors the industry group that has greater political clout. We have $\tau_i / \tau_i^* > 1$ when the first bracketed term on the right-hand side exceeds the second and $\tau_i / \tau_i^* < 1$ when the second exceeds the first. Since $\tau_i / \tau_i^* = 1$ in free trade and the home (foreign) domestic price is an increasing (decreasing) function of τ_i / τ_i^*, it is the politically stronger industry that winds up with greater profits under the agreement as compared to free trade.

Several components enter into the measurement of political power. First and foremost, political power derives from representation in the political process. If the specific factor owners in industry *i* are organized in one country and not in the other, then the organized group always secures from the trade agreement a gain relative to free trade. When both countries' specific factor owners are organized in some industry, then the more powerful group is the one with the greater stake in the negotiation (i.e., X_i versus X_i^*), the one with the government that places less weight on average welfare (i.e., a versus a*), and the one in the country where a smaller fraction of the voting population bids for policies (i.e., α_L versus α_L^*). Also, an industry interest group at home gains a political advantage relative to its foreign counterpart if the home import demand or export supply is less price sensitive than that abroad. A high price sensitivity raises the cost to a government of distorting prices and thus makes the government less open to the industry's bids for protection.

When the interest groups in industry *i* enjoy equal political power in the two countries, a negotiated agreement gives rise to equal rates of import tax and export subsidy. In the event, internal prices, world prices, and industry outputs and profit levels will be the same as in free trade. This finding points to the conclusion that whatever aggregate efficiency losses result from the negotiated trade agreement, they stem not from the mere existence of special interest politics in the two countries, but

---

[25] We can also show that no lobby can improve its lot by deviating to an arbitrary contribution function $C_i(\tau,\tau^*,R)$ in place of the one with the form $\tilde{C}_i(\tau,\tau^*)+\lambda_i R$.

from differences in the extent of the political pressures that the interest groups can bring to bear. A trade negotiation pits the powerful lobbies in one country against those in another, and thereby neutralizes (to some extent) the power of each one.

Notably absent from the formula in (25) is any measure of the relative market power of the two countries. That is, the foreign trade elasticities – which fully determine the Johnson equilibrium and appear as components of the trade war equilibrium discussed in Section 4 – are neglected by the hypothetical mediator of the trade agreement. As is well known, policy induced terms-of-trade movements benefit one country at the expense of the other and impose a deadweight loss on the world economy. An efficient negotiation will eliminate this source of deadweight loss while perhaps compensating the party that otherwise would have captured the benefits.

It is time now to introduce a specific bargaining procedure, in order to show how this determines the division of surplus between the two negotiating parties. For illustrative purposes, we adopt the Rubinstein (1982) bargaining model, as extended by Binmore et al. (1986) and Sutton (1986) to incorporate the risk that negotiations might break down at any moment when an agreement has not yet been reached.

Suppose that the two governments meet at the bargaining table with the trade war equilibrium of Section 4 as the status quo ante. The governments take turns proposing vectors of trade policies τ and τ^* to replace those in the non-cooperative equilibrium. When one government makes an offer, the other can accept or reject. If it accepts, the agreement goes into effect immediately. If it rejects, then a period of time passes during which the policies given in (16) and (16*) remain in force. At the end of this period, the talks may terminate exogenously or else the second government will get an opportunity to make a counterproposal. Termination happens with probability $\left(1-e^{-\beta\Delta}\right)$, where Δ represents the length of a bargaining period and β is a parameter measuring the likelihood of a breakdown per unit time. The process of alternating proposals continues until either an agreement is reached or a breakdown occurs. In the event of the latter, the non-cooperative equilibrium continues indefinitely.

In this setting, the cost of failing to reach an immediate agreement is twofold. First, the non-cooperative equilibrium applies during the bargaining period. Second, the parties face the risk that the talks will come to an end. To capture the cost of delay, we introduce discount rates ρ and ρ^* for the two governments. These could arise, for example, if politicians and factor owners have the same discount rates and if the politicians did not collect their promised gifts until after the talks were completed.[26] The discount rates imply that the home government perceives the value of an agreement reached after k rounds of bargaining to be $e^{-\rho\Delta(k-1)}$ times as great as the value of an agreement with identical provisions that is signed immediately.

In this bargaining game neither government has an incentive to offer a set of policies when another set would provide strictly greater welfare to both governments. In other words, the offers must maximize the right-hand size of (20). Let the maximal value for this expression be $\overline{G}$. Then we can think of the governments as bargaining directly over the instantaneous welfare levels G and G^* subject to the constraint that $a^*G + aG^* = \overline{G}$. Once a distribution of welfare has been agreed upon, the governments can implement the agreement by choosing policies that satisfy (25) and that divide the trade tax revenues as required by the agreement.

We can solve the bargaining game in the manner suggested by Sutton (1986). Let the home country make the first offer and denote its proposed division of the surplus by (G_H, G_H^*). Of course the proposal must satisfy

$$a^*G_H + aG_H^* = \overline{G} \tag{26}$$

Moreover, the offer will be such as to induce immediate acceptance while leaving the foreign government with no extra surplus relative to what it could achieve by refusing the offer. If the foreign government accepts, it receives G_H^* forever. If it rejects, the non-cooperative equilibrium continues on for a period of at least Δ.

---

26 The governments' discount factors also reflect the fact that the incumbent politicians may not remain in power forever. We view the discount factors as a simple way to capture whatever costs the governments perceive to be associated with delay in reaching an agreement.

Then, with probability $(1-e^{-\beta\Delta})$ the negotiations end and the non-cooperative equilibrium persists forever; and with probability $e^{-\beta\Delta}$ the foreign government gets the opportunity to make a counteroffer, which we denote by $(G_F,\ G_F^*)$. The foreign government would always choose an offer that would (just) be accepted, so it can count on a flow of utility G_F^* after the delay of Δ, if the talks do not break down. The home offer that makes the foreign government just indifferent between accepting and rejecting satisfies

$$\frac{G_H^*}{\rho^*}=\frac{1-e^{-\rho^*\Delta}}{\rho^*}G_N^*+\left[\frac{(1-e^{-\beta\Delta})e^{-\rho^*\Delta}}{\rho^*}G_N^*+\frac{e^{-\beta\Delta}e^{-\rho^*\Delta}}{\rho^*}G_F^*\right],$$

where G_N^* is the flow of utility to the foreign government in the non-cooperative equilibrium of Section 3. The two terms on the right-hand side represent, respectively, the present value of the utility flow during the period before the first possible counteroffer (from time 0 to time Δ), and the expected value of the flow from that time onward. Rearranging this equation gives

$$G_H^*=\left[1-e^{-(\beta+\rho^*)\Delta}\right]G_N^*+\left[e^{-(\beta+\rho^*)\Delta}\right]G_F^* \quad . \tag{27}$$

We derive now the offer that the foreign government would make were it to reach the stage of counterproposing. The counteroffer $(G_F,\ G_F^*)$ satisfies

$$a^*G_F+aG_F^*=\overline{G} \tag{26*}$$

and it provides the home politicians with just enough utility to make them indifferent between accepting the offer and waiting for the chance of still another bargaining round. This indifference condition implies

$$G_F = \left[1 - e^{-(\beta+\rho)\Delta}\right] G_N + \left[e^{-(\beta+\rho)\Delta}\right] G_H \quad , \tag{28}$$

where G_N is the flow of utility to the home government in a trade war.

We solve the four equations (26), (26*), (27) and (28) for the offer $(G_H,\ G_H^*)$ and the counteroffer $(G_F,\ G_F^*)$. Since the initial offer always is accepted, we can readily calculate the division of surplus in the modified Rubinstein game. As is usual in such games, the outcome of the bargaining depends on which government can make the initial offer. However, the advantage from going first disappears as the time between offers shrinks to zero. With continuous bargaining (i.e., $\Delta \to 0$), the equilibrium trade pact yields the following flows of utility to the two governments:

$$G = \frac{1}{2+\gamma+\gamma^*}\left[\frac{1+\gamma^*}{a^*}\overline{G} + (1+\gamma)G_N - \frac{a}{a^*}(1+\gamma^*)G_N^*\right] \quad ; \tag{29}$$

$$G^* = \frac{1}{2+\gamma+\gamma^*}\left[\frac{1+\gamma}{a}\overline{G} + (1+\gamma^*)G_N^* - \frac{a^*}{a}(1+\gamma)G_N\right] \quad ; \tag{29*}$$

where $\gamma = \rho / \beta$ and $\gamma^* = \rho^* / \beta$. Here, the division of surplus depends on the fallback positions. That is, the more each government captures of the gains from cooperation the greater is its measure of political welfare in the trade war equilibrium. As usual, higher welfare in the status quo ante gives a negotiator a stronger position at the bargaining table. Also, the more each government gains from the trade agreement the more patient it can be while bargaining. Patience gives a negotiator a credible threat to decline a low offer, and thus his rival must offer more to ensure an agreement without delay.

6. Conclusions

In this paper we have introduced special interest politics into the analysis of international trade relations. Our model features campaign contributions by industry lobbies which induce policy preferences in self-interested politicians. We have used the model to study policy formation in cooperative and non-cooperative international settings.

Our approach rests on the key assumption that interest groups contribute to politicians with the intention of influencing their policy choices. This assumption finds support in the evidence presented by Magelby and Nelson (1990) and Snyder (1990). Moreover, econometric studies of Congressional voting behavior suggest that such investments bear fruit. For example, Baldwin (1985) found that a Congressperson was the more likely to vote against the Trade Act of 1974 the greater the contributions he or she received from major labor unions opposed to the bill, while Tosini and Tower (1987) found a positive association between a vote in favor of the protectionist Textile Bill of 1985 and the size of donations received from companies and unions in the textiles and apparel industries.

When governments set their trade policies non-cooperatively, each party neglects the impact of its policies on factor owners and politicians abroad. Our model predicts that in such circumstances higher tariff rates will emerge in industries that are politically organized, all else equal. Rates of protection should vary positively with the stake of the specific factor in trade policy relative to that of the average voter (i.e., with the ratio of output to imports), and inversely with the sizes of the elasticities of foreign export supply and home import demand.

It is difficult to evaluate how well these predictions are borne out by the empirical evidence. While there have been many econometric studies of the determinants of protection across industries, most suffer from a number of serious shortcomings. First, it has been common practice to include a long list of regressors when "explaining" the level of protection in an industry. Often each regressor bears only a loose relationship to some theoretical concept and different interpretations can be ascribed to the same right-hand side variable. Second, many of the (collinear) regressors are intended to proxy the same thing, so it is difficult to give meaning to the coefficient on one of them when others are implicitly being held constant. Third, almost all of the regressions have been estimated by ordinary least squares, despite the fact that levels of protection clearly influence many of the supposedly exogenous right-hand-side variables.[27] Finally, none of the studies includes any regressors relating to foreign political and economic conditions and thus they implicitly assume that international interdependence is unimportant or that foreign industry conditions are uncorrelated with those at home.

With these caveats in mind, the evidence does suggest a positive association between levels of protection and the extent to which an industry is politically organized. Lavergne (1983), Baldwin (1985), and Trefler (1993) have proxied political activism by the economic and geographic concentration of firms, since these presumably affect the ease of organizing politically. They find one or both of these variables to be a positive and significant influence on the levels of tariffs or non-tariff barriers. As for our prediction that tariffs will be higher in industries with more to gain from protection, the evidence here is ambiguous. Riedel (1977), Baldwin (1985) and others find that protection is higher in industries with greater levels of employment. While consistent with our prediction (more employment means a larger stake, all else equal), this result is difficult to interpret, because these same authors include the share of labor in value added and the import-penetration ratio as separate explanatory variables. Several studies find that import-penetration ratios are positively related to the level of protection. Our model predicts that the opposite should be true, but again it is difficult to know what the empirical results mean, both because import penetration should really be treated as endogenous and because the regressions hold constant several variables related to the size of the domestic industry. Finally, as for the effects of the elasticities of import demand and export supply, these have not been examined in any of the existing empirical work.

Our model also yields predictions about the outcome of trade negotiations. For example, when governments bargain efficiently, the resulting trade policies for a given industry should not reflect the countries' market power in trade. In other

---

[27] An exception to this rule is Trefler (1993), who estimates an equation explaining the level of non-tariff barriers jointly with one explaining the pattern of trade. He finds substantial evidence of simultaneity in these two equations.

words, the foreign export supply elasticities that should enter into each country's tariff rates in a non-cooperative equilibrium should have no bearing on these rates in a cooperative settlement. With international bargaining, rates of protection should reflect not only the political strength of the special interest group at home – as indicated by the extent of its political activism, by the ratio of domestic output to net trade, and by the size of the home import demand or export supply – but also by the political strength of the interest group in the same industry abroad. Protection should be especially high where the home interest group is strong and the foreign group in the same industry is weak. When both are equally strong, their political influences will cancel, and international prices under a trade agreement should be equal to those that would prevail under totally free trade.

There is some scant evidence that such international bargaining considerations do affect U.S. trade policies. For example, Lavergne (1983) finds that U.S. tariff cuts have been largest in industries in which Canadian producers enjoy the biggest U.S. market share. He interprets this as reflecting the outgrowth of pressures brought by the Canadian government on behalf of its industry interests and the willingness of the U.S. government to concede in the light of corresponding concessions offered to U.S. exporters. Still, much remains to be done in testing whether and how the policies prescribed by trade treaties reflect the political pressures that the governments faced when they negotiated the pacts.

References

Baldwin, Robert E. (1985), *The Political Economy of U.S. Import Policy.* MIT Press, Cambridge, Mass.

Bernheim, B. Douglas and Michael D. Whinston (February 1986), "Menu Auctions, Resource Allocation, and Economic Influence", *Quarterly Journal of Economics* 101, pp. 1-31.

Binmore, Ken, Ariel Rubinstein and Asher Wolinsky (Summer 1986), "The Nash Bargaining Solution in Economic Modeling", *Rand Journal of Economics* 17, pp. 176-188.

Brock, William A. and Stephen P. Magee (May 1978), "The Economics of Special Interests: The Case of the Tariff", *American Economic Review* 68, pp. 246-250.

Cowhey, Peter F. (1990), "'States' and 'Politics' in American Foreign Policy", in: Odell, J.S. and T.D. Willett (eds.): *International Trade Policies: Gains from Exchange between Economics and Political Science*, The University of Michigan Press, Ann Arbor.

Fershtman, Chaim and Kenneth L. Judd (December 1987), "Equilibrium Incentives in Oligopoly", *American Economic Review* 77, pp. 927-940.

Findlay, Ron, and Stanislaw Wellisz (1982), "Endogenous Tariffs, The Political Economy of Trade Restrictions, and Welfare", in: Bhagwati, J. (ed.): *Import Competition and Response*, University of Chicago Press.

Grossman, Gene M. and Elhanan Helpman (September 1994), "Protection for Sale", *American Economic Review* 84, pp. 833-850.

Hillman, Arye L. (December 1982), "Declining Industries and the Political-Support Motive for Protection", *American Economic Review 72*, pp. 1180-1187.

Hillman, Arye L. and Peter Moser (1995), "Trade Liberalization as Politically Optimal Exchange of Market Access", in: Canzoneri, Matthew et al. (eds.): *The New Transatlantic Economy*, Cambridge University Press, Cambridge, U.K.

Johnson, Harry G. (1953/54), "Optimal Tariffs and Retaliation", *Review of Economic Studies* 21, pp. 142-153.

Katz, Michael L. (Autumn 1991), "Game Playing Agents: Unobservable Contracts as Precommitments", *Rand Journal of Economics* 22, pp. 307-328.

Kennan, John and Ray Riezman (February 1988), "Do Big Countries Win Tariff Wars", *International Economic Review* 29, pp. 81-85.

Kuga, Kiyoshi (November 1973), "Tariff Retaliation and Policy Equilibrium", *Journal of International Economics* 3, pp. 351-366.

Lavergne, Real P. (1983), *The Political Economy of U.S. Tariffs: An Empirical Analysis*. Academic Press, Toronto.

Long, Ngo Van, and Neil Vousden (February 1991), "Protectionist Responses and Declining Industries", *Journal of International Economics* 30, pp. 87-103.

Magee, Stephen P., William A. Brock and Leslie Young (1989), *Black Hole Tariffs and Endogenous Policy Formation*. The MIT Press, Cambridge, Mass.

Magelby, David B. and Candice J. Nelson (1990), *The Money Chase: Congressional Campaign Finance Reform*. The Brookings Institution, Washington, DC.

Mayer, Wolfgang (March 1981), "Theoretical Considerations on Negotiated Tariff Adjustments", *Oxford Economic Papers* 33, pp. 135-153.

Pelzman, Sam (August 1976), "Toward a More General Theory of Regulation", *Journal of Law and Economics* 19, pp. 211-240.

Putnam, Robert (Summer 1988), "Diplomacy and Domestic Policy: The Logic of Two Level Games", *International Organization* 43, pp. 427-460.

Reidel, James (May 1977), "Tariff Concessions in the Kennedy Round and the Structure of Protection in West Germany: An Econometric Assessment", *Journal of International Economics* 7, pp. 133-144.

Riezman, Ray (January 1982), "Tariff Retaliation from a Strategic Viewpoint", *Southern Journal of Economics* 48, pp. 583-593.

Rubinstein, Ariel (January 1982), "Perfect Equilibrium in a Bargaining Model", *Econometrica* 50, pp. 97-109.

Snyder Jr., James M. (December 1990), "Campaign Contributions as Investments: The U.S. House of Representatives, 1980-86", *Journal of Political Economy* 98, pp. 1195-1227.

Stigler, George J. (Spring 1971), "The Theory of Economic Regulation", *Bell Journal of Economics and Management Science* 1, pp. 1-21.

Sutton, John (October 1986), "Non-cooperative Bargaining Theory: An Introduction", *Review of Economic Studies* 53, pp. 709-724.

Tosini, Suzanne C. and Edward Tower (1987), "The Textile Bill of 1985: The Determinants of Congressional Voting Patterns", *Public Choice* 54, pp. 19-25.

Trefler, Daniel (February 1993), "Trade Liberalization and the Theory of Endogenous Protection: An Econometric Study of U.S. Import Policy", *Journal of Political Economy* 101, pp. 138-161.

Trade Liberalization, Privatization, and Restructuring Incentives

Arye L. Hillman,

Manuel Hinds,

Branko Milanovic and

Heinrich W. Ursprung*

Introduction and Outline

This paper presents a model describing the policy decision framework confronting governments seeking to effect transition of their economies from prior socialism to a free-market private-property economy. Fundamental elements of this transition are (i) change from the socialist trade regime under which domestic enterprises did not confront import competition (nor domestic competition for that matter), and (ii) privatization of the formerly socialist enterprises. We consider circumstances where governments have as an objective a liberal trade regime, sought because of the traditional efficiency case for an open economy – with the additional benefit, not present when the domestic market is competitive, from exposure of a sole domestic producer to discipline of import competition. The government that we model bases its policies on broadly consensual economic principles and policy advice. Government officials do not seek to take advantage of incumbency to provide policy favors in exchange for political support or personal remuneration, and the pursuit of efficiency objectives is not compromised by political competition that can lead to

* We thank seminar participants at The World Bank, Bar-Ilan University, the University of Konstanz, Australian National University, and the European Workshop in International Trade (Rotterdam, 1993) for helpful observations. The views expressed and positions taken in this paper do not necessarily reflect the views of the World Bank or any of its affiliates, its Board of Directors, management, or member countries.
Financial support by the Deutsche Forschungsgemeinschaft through the Sonderforschungsbereich 178 "Internationalisierung der Wirtschaft" is gratefully acknowledged.

policies favoring domestic interest groups. Nonetheless, as we shall elaborate, the formulation of policy is subject to the need to maintain a minimum level of electoral support. A substantial literature motivated by real-world observation views policies as endogenous to the political process via the self-interest motives of policy makers.[1] We adopt our view of government so as not to bias policy outcomes away from efficiency because of political and personal objectives, rather than as a statement of the necessary manner of government conduct.

The domestically produced good is technologically inferior to imported foreign substitutes.[2] Domestic demand is segmented by income, with those domestic consumers that can "afford to", purchasing the higher-quality import, and the remainder the lower-quality domestically produced substitute. The capability to improve the quality of domestic output rests with foreign investors, to whom the government can sell a share of the enterprise as part of its privatization policy. That share of the enterprise not sold to a foreign investor is distributed by vouchers free of charge to the domestic population. Restructuring is thus linked to privatization. Only a foreign investor (who requires a minimum controlling interest in ownership) has the means of improving domestic quality by restructuring.

The foreign investor, however, has an interest in protection of the domestic enterprise from import competition, as do domestic shareholders who have received shares via a voucher scheme; since domestic shareholders together with the foreign investor are the residual claimants who benefit from the increased profits facilitated by protection. Protection is also to the advantage of workers employed in the domestic enterprise. The protectionist interest of workers is further enhanced if they are also shareholders via the allocation of shares. The presence of these domestic protectionist interests does not compromise the policy objectives of the principled government, which seeks the efficiency of a free-trade regime.

---

1. For example, with respect to trade policy, see the surveys by Hillman (1989), Magee et al. (1989), and Magee (1994).

2. Since socialist enterprises did not confront competition, they could produce with technologies inferior to those of western competitors. See for example Hillman and Milanovic (1992).

By liberalizing trade, the government provides an incentive for the foreign owner to invest in upgrading the quality of domestic output, to counter the lower-priced competition from higher-quality imports; and should restructuring occur, domestic consumers are able to purchase a higher-quality domestic product, and at a lower price. Again, however, a foreign investor would prefer protectionist policies, which would not oblige him to invest in upgrading the domestic enterprise as a counter to the higher-quality import competition. But if the government simply went ahead and liberalized trade, profit maximization by the investor would entail restructuring and quality improvement in face of import competition. And, with some additional commentary on how the enterprise might be valued for sale to the foreign investor given the expectation of exposure to import competition, that would be the end of the story.

This end to the story, however, leaves out of account the political feasibility of government policy. In the democracies of the post-communist societies, governments require a minimal level of political support, even if – or as a consequence of – pursuing principled policies. To reflect this aspect of the policy environment, we model a government's policies as feasible only if the distributional consequences of policies permit a minimum political-support constraint to be satisfied.

Both trade policy and privatization policy affect political support in ways that have been independently studied.[3] The model that we shall formulate introduces the interdependence between the two policies in affecting political support. With the new post-privatization owners and workers employed in the domestic enterprise favoring protection, and consumers at large favoring free trade, the traditional political trade-off underlying protectionist policies is present. The form of privatization also affects political support, via the division between the share of the enterprise sold to the foreign investor and the part freely allocated to the domestic population. Since domestic shareholders benefit from the investment in restructuring undertaken by the foreign investor, their interest is not in voucher allocation of all shares in the enterprise, but in a division which gives them a share while providing the incentive for upgrading of the enterprise by a foreign investor. The investor's incentive to restructure, and consequently domestic shareholders' preferred means of privatization, in turn depends on how liberal trade policy is, since trade policy

[3] On privatization, see Milanovic (1992).

determines the price at which higher quality competitive imports enter the domestic market. A political support function encompassing both the interests of domestic agents in trade policy and the means of privatization is, because of these considerations, somewhat complex, but, as we shall see, not unmanageable. We shall employ such a political-support function to specify the requirement of policy feasibility.

The extent of trade liberalization affects an investor's decision to upgrade the enterprise (more upgrading being evoked as the domestic enterprise is exposed to increasingly greater import competition). There is also a reverse relationship present, since the more investment in restructuring that occurs, the further the government can proceed to liberalize trade. Upgrading of the enterprise reduces the political liabilities incurred in exposing the enterprise to import competition, since the higher the quality of domestic output in the face of technologically superior imports, the more capable is the enterprise of withstanding increased import competition.

However, by refraining from restructuring, foreign investors inhibit trade liberalization, because of the higher political cost of exposing the non-restructured enterprise to import competition. And one may anticipate that foreign investors will realize that restructuring enhances the political feasibility of trade liberalization, that is, that trade policy is endogenous in this manner.

Our model is directed at establishing the nature of equilibria in such situations, where a principled but politically constrained government wishes to liberalize trade, but the prospects for politically feasible trade liberalization are determined by the form of privatization chosen for the enterprise, and by the associated incentives of a foreign investor to invest in restructuring to improve product quality – or not to do so. The question to which we seek an answer is whether a government can hope to succeed in basing political feasibility of trade liberalization on privatization and restructuring by an investor, or whether liberalization objectives will be countered by investors' realizations that the profits from investments in restructuring will be dissipated by a more liberal trade policy.

The following example is illustrative of the type of policy problem we are modelling:

> After Germany's Mercedes-Benz AG announced plans to forge a joint venture with a Czech truck maker, a government official complained that German

> conditions were "totally unacceptable". Mercedes wants tariff protection (in exchange for investment of) 350 million marks into updating the plant (an initial stake of 31% in the venture). Both sides have agreed to make the venture contingent on government approval. "We shall negotiate as long as it takes to bring us together" (said a government official). Mercedes officials said this showed the East European government was willing to make concessions.[4]

Here the foreign investor wants protection as a condition for restructuring. But once protection has been granted and privatization has occurred, does the investor still have an incentive to follow through with original restructuring intentions? Restructuring would make liberalization politically attractive. In the absence of restructuring, trade liberalization would disadvantage domestic shareholders in the privatized enterprise and the enterprise's workers, thereby making trade liberalization politically costly and so inhibiting liberalization.

Formally, we have a game between governments and foreign investors. The ability of a government to credibly commit to maintain an announced policy is critical to determining the equilibrium, as is awareness by foreign investors of the political endogeneity of trade policy via the link between restructuring and feasible liberalization. We shall consider circumstances where governments can and cannot make credible commitments to maintain trade policies, and where investors are respectively naive and sophisticated regarding the relation between restructuring and politically feasible trade policies. An equilibrium characterized by trade liberalization and restructuring arises, when (implausibly) investors are not aware of the political endogeneity of trade liberalization, or (more plausibly) a government can credibly limit its discretion to revise announced trade policies, via international trade agreements or international-agency policy conditionality.

The model also demonstrates the interconnections between the means of privatization and trade policy. Thus, if a government anticipates that privatization by sale to a foreign investor will not result in enterprise restructuring – and that thereby trade liberalization objectives will not be furthered – the government may prefer to privatize by a more politically popular distribution of shares to domestic citizens and/or workers and management, rather than follow the generally politically more

---

4 Wall Street Journal, European edition, August 1, 1992.

controversial procedure of sale to foreigners, with all that entails in terms of asset valuation and the quest to establish correct privatization prices.[5]

The paper proceeds as follows. Section 1 sets out a model of an enterprise confronted with import competition from technologically superior foreign goods, and derives the profit function for investors contemplating restructuring to improve domestic quality. Section 2 sets out the political model describing government policy objectives and constraints establishing politically feasible trade and privatization policies. The models of these first two sections are then superimposed on one another to consider equilibria when, respectively, credible commitment to sustain announced trade policy is feasible (section 3) and is not (section 4). The final section provides a concluding summary and relates the model to other literature.

1. The Enterprise

1.1 The domestic market

We consider an enterprise which is the sole domestic producer of a good that is inferior in quality to imported substitutes. The primary factors of production employed by the enterprise are intersectorally (or geographically) immobile. Labor is immobile in that if dismissed, subsequent new employment may only be found after a period of unemployment, if at all. Labor therefore resists being obliged to leave its present employment. Capital is sector-specific, and consists of capital equipment inherited from the socialist past and/or capital which embodies western technology and facilitates improved-quality production. Western capital is provided by foreign investors in the course of restructuring the privatized enterprise. In the absence of sale of a controlling interest to foreign investors, no restructuring occurs.

We adopt a specification of demand which portrays consumers as not buying the domestic good if they can "afford" the imported substitute. With consumption of domestically produced and imported goods denoted by x and x^*, and domestic prices

---

[5] On the political considerations associated with allocation of shares to citizens rather than sale to foreigners, see Hillman (1994), and for considerations pertaining to workers, see Želko Bogetic(1993).

of the two goods by P and P^*, domestic demand functions for domestic and imported goods are,

$$x = [a\gamma + (2-\gamma)P^* - 2P] / 2b \geq 0 \tag{1}$$

$$x^* = (a - P^*)(2-\gamma) / 2b \geq 0 \tag{2}$$

where a, $b > 0$, and the parameter $\gamma(0 \leq \gamma \leq 1)$ indicates the quality differential between the domestically produced and imported goods. When $P^* > a$, there is of course no domestic demand for imports. The demand functions have the asymmetric property that demand for the domestic good depends on the price of the imported good, whereas demand for the imported good does not depend on the price of the domestic good; that is, those consumers who "can afford to" do so, simply ignore the domestic good and purchase the higher-quality imports. We assume that at the upper limit of domestic quality, where $\gamma(=1)$, the domestic and foreign goods remain imperfect substitutes, with the foreign good maintaining the higher quality.

Circumstances of no restructuring are described by $\gamma = 0$, in which case the demand functions reduce to

$$x = (P^* - P) / b \geq 0 \tag{3}$$

$$x^* = (a - P^*) / b \geq 0 \ . \tag{4}$$

Figure 1 depicts these functions with demand partitioned at R between domestic products and imports. Consumers whose valuation equals or exceeds the price of imports P_1^* (equal to a world price converted to domestic currency P^W plus a duty or quota-equivalent t [6]) purchase the higher-quality imported good (in quantity x_1^*), leaving (residual) demand for the lower-quality domestic good as RS. If $P^* \geq a$, so that no consumers are willing, or can afford, to purchase the imported good, residual domestic demand is $x = (a - P) / b$ which is then entire domestic demand.

---

[6] We assume an import duty as the means of protection. Protection can of course take other forms (quotas, tariff-quotas, and administrative controls). See the World Bank (1992), pp. 131-132.

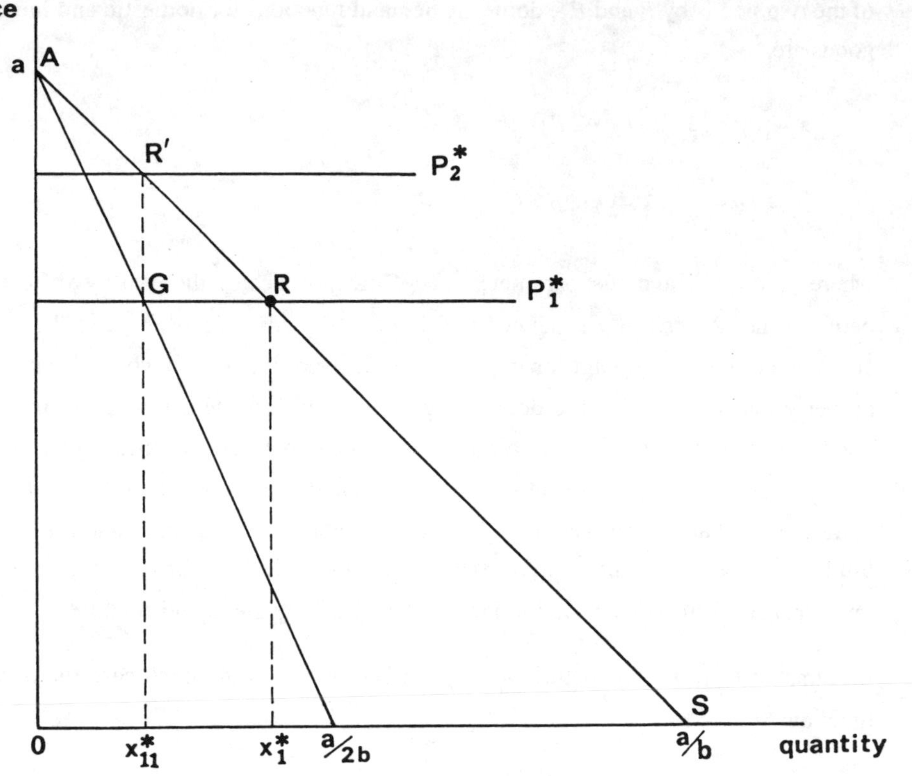

Figure 1

Investment in upgrading domestic quality increases γ. At $\gamma = 1$ (the upper limit), demand functions for domestic goods and imports are

$$x = (a + P^*) / 2b - P / b \geq 0 \tag{5}$$

$$x^* = (a - P^*) / 2b \geq 0 \ . \tag{6}$$

In Figure 1, an increase in γ from 0 to 1 shifts demand for the domestic good from *RS* to *R'S*, and shifts the import demand function from *AR* to *AG*. Substitution takes place in consumption, with imports declining and consumption of the domestic good increasing by the amount $(x_1^* - x_{11}^*)$. This same substitution could take place if the relative price of imported substitutes were to increase, with no change in domestic quality, that is, if γ were maintained at zero, and an increase in the price of imported goods from P_1^* to P_2^*. For marginal improvements in domestic quality (for $0 \leq \gamma < 1$), substitution in domestic consumption is expressed by

$$\frac{\partial x}{\partial \gamma} = \frac{1}{2b}(a - P^*) = -\frac{\partial x^*}{\partial \gamma} \tag{7}$$

This substitution effect indicates that investment in restructuring permits trade to be liberalized, while maintaining demand for domestically produced output.

1.2 Profit maximization by investors

Restructuring decisions are made by foreign investors, to whom the enterprise would be privatized. Investors bear the cost of restructuring. The unit cost of western capital is denoted by *r*, and the capital infusion by *K*. Western capital increases domestic quality, via $\gamma = \xi K^{1/2}$, $\xi > 0$, reflecting diminishing returns from restructuring. Upon privatization, investors impose a profit-maximization objective and establish a minimized (constant) per unit cost of production *c*.[7] Enterprise profits gross of restructuring costs are $\Pi = (P - c)x$.

[7] This cost of production is distinct from the investment in restructuring born by investors.

Privatization policy is specified with respect to a value s denoting the foreign investors' share in ownership of the privatized enterprise. s is subject to a lower bound establishing a controlling interest. The remaining share $(1-s)$ of shares in the enterprise is allocated free of charge to domestic citizens.

Given s, the investors' profits net of restructuring costs are

$$\Pi^{f}(P,K\,|a,b,c,r,\xi;\,s,P^{*}) = s\Pi - rK$$
$$= s(P-c)\left[a\xi K^{1/2} + (2-\xi K^{1/2})P^{*} - 2P\right]/2b - rK\,. \qquad (8)$$

Investors maximize profits by choosing the domestic price P and investment in restructuring K, given domestic demand and cost of production (reflected in a, b and c), and subject to the cost and effectiveness of restructuring, respectively, r and ξ.

Investors' profits as specified by (8) depend on the decision taken by the government regarding (i) the share s of the enterprise to be privatized by sale rather than by allocation to the population or workers, and (ii) trade policy which determines the domestic price P^{*} of competitive imports. We turn now to consider the government's policy decisions.

2. The Political Model

2.1. Policy objectives and policy feasibility

We shall model the behavior of a government which views, as requisites of the transition, privatization of state enterprises and exposure of the privatized enterprises to a liberal trade regime. The government has no preferences regarding the post-privatization pattern of ownership, and is concerned with the choice between sale to foreign investors and distribution of shares to the population (i.e., s), only insofar as this furthers the objective of trade liberalization. The government's policy objective can be simply stated as

$$\min t \qquad (9)$$

where t is, as previously specified, the level of protection provided to the privatized enterprise.

Trade and privatization policies are, however, in conjunction, required to ensure a minimal level of political support for the government. Political feasibility of policy is described by

$$(t,s) \geq V_{\min} \quad , \tag{10}$$

where (t,s) is the level of political support associated with the policies t and s, and $_{\min}$ is the minimum required level of political support.

The function (t,s) is a reduced form derived from the manner in which policies affect different interest groups in the economy. Groups with a direct identifiable interest in trade and privatization policies are:

- domestic shareholders, who are allocated the shares not sold to investors, and who as owners of industry-specific capital benefit (along with investors) from protection;
- workers whose job security is threatened by trade liberalization, and who – if shareholders – also benefit from protection via their share holdings;
- consumers at large who are beneficiaries of trade liberalization;
- citizens who as a matter of principle are averse to foreign ownership;
- the government treasury, which is the recipient of revenue, consisting of proceeds from privatization and import duties paid.

Incorporating these different interests in a linear specification for political support,[8] we have

$$(t,s) = \alpha(1-s)\Pi + \beta cx + \delta t^2 + \varepsilon s^2 + \varphi_1 R_1 + \varphi_2 R_2 \geq V_{\min} \tag{11}$$

[8] The linear specification follows Sam Peltzman (1976). Linearity implies absence of cross effects that reflect envy or dissatisfaction with political benefits provided to others (see Hillman, 1989, chapter 2).

$\alpha\ (>0)$ is the political weight of domestic shareholders, who benefit from increases in their share of enterprise profits $(1-s)\Pi$, and from protection (which increases profits Π); as s increases, domestic shareholders receive a smaller share of the enterprise, but also a smaller s reduces the incentive of an investor to restructure, hence there exists for domestic shareholders a value maximizing privatization policy.

$\beta\ (>0)$ is the political weight of workers, whose employment opportunities increase with total output or cost of production cx.

$\delta\ (<0)$ is the political weight of consumers at large as beneficiaries of trade liberalization – we adopt here a quadratic specification so as to reflect increasing consumer dissatisfaction as protection becomes higher and more visible.[9]

$\varepsilon\ (<0)$ is the weight on populist discontent when foreign investors secure ownership of privatized enterprises; we adopt a quadratic specification to reflect increasing discontent as foreign ownership increases.

φ is the weight on privatization revenue R_1; investors pay for their share of the enterprise a proportion of the present value of profits $(s\Pi - rK)$.

φ_2 is the weight on revenue from trade taxes, $R_2(=tx^*)$.

These latter two revenue weights could of course be equal. The weights would differ if privatization proceeds were payable in convertible foreign currency, with tariff revenue payable in domestic currency. While governments certainly have revenue needs, we choose here to assume that revenue considerations are not primary concerns in the government's decisions regarding trade policy and the means of privatization, and consequently $\varphi_1 \approx 0$ and also $\varphi_2 \approx 0$.

---

[9] The quadratic specification is suggested by Magee's notion of optimal obfuscation: see Magee, Brock, and Young (1989), chapter 18.

2.2 Trade policy and political support

With the means of privatization reflected in a given value, s_0, we consider now how trade policy is related to political support. The following proposition can be readily established:

In the neighborhood of the government's constrained politically feasible trade policy, for any choice of privatization program, if political support can be increased at all, this will be achieved by increasing protection.

That is, in non-pathological cases, increased protection is always a solution to the problem of inadequate political support; this would of course not be the case were the government choosing policies to maximize political support, since then any deviation from the chosen policy could only reduce political support.

Proof: To prove this above proposition, we observe that in the neighborhood of the chosen t, protection affects political support via

$$\frac{\partial V(t|s_0)}{\partial t} = \alpha(1-s)\frac{\partial P}{\partial t} + \beta c\frac{\partial x}{\partial t} + 2\delta t + \varphi_2\frac{\partial R_2}{\partial t}$$

$$= \alpha(1-s)(2-\gamma)\frac{A}{8b} + \beta c\frac{(2-\gamma)}{4b} + 2\delta t + \varphi_2\frac{(2-\gamma)(a-P^W-2t)}{2b} > 0. \tag{12}$$

The term A in this above expression is defined by demand for the domestic good

$$x = \left[a\gamma + (2-\gamma)(P^W + t) - 2c\right]^2 / 4b = A^2 / 4b \quad .$$

The first term in (12) reflects the change in political support from domestic share-holders as protection increases (and is thereby positive). The second term reflects workers' interests, and is also positive, since employment increases with protection. The third term reflects consumer dissatisfaction with increased protection, and is thus negative. Whether the final term is positive or negative depends upon whether the maximum tariff revenue, here $(a - P^W)/2$, has been attained. Figure 2 depicts two

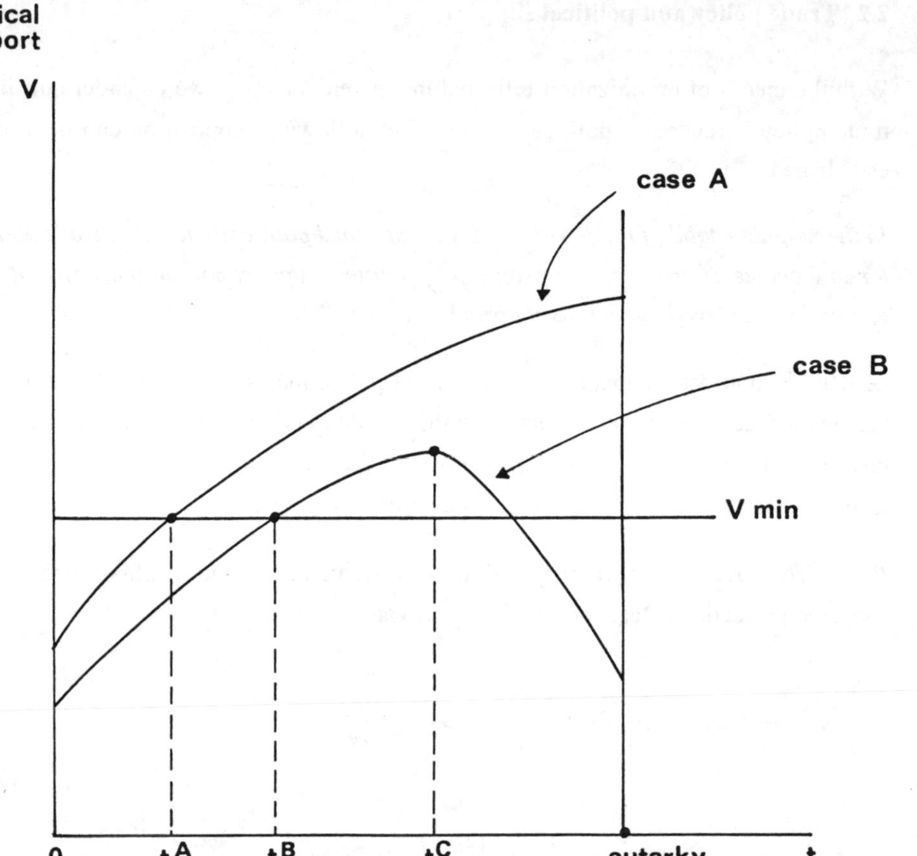
political support
V
case A
case B
V min
0
t^A
t^B
t^C
autarky
t
protection

Figure 2

possibilities implied by (12) for the political support function $(t|s_0)$. In case *A*, political support is globally increasing with protection; in case *B* there is an interior political-support-maximizing trade policy at t^C.

Hence, in case *A*, appeasing domestic shareholders and workers by increased protection persistently dominates at the margin the political benefit of catering to the broad consumer-based coalition of losers from protection; maximal politically feasible trade liberalization is t^A.

In case *B*, there is an interior solution for political-support maximizing protection at t^C, and maximal politically feasible trade liberalization entails a tariff of t^B.

Whether at t^A or t^B, an increase in protection increases political support.

2.3 Restructuring and political support

The effect on political support of increased investment in restructuring follows from (11) as

$$\frac{\partial V}{\partial K} = \alpha(1-s)\frac{\partial \Pi}{\partial K} + \beta c \frac{\partial x}{\partial K} + \varphi_2 \frac{\partial R_2}{\partial K} \tag{13}$$

$$= \alpha(1-s)\frac{A\,\xi(a-P^W-t)}{16b\sqrt{K}} + \beta c \frac{\xi(a-P^W-t)}{8b\sqrt{K}} - \varphi_2 \frac{\xi t(a-P^W-t)}{4b\sqrt{K}} > 0,$$

$$\text{for } \varphi_2 \approx 0 .$$

There can be no domestic losers from restructuring, which improves domestic quality and thereby increases demand for domestically produced output at the expense of imports. Domestic shareholders are thereby made better off, as are workers for whom employment opportunities expand, as well as consumers who purchase the now higher-quality domestic product.

3. Policy Equilibria

3.1. The government

We turn now to the strategic interaction between governments and investors. We have established that both increased protection and increased investment in restructuring increase political popularity. A trade-off for the government is therefore implied, indicating that *the government's response to increases in investment in restructuring is to liberalize trade.*

This is illustrated in Figure 3, where (with s given) an increase in investment in restructuring from K_0 to K_1 moves the political support function upward, with $(t, K_1) > V(t, K_0)$, so permitting the minimum political-support constraint to be satisfied at a lower level of protection. Protection is thus reduced from t_0 to t_1.

The behavior of the government in adjusting protection to maintain $= V_{\min}$ defines the government's reaction function *GH* in Figure 4. Below *GH*, where $< V_{\min}$, the government increases protection to attain $_{\min}$; above *GH*, where $> V_{\min}$, trade is liberalized until $_{\min}$ is attained.

3.2 Investors

The behavior of investors depends on whether they perceive the link between their restructuring decisions and trade policy. If so, investors do exhibit awareness that governments change trade policies in response to restructuring of privatized enterprises, the marginal profitability of investment in restructuring is correctly perceived to be

$$\frac{d\Pi^f}{dK} = \left[\frac{\partial\Pi^f}{\partial K} - r\right] + \frac{\partial\Pi^f}{\partial t}\frac{dt}{dK} \tag{14}$$

The second term here reflects the decline in profits due to reduced protection.

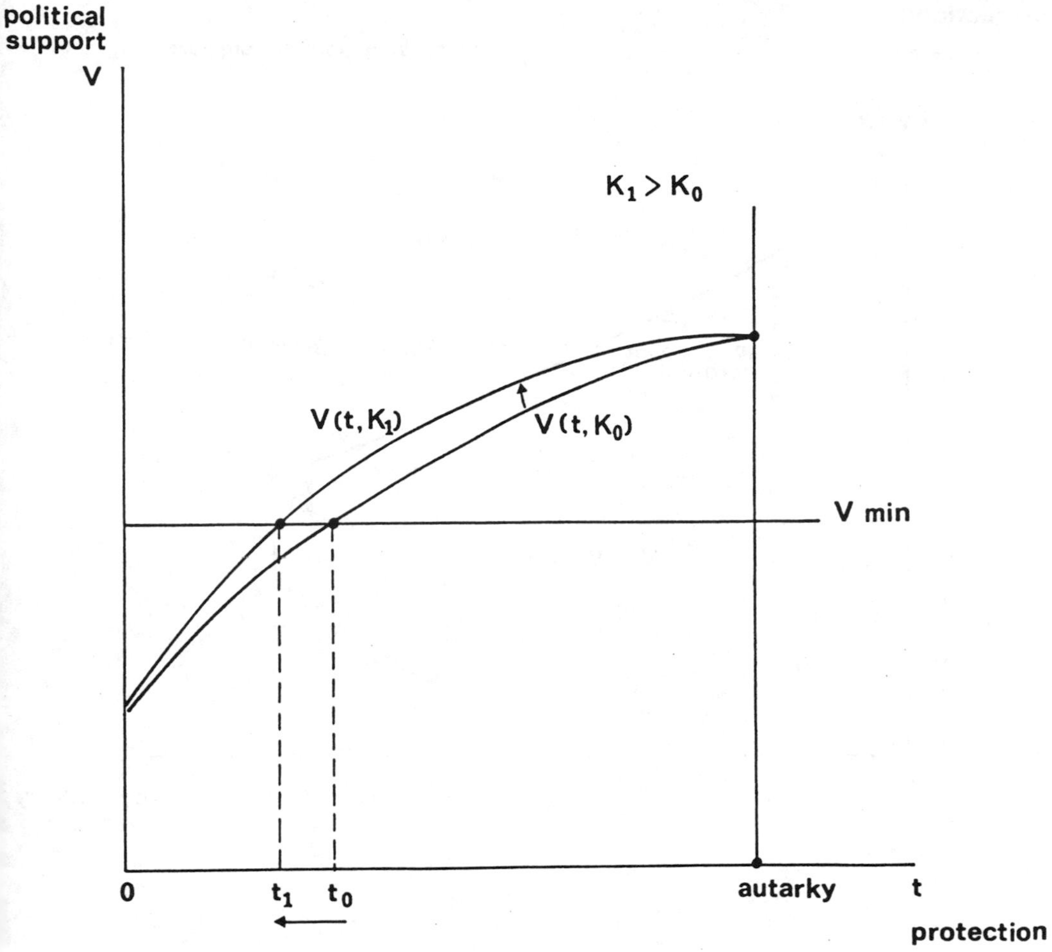

political
support
V
$K_1 > K_0$
$V(t, K_1)$
$V(t, K_0)$
V min
0
t_1
t_0
autarky
t
protection

Figure 3

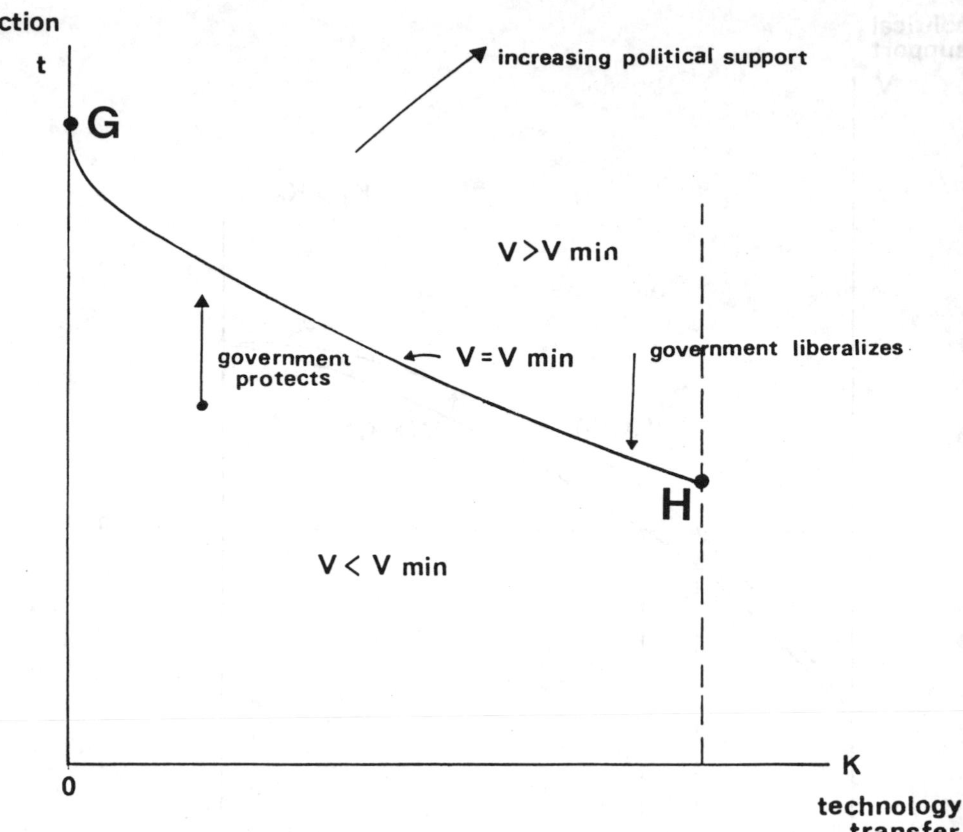
protection
t
G
increasing political support
V>V min
government protects
V = V min
government liberalizes
H
V < V min
0
K
technology transfer

Figure 4

Investors who view trade policy as exogenous to their restructuring decisions perceive in place of (14) simply,

$$\frac{d\Pi^f}{dK} = \frac{\partial \Pi^f}{\partial K} - r \quad . \tag{14a}$$

3.3 Non-sophisticated investors

Figure 5 depicts the government's reaction function *GH* and the reaction function *AC* of the latter investors. The reaction function of the investors is

$$K(t) = \left[\frac{2\xi(P^* - c)(a - P^*)}{16b\frac{r}{s} - \xi^2 (a - P^*)^2} \right]^2 \tag{15}$$

and has a negative slope, since investors upgrade quality to counter greater exposure to import competition.

To establish the equilibrium, the government moves first, to set t. The government's preferred outcome along *AC* is at the endpoint *C* where $t = 0$ and where investors choose K_m. However, the outcome at *C* is not politically feasible, since points below the government's reaction function *GH* do not satisfy the government's minimum-political-support constraint. The government consequently revises trade policy, and increases protection, to $t_m^{'}$ on *GH*. The government's original policy was therefore not time consistent. Investors benefit from the revised policy, but they nonetheless have reason for regret, since had they anticipated protection at $t_m^{'}$, they would have undertaken the smaller investment in restructuring $K_m^{'}$, which would have sufficed in the more protected domestic market.[10]

---

[10] It is possible for the reaction function *AC* to have a positively sloped range for low values of t, so that the government's trade policy revision may entail liberalizing trade.

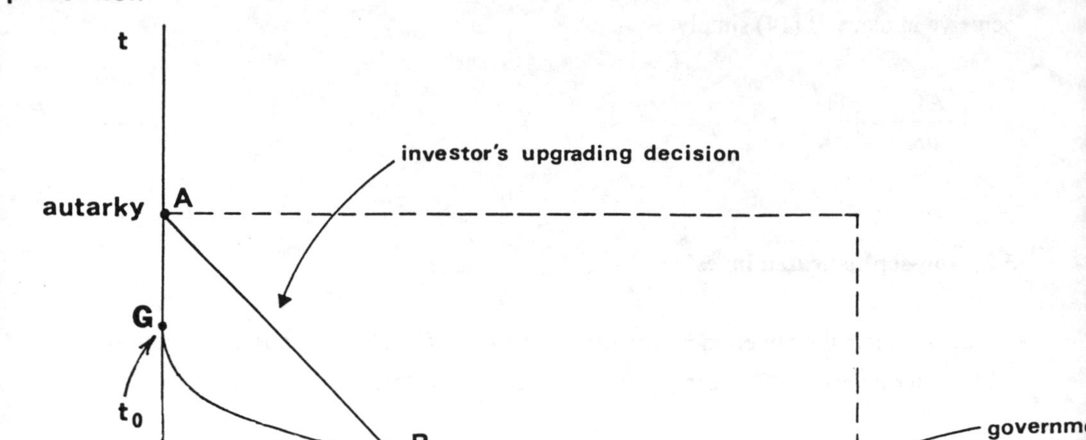
protection
t
autarky
A
investor's upgrading decision
G
t_0
B
governm
t'_m
H
t_m
C
K
0
K'_m
K_m
K^{max}
technology
transfer

Figure 5

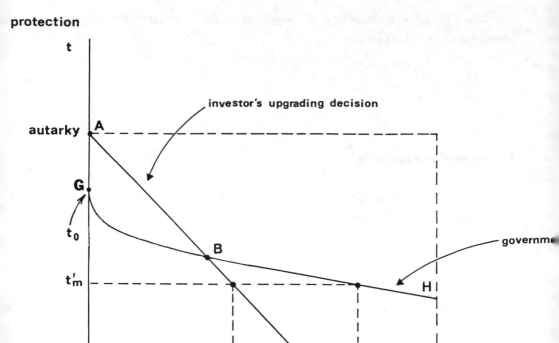

3.4 Sophisticated investors

More reasonably, investors can be expected to be sufficiently astute to be aware that their restructuring decisions affect the government's feasible trade liberalization possibilities, and to recognize therefore that the marginal profitability of investment in restructuring is given by (14) and not (14a). This awareness changes the nature of the strategic interaction between the government and investors. Investors can choose (as Stackelberg leaders) profit-maximizing investment in restructuring, subject to the (predictable) reaction of the government (as Stackelberg follower) with regard to trade policy. Under these conditions, investors' profits are maximized at the point G in Figure 5, where $(t, K) = (t_0, 0)$. We are able to conclude therefore:

Proposition 1

When investors take account of government policy intentions, the equilibrium is – independently of the share of the privatized enterprise which the investor owns – that no investment in restructuring takes place, and because of the political costs of exposing a non-restructured enterprise to import competition, governments are inhibited from liberalizing trade.

Proof:

Profit-maximizing investment in restructuring is determined by

$$\frac{d\Pi^f}{dK} = \left[\frac{\partial \Pi^f}{\partial K} - r\right] + \frac{\partial \Pi^f}{\partial t}\frac{dt}{dK}\begin{cases} = 0, & \text{if } K > 0 \\ \leq 0, & \text{if } K = 0 \end{cases} \tag{16}$$

Incorporating into (16) the government's policy reaction to restructuring

$$\frac{\partial t}{\partial K} = -\frac{\dfrac{\partial V}{\partial K}}{\dfrac{\partial V}{\partial t}}, \quad \text{where} \quad \frac{\partial V}{\partial K} > 0, \quad \frac{\partial V}{\partial t} > 0, \tag{17}$$

establishes

$$\frac{d\Pi^f}{dK} = \frac{s}{\left(\dfrac{\partial V}{\partial t}\right)}\left[2\delta t\frac{\partial \Pi}{\partial K} + \varphi_2\left(\frac{\partial R_2}{\partial t}\frac{\partial \Pi}{\partial K} - \frac{\partial R_2}{\partial K}\frac{\partial \Pi}{\partial t}\right)\right] < 0. \tag{18}$$

The solution to (16) is thus $K=0$; that is, investment in restructuring is not profitable.[11]

3.5 The means of privatization

These above results hold for any (positive) s. Now consider the *choice* of s. Since in an equilibrium with sophisticated investors no restructuring takes place, the political-support constraint confronting the government is

$$(s,t_0)\big|_{K=0} = V_{\min} \tag{19}$$

where t_0 denotes a level of protection which the government chooses in the absence of restructuring. From (19) we derive the expression,

$$\frac{dt_0}{ds} = -\frac{1}{\left(\frac{\partial V}{\partial t}\right)}\left[\frac{(\varphi_1\lambda-\alpha)(P^W+t_0-c)^2}{4b}+2\varepsilon s\right] \tag{20}$$

which expresses the trade-off between s and t when political support is maintained at ${}_{\min}$. Since no restructuring occurs, revenue is the sole source of benefit to the government from sale to investors, to be balanced against two elements of political support, (i) popular dissatisfaction of the public in not receiving allocations of shares and (ii) populist sentiment against foreign ownership. If these combined effects dominate the benefits of revenue, (20) is positive, and the government in order to achieve maximal trade liberalization privatizes by allocation of shares to the public (i.e., by choosing $s = 0$); should revenue dominate, (20) is negative, and maximal trade liberalization is facilitated by privatizing via sale to foreign investors .

---

[11] Notice that $\partial\Pi/\partial K$ exceeds all bounds when K converges to zero. One might therefore infer that $d\Pi^f/dK$ is positive for $K=0$, which would imply a positive optimal value of K. However, $-dt/dK$ also exceeds all bounds for $K=0$ (see equation (13)) and the result is nevertheless $K=0$. Moreover, notice that to derive equation (18) we make use of the fact that

$$\frac{\partial\pi}{\partial K}\frac{\partial x}{\partial t} = \frac{\partial\pi}{\partial t}\frac{\partial x}{\partial K}\quad .$$

4. Credible Non-discretionary Trade Policies

4.1 The time-consistent policy with credible commitment

Whatever the means of privatization chosen, the outcome indicated in proposition 1 is not favorable for the government, since with no investment in restructuring taking place, trade liberalization is not politically feasible. However, if trade policy could be made credibly non-discretionary after policy announcements have been made, the strategic roles of governments and investors are reversed. As in the case of non-sophisticated investors, governments are then Stackelberg-leaders and investors followers. For any s, the government chooses trade policy recognizing that investors' best responses lie on the reaction function AC in Figure 5. On AC, politically feasible policies lie on AB (on or above GH). Since the government's objective is to liberalize trade, it chooses trade policy at the point B, where t is minimized subject to the political-support constraint. We conclude therefore:

Proposition 2

When governments can commit to make trade policy non-discretionary, investors are led to restructure privatized enterprises and more liberal trade policies are achievable, than when investors are aware that trade policy is discretionary.

The same outcome as in proposition 2 obtains as a Nash rather than Stackelberg equilibrium, if investors cannot commit to implement announcements regarding restructuring and governments cannot commit to maintain announced trade policies. A Nash equilibrium would arise, if governments, before deciding upon trade policy, were unable to observe the level of investment in restructuring which had taken place. Investors then could not credibly indicate that no investment in restructuring had occurred, and consequently investors would have no credible means of indicating to governments that failure to protect the enterprise would result in exposure of low-quality domestic output to high-quality import competition, with the attendant political costs.

4.2 Privatization

Now consider the associated privatization decision. Since investment in restructuring takes place, the government benefits from sale to foreigners, beyond the revenue thereby attained. The government's problem is to:

$$\text{minimize} \quad t \tag{21}$$

$$\text{subject to} \quad [s, t, K(s,t)] = V(s,t) \geq V_{\min} , \tag{22}$$

where (22) encompasses the investors' reaction function *K*(*s*, *t*). Figure 6 depicts an equilibrium. Iso-political support contours emanate from the point *D*, which depicts the policies which the government would choose, were it seeking to maximize political support. The policy equilibrium is at the point *B*, where maximal trade liberalization is achieved subject to the political constraint of maintaining at least $_{\min}$. The point *B* establishes the unique value of *s* which is the associated preferred combination of sale to investors and allocation of shares to the population.

4.3 Policy equilibria when governments care about the means of privatization

One could further envisage that, rather than being indifferent regarding *s* as we have supposed, governments themselves have preferences regarding the form that they prefer privatization to take. Such preferences can readily be imposed in Figure 6.

For a government with a preference for privatization via allocation of shares to domestic shareholders, policy preferences yield an equilibrium such as at the point *A*, and for a government with a preference for sale to investors, policy preferences yield an equilibrium such as at the point *C*. In both of these cases, governments trade off pursuit of trade liberalization to achieve a privatization program more to their liking than the outcome at *B*, which is the equilibrium when governments are indifferent regarding the means of privatization.

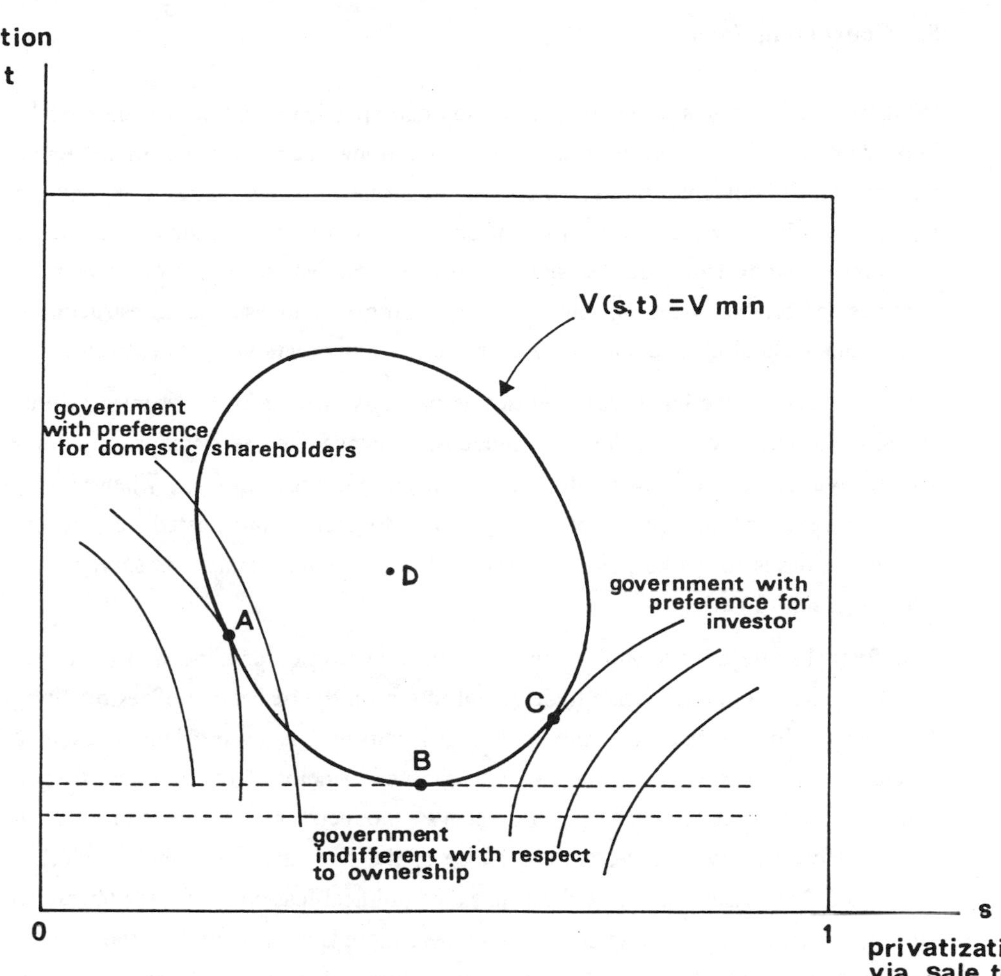
rotection
t
V(s,t) =V min
government
with preference
for domestic shareholders
D
A
government with
preference for
investor
C
B
government
indifferent with respect
to ownership
0
1
s
privatization
via sale to
investor

Figure 6

5. Concluding Remarks

We have sought in this paper to capture the interdependence in the transition exhibited by privatization, enterprise restructuring, and trade policy. A liberal trade regime exposes to the competitive discipline of international markets domestic enterprises that previously were not obliged to confront competition; privatization is central to the transformation from socialist industry to economic activity based on market incentives and private ownership; and, for many enterprises, investment in restructuring to upgrade technology and quality is a prerequisite to international competitiveness.

The model which we have presented in this paper is distinct in its assumed institutional environment of transition. The model is, however, in the tradition of studies which have investigated how institutions can facilitate manipulative policy behavior by beneficiaries of protection, by private agents endogenizing anticipated government policy responses to evoke policies to their advantage (the literature is surveyed by Michael Leidy, 1994).

Our focus has been on identifying whether, or under which conditions, a politically feasible policy can entail basing trade liberalization on the realization of restructuring by investors in privatized enterprises. The government's policy problem is rendered tractable when investors are not aware of the endogeneity of trade policy, that is, when they are not aware that the government's announced trade policy is time inconsistent. However, when investors are aware of the fact that the extent to which a privatized enterprise is upgraded determines the political feasibility of trade liberalization, governments confront an equilibrium where there is no incentive for the investor to restructure, and where therefore trade liberalization is preempted; the time inconsistency is then on the part of the investor, who may declare his intention to restructure, but does not find it to his benefit to do so. We have further an example where containing government discretion to formulate policy facilitates efficient free-market outcomes. When investors are aware of the political endogeneity of trade policy, but a government's declaration that its policies are not subject to revision is credible, the profit-maximizing response for the investor is to restructure. Our model therefore highlights the role of extra-national commitments. Such commitments, by limiting the policy flexibility of the national government, allow a principled government to conduct efficiency-based policies subject to the political feasibility constraints that derive from the distributional consequences of policy.

The transition encompasses, of course, much broader policy dimensions than our model.[12] For example, undervalued currencies have often provided exchange-rate protection for the entire traded-goods sector, whereas we have been concerned with differential advantages sought by a particular enterprise (or industry) via selective policies (as in our introductory example). We have also assumed that the domestic enterprise, even when restructured, does not export; this assumption has been purely expository, and it is a small extension to introduce profits from prospective export sales.[13] We have also not considered government subsidies to encourage investors to restructure;[14] such policies appear particularly out of place in economies in transition where the government is withdrawing from prior centralized control over investment.[15]

We conclude with an observation on the view of government taken in this paper. Past literature has traditionally portrayed governments as being able to focus on efficiency objectives by having at hand lump-sum taxes to achieve income distribution objectives. Other models seeking a more realistic picture of political motives and policy feasibility have presented a view of governments and politicians as self-interested agents choosing policies to maximize probabilities of election.[16] Our formulation has differed from both of these perspectives. We have presented a picture of a government which does not set policies for the personal gain of its officials and which does not seek blindly to maximize reelection prospects, but which is cognizant of the political-support implications of its policies and the need to maintain a minimal level of political support if policies are to be implementable.[17] The model thereby reflects the political altruism of the (early?) transition.

---

[12] For broad overviews, see for example Horst Siebert (1992) and Michael Keren and Gur Ofer (1992).

[13] This in turn raises important issues of foreign market access. See for example Ludger Schuknecht (1992).

[14] See Neil Vousden (1990, chapter 6) and Leonard Cheng (1988).

[15] See Mark Schaffer (1989) on associated principal-agent problems. As Aaron Tornell (1991b) has stressed, investment-contingent subsidies that can potentially resolve the time-inconsistency problems are in practice not feasible and become in effect bail-out payments evoked by the (endogenous) distress of the protected enterprise. See also Tornell (1991b).

[16] See Dennis Mueller (1989), and with particular reference to trade policy Hillman (1989).

[17] See also Kanbur and Myles (1992).

References

Bogetić, Željko (1993), "The Role of Employee Ownership in Privatization of State Enterprises in Eastern and Central Europe," *Europe-Asia Studies*, 45, 463-481.

Cheng, Leonard (1988), "Assisting Domestic Industries under International Oligopoly: The Relevance of the Nature of Competition to Optimal Policies," *American Economic Review*, 78, 746-758.

Hillman, Arye L. (1989), *The Political Economy of Protection*, Harwood Academic Publishers, Chur.

Hillman, Arye L. (1994), "The Transition from Socialism: An Overview from a Political-economy Perspective," *European Journal of Political Economy*, 10, 191-225.

Hillman, Arye L. and Branko Milanovic (1992), (editors), *The Transition from Socialism in Eastern Europe: Domestic Restructuring and Foreign Trade*, The World Bank, Washington, D.C.

Kanbur, S.M.R. and G.D. Miles (1992), "Policy Choice and Political Constraints," *European Journal of Political Economy*, 8, 1-29.

Keren, Michael and Gur Ofer (1992), (editors), "Trials of Transition: Economic Reform in the Former Soviet Bloc", *Westview Press*, Boulder.

Leidy, Michael (1994), "Trade Policy and Indirect Rent Seeking: A Synthesis of Recent Work," *Economics and Politics*, 6, 97-118.

Magee, Stephen P., William A. Brock, and Leslie Young (1989), *Black Hole Tariffs and Endogenous Policy Theory: Political Economy in General Equilibrium*, Cambridge University Press.

Magee, Stephen (1994), in: Greenaway (ed.): *"Surveys of International Trade"*, Oxford.

Milanovic, Branko (1991), "Privatization in Post-communist Societies," *Communist Economies and Economic Transformation*, 3, 5-39.

Mueller, Dennis (1989), *Public Choice*, Cambridge University Press.

Peltzman, Sam (1976), "Toward a More General Theory of Regulation," *Journal of Law and Economics*, 19, 211-240.

Schaffer, Mark (1989), "The Credible Commitment Problem in the Center-Enterprise Relationship," *Journal of Comparative Economics*, 13, 359- 382.

Schuknecht, Ludger (1992), *Trade Protection in the European Community*, Harwood Academic Publishers, Chur.

Siebert, Horst (1992), (editor), *The Transformation of Socialist Economies*, J.C.B. Mohr (Paul Siebeck), Tübingen.

Siebert, Horst (1993), "The Big Bang with the Big Brother," Kiel Discussion Paper number 211, Kiel Institute of World Economics.

Tornell, Aaron (1991a), "Time Inconsistency of Protectionist Programs," *Quarterly Journal of Economics*, 106, 963-974.

Tornell, Aaron (1991b), "On the Ineffectiveness of Made-to-Measure Protectionist Programs," in: Elhanan Helpman and Assaf Razin (eds.): *International Trade and Trade Policy*, MIT Press, Cambridge, 66-79.

Vousden, Neil (1990), *The Economics of Trade Protection*, Cambridge University Press.

World Bank (1992), *Russian Economic Reform: Crossing the Threshold of Structural Change*, Washington, DC.

The Internationalisation of Economic Activity and Tariff Policy*

Albert G. Schweinberger and

Hans-Jürgen Vosgerau**

Abstract

Optimal tariffs in the presence of foreign factor ownership are derived and interpreted. Three types of optimal tariffs are considered: the analogue (with foreign factor ownership) of the standard optimal tariff (terms of trade improvement), the second best optimal tariff (distortion reducing) and the general optimal tariff. The general optimal tariff is equal to the analogue of the standard optimal tariff if foreigners do not own factors in the home country. In this case the optimal tariff is negative if and only if trade pattern reversals occur. The general optimal tariff may be positive in the presence of foreign factor ownership in the home country even if trade pattern reversals occur. Foreign factor ownership may explain the existence of import or export subsidies in many countries. This explanation is an alternative to rent shifting or the existence of a foreign monopoly which supplies the domestic market.

---

* A slightly different version was first published in *"Review of International Economics"*, February 1997. This chapter is printed with the permission of Blackwell Publishers Co., U.K.

** We gratefully acknowledge comments by Karlhans Sauernheimer on an earlier version. Of course, the usual caveat applies.
Financial support by the Deutsche Forschungsgemeinschaft through the Sonderforschungsbereich 178 "Internationalisierung der Wirtschaft" is gratefully acknowledged.

1. Introduction

Foreign factor ownership is associated with many forms of internationalisation (globalisation) of economic activity. The latter, as is well known, has risen phenomenally in the last forty odd years [see e.g. Harris (1992)]. During the same period dramatic changes have occurred in the tariff policies of many countries. It therefore seems natural to ask if the two phenomena are causally linked. Intuitively one would expect this to be the case. Foreign factor ownership entails income flows between countries and clearly these are affected by changes in tariffs. Rather surprisingly, the causal relationship between foreign factor ownership and tariff policy has received remarkably little attention in the literature. This is in sharp contrast to the large literature on the welfare effects of direct foreign investment (purchase or sales of foreign factors) in the presence of given tariffs [see e.g. Johnson (1967), Alejandro-Diaz and Brecher (1977) or Schweinberger (1989)].

The seminal paper on welfare analysis in an open economy in the presence of foreign owned factors of production is Bhagwati and Brecher (1980). Bhagwati and Brecher have shown that a country may lose from free goods trade in the presence of foreign owned factors. Furthermore, in assessing the welfare effects of terms of trade improvements, foreign factor ownership may overturn the standard results (without foreign factor ownership).

These conclusions hinge on the assumption that the economy is in a short run equilibrium: the ownership pattern of factors of production is exogenous. In this case, free trade is optimal from the point of view of a trading world but not from the point of view of each country.[1] The key contribution by Bhagwati and Brecher (op.cit.) is to have shown that in the presence of foreign owned factors there may be *trade pattern reversals*.[2] A country may export good 1 and import good 2 if only goods flows between countries are taken into account. However, this may not be the "true" trading pattern. The latter also has to consider the flows of factor incomes between

---

1 It is well known (from the standard optimal tariff literature) that free trade is not necessarily optimal from the point of view of a country even in the presence of foreign retaliation.

2 Bhagwati and Brecher (op.cit.) refer to this as the "differential trade pattern phenomenon".

countries. Taking income flows into consideration good 1 may be imported (rather than exported) and good 2 exported (rather than imported). The welfare effects of exogenous product price changes are, as is well known, sensitive to changes in the trading pattern.

Apart from Bhagwati and Brecher's contribution there is, to the best of our knowledge, only one other article concerned with the effect of foreign factor ownership on tariff policy. This is Levinson (1989). However, Levinson's main aim is rather different from ours. He examines the equivalence (or lack thereof) between quotas and tariffs under imperfect competition with foreign factor ownership in a simple partial equilibrium model.

The present paper extends the analysis of Bhagwati and Brecher in several directions:

(1) Bhagwati and Brecher assume a two factor and two good economy. We relax this assumption. In fact all our results can be shown to hold whatever the finite number of factors and goods.

(2) We derive various kinds of optimal tariffs: tariffs which are optimal in the sense of improving the terms of trade (analogues of standard optimal tariffs), tariffs which are second best optimal, i.e.: tariffs which are used to reduce the foreign factor income and generally optimal tariffs. Apparently this distinction, which is fundamental to all tariff analysis in economies with income flows due to foreign factor ownership and endogenous terms of trade, is novel. It acquires particular significance in the context of political economy approaches (see footnote 7 below).

(3) A necessary and sufficient condition for the analogue of the standard optimal tariffs to be negative is derived and interpreted. This is contrasted with the result which is obtained if tariffs are used to reduce (optimally) the foreign factor income.

(4) All the results are shown to be sensitive to changes in the assumptions regarding the pattern of foreign factor ownership.

The analysis of the relationship between endogenous tariff policy and foreign factor ownership seems interesting for several reasons.

Firstly, it is related to the theory of rent and profit shifting. As is well known, there is a huge literature on the desirability of export subsidies in the case of imperfect competition [see e.g. Brander and Spencer (1981)]. If the home country owns factors abroad it can use tariff policy to shift income from the factors owned by the foreign country to the factors owned by the home country. Proposition 1 below states a necessary and sufficient condition under which the relevant tariff is negative. This may be regarded as an alternative explanation of the existence of export subsidies in certain countries.[3]

Secondly, there is the interesting literature on the effects of tariff policy of a foreign monopoly producer which supplies the domestic market [see e.g. De Maza (1979), Brander and Spencer (1984), Jones (1987) and Jones and Takemori (1989)]. If import demand curves are of a certain curvature it can be shown that the imposition of a tariff by a small country (small in the sense that its trade has negligible effects on the world market) may entail a rise rather than a fall in the foreign supply price of the imported good. In this case too there are income flows from the home country to the foreign country which can be influenced by tariffs. It is therefore not surprising that yet again trade subsidies may be used to shift income from the foreign monopoly to domestic factors of production.

At this point we should emphasize that we regard foreign factor ownership as only one aspect of the problem of explaining tariff policy. There are certainly many other equally or more important aspects, such as lobbying, distributional considerations in its many different forms, unemployment and declining industries (because of high retraining costs) etc. The importance of foreign factor ownership can, of course, only be evaluated if all the other potential explanations of tariff policy are considered as well. Our claim is only that foreign factor ownership merits (inter alia) careful consideration.

---

3 Export subsidies can also be explained by the existence of general or Harris-Todaro involuntary unemployment [see e.g. Batra and Naqvi (1987)].

The paper is structured as follows. In the following part 2 the main results of the paper are proven within the framework of a simple Ricardo-Viner model. In this framework it is easy to obtain an intuitive grasp of the main results.

Part 2 is subdivided into sections 2.1, 2.2 and 2.3. In 2.1 the analogue of the standard optimal tariff is derived and interpreted. In section 2.2 we focus on the second best optimal tariff. Finally in section 2.3, the analogue of the standard optimal tariff and the second best optimal tariff are related to each other and a general optimal tariff is derived and interpreted. Directions for further research as well as a summary of the main conclusions can be found in part 3.

2. The Main Results within a Simple Ricardo-Viner Model

We make all the assumptions of a simple (two good) Ricardo-Viner or specific factor model, except that we allow for the home country to own factors abroad and the foreign country to own factors in the home country. Foreign factor ownership extends only to sector specific factors (not to the mobile factors). The two goods are denoted by good 1 and good 2. Good 2 is assumed to be imported by the home country and good 1 is exported.

Since there are no distortions other than a given pattern of foreign factor ownership we can make use of the following revenue functions of the home and foreign countries.

$$g^I = g^I(1,\ p_2,\ K_1,\ K_2,\ L) \tag{1}$$

and

$$g^{II} = g^{II}\left(1,\ p_2^*,\ K_1^*,\ K_2^*,\ L^*\right) \tag{2}$$

where the stars denote the foreign country and good 1 has been chosen as the tax-free numéraire.

The amounts of K_1 and K_2 owned by foreign households are $\alpha_1^* K_1$ and $\alpha_2^* K_2$ respectively. Similarly, the amounts of K_1^* and K_2^* owned by households of the home country are $\alpha_1 K_1^*$ and $\alpha_2 K_2^*$.

In the present context it is convenient to use indirect trade utility functions [see Woodland (1982)], to derive optimal tariff rates.

$$U^I = U^I\Bigg[1,\, p_2,\, g^I(1,\, p_2,\, K_1,\, K_2,\, L) + \alpha_1 \frac{\partial g^{II}}{\partial K_1^*} K_1^* + \alpha_2 \frac{\partial g^{II}}{\partial K_2^*} K_2^* \ldots$$

$$\ldots - \alpha_1^* \frac{\partial g^I}{\partial K_1} K_1 - \alpha_2^* \frac{\partial g^I}{\partial K_2} K_2 + (p_2 - p_2^*)\,(y_2^* - x_2^*)\Bigg] \tag{3}$$

where:

$$y_2^* = \frac{\partial g^{II}}{\partial p_2^*}\left(1,\, p_2^*,\, K_1^*,\, K_2^*,\, L\right),$$

and

$$x_2^* = x_2^*\left[1,\, p_2^*,\, g^{II}(\cdot) + \alpha_1^* r_1\, K_1 + \alpha_2^* r_2\, K_2 - \alpha_1 r_1^* K_1^* - \alpha_2 r_2^* K_2^*\right]$$

y_2^* stands for the supply of good 2 abroad and

$x_2^*(\cdot)$ represents a Marshallian demand function for good 2 abroad.

Expression (3), the indirect trade utility function, is obtained by substituting the sum of income from production, net foreign factor ownership and governmental revenue into the indirect utility function of the household of the home country.

From standard duality theory:

$$\frac{\partial g^{II}}{\partial K_2^*} = r_2^*\left(1,\, p_2^*,\, K_1^*,\, K_2^*,\, L^*\right) \tag{4}$$

$$\frac{\partial g^{II}}{\partial K_1^*} = r_1^*\left(1,\, p_2^*,\, K_1^*,\, K_2^*,\, L^*\right) \tag{5}$$

$$\frac{\partial g^{II}}{\partial K_2} = r_2\left(1,\, p_2,\, K_1,\, K_2,\, L\right) \tag{6}$$

$$\frac{\partial g^{II}}{\partial K_1} = r_1\left(1,\, p_2,\, K_1,\, K_2,\, L\right) \tag{7}$$

Factor prices are not equalised. Since the ownership pattern of factors is exogenous, the equilibrium is short run. This can be explained in terms of a rationing of purchases or sales of factors in foreign countries. This rationing is the essence of the distortion present in the model.[4] If the purchases and sales of all factors were fully endogenous (and unconstrained) all the standard welfare results have to hold because the distinction between goods and factors is immaterial from the point of view of normative general equilibrium analysis.

4 It is well known that rationing of the imports or exports of goods in a *small* country implies a second best or constrained Pareto efficient equilibrium, see for example Corden and Falvey (1985). This is not generally the case with constraints on factor purchases or sales. Tariffs on the imports or exports of goods can affect income flows between countries because they can change factor prices in the home country.

We are now in a position to derive three different kinds of optimal tariffs: (a) the analogue of the standard optimal tariff, (b) the second best optimal tariff and (c) the general optimal tariff.[5]

2.1 The analogue of the standard optimal tariff

To solve for this tariff the indirect utility function is partially differentiated with respect to $\overset{*}{p}_2$. This yields the following first order condition:

$$\alpha_2 \frac{\partial \overset{*}{r}_1}{\partial \overset{*}{p}_2} \overset{*}{K}_1 + \alpha_2 \frac{\partial \overset{*}{r}_2}{\partial \overset{*}{p}_2} \overset{*}{K}_2 + \left(p_2 - \overset{*}{p}_2\right)\left(\frac{\partial \overset{*}{y}_2}{\partial \overset{*}{p}_2} - \frac{\delta \overset{*}{x}_2}{\delta \overset{*}{p}_2}\right) - \left(\overset{*}{y}_2 - \overset{*}{x}_2\right) = 0 \tag{8}$$

Expression (8) is an equation in p_2 and $\overset{*}{p}_2$. To solve for the analogue of the standard optimal tariff we also need the following world market equilibrium condition for good 2.

$$y_2(\cdot) + \overset{*}{y}_2(\cdot) = x_2(1, p_2, Y^I) + x_2(1, \overset{*}{p}_2, Y^{II}) \tag{9}$$

where

$$Y^I = g^I(\cdot) + \alpha_1 \overset{*}{r}_1 \overset{*}{K}_1 + \alpha_2 \overset{*}{r}_2 \overset{*}{K}_2 - \overset{*}{\alpha}_1 r_1 K_1 - \overset{*}{\alpha}_2 r_2 K_2 + (p_2 - \overset{*}{p}_2)(\overset{*}{y}_2 - \overset{*}{x}_2)$$

and

$$Y^{II} = g^{II}(\cdot) + \overset{*}{\alpha}_1 r_1 K_1 + \overset{*}{\alpha}_2 r_2 K_2 - \alpha_1 \overset{*}{r}_1 \overset{*}{K}_1 - \alpha_2 \overset{*}{r}_2 \overset{*}{K}_2 \quad .$$

In the derivation of the analogue of the standard optimal tariff the optimising variable is the terms of trade, in this case $\overset{*}{p}_2$. The role of p_2 the home price of good 2, is to equilibrate the world market for good 2. In other words p_2, the home price of

---

5 As will become clear further below only the imposition of a general optimal tariff guarantees, in the absence of foreign retaliation, a welfare improvement relative to the free trade equilibrium (if certain regularity conditions are satisfied).

the imported good, acts in an accommodating fashion. To be precise, in a general equilibrium approach p_2 and p_2^* are of course determined simultaneously by equations (8) and (9).

To gain more insights, expression (8) is rewritten as follows:

$$\alpha_1 \frac{\partial r_1^*}{\partial p_2^*} K_1^* + \alpha_2 \frac{\partial r_2^*}{\partial p_2^*} K_2^* + \frac{(p_2 - p_2^*)}{p_2^*} \frac{\partial X_2^*}{\partial p_2^*} p_2^* = X_2^* \tag{10}$$

where $X_2^* = y_2^* - x_2^*$

or

$$\alpha_1 \frac{\partial r_1^*}{\partial p_1^*} K_1^* + \alpha_2 \frac{\partial r_2^*}{\partial p_2^*} K_2^* + X_2^* \frac{(p_2 - p_2^*)}{p_2^*} E_x^* = X_2^* \tag{11}$$

where E_x^* is the foreign supply elasticity of exports.

Making use of the technique of imputing economy outputs to factors, developed in Lloyd and Schweinberger (1988), we define:

$$\frac{\partial r_1^*}{\partial p_2^*} K_1^* = \tilde{y}_{2}^*, K_1 \qquad \text{and} \qquad \frac{\partial r_2^*}{\partial p_2^*} K_2^* = \tilde{y}_{2}^*, K_2 \tag{12}$$

where: $\tilde{y}_2^*, K_1$ is defined as the output of good 2 *imputed* to factor K_1 abroad and

$\tilde{y}_2^*, K_2$ as the output of good 2 *imputed* to factor K_2 abroad.

That these definitions are meaningful and consistent can be seen by differentiating partially the following identity with respect to p_2^*:

$$g^{II}(1, p_2^*, K_1^*, K_2^*, L) = r_1^*(\cdot)K_1^* + r_2^*(\cdot)K_2^* + w^*(\cdot)L^* \tag{13}$$

This yields:

$$y_2^* = \tilde{y}_2^*, K_1 + \tilde{y}_2^*, K_2 + \tilde{y}_2^*, L \tag{14}$$

The aggregate output of good 2 is *imputed* to the factors K_1^*, K_2^* and L^*. Imputed outputs may be positive or negative.

An analogous expression holds for the output of good 2 in the home country:

$$y_2 = \tilde{y}_2, K_1 + \tilde{y}_2, K_2 + \tilde{y}_2, L \tag{15}$$

In this very simple model it is well known that:

$$\tilde{y}_2, K_1, \; \tilde{y}_2^*, K_1 < 0 \quad \text{and} \quad \tilde{y}_2, K_2, \; \tilde{y}_2^*, K_2 > 0$$

Making use of the concept of imputed outputs, expression (11) can be rewritten as follows:

$$\frac{(p_2 - p_2^*)}{p_2^*} E_x^* = I - \frac{\alpha_1 \tilde{y}_2^*, K_1 + \alpha_2 \tilde{y}_2^*, K_2}{X_2^*} \tag{16}$$

Defining $\alpha_1 \tilde{y}_2^*, K_1 + \alpha_2 \tilde{y}_2^*, K_2$ as the outputs imputed to the home country on account of its ownership of foreign factors we are in a position to explain the concept of trade pattern reversals due to foreign factor ownership [see also Bhagwati and Brecher (1980)]:

Definition A:

There are trade pattern reversals if $(y_2^* - x_2^*)$ is positive but $y_2^* - x_2^* - \alpha_1 \tilde{y}_2^*, K_1 - \alpha_2 \tilde{y}_2^*, K_2$ negative.

In the light of definition A and the preceding analysis we can now state and prove proposition I:

Proposition I

Assume that the analogue (with foreign factor ownership) of the optimal tariff/subsidy exists in a simple Ricardo-Viner model. Then the *standard* optimal tariff is negative if and only if trade pattern reversals occur. For a definition of trade pattern reversals, see Definition A.

Proof:

From the standard assumption that the foreign export supply elasticity is positive, i.e. $E_x^* > 0$ and the occurrence of trade pattern reversals it follows from expression (16) that $\frac{p_2 - p_2^*}{p_2^*}$ is negative.[6] Q.E.D.

The economic meaning of proposition I is straightforward. Whilst in a model without foreign factor ownership the welfare effects of changes in foreign prices depend upon the actual trading pattern, they depend now upon the *imputed* trading pattern. If trade pattern reversals occur, the actual and the imputed trading patterns are different. In the present case good 2 is actually exported by the foreign country but in *imputed* terms it is imported by the foreign country.

It will be shown below that the general optimal tariff is equal to the analogue of the standard optimal tariff if foreigners do not own factors of production in the home country.

---

6 It should be carefully noted that the indirect trade utility function cannot be shown to be a concave or even quasi concave function of p_2^*. Expression (8) is only a first order necessary condition for the existence of a standard optimal tariff. This is a well known problem in the literature on optimal taxation [see e.g. Dixit and Norman (1980, p.174)].

2.2 The second best optimal tariff

In the derivation of the standard optimal tariff the optimising variable was p_2^*, the terms of trade. However, this is not to be taken for granted in the present context. The role of p_2^* could be accommodating, i.e: it could equilibrate markets, see expression (9), and the optimising variable could be p_2 instead of p_2^*.

Foreign factor ownership adds a new dimension to the derivation of optimal tariffs for the following reason: if optimal tariff rates are derived without foreign factor ownership the derivation of $U^I(\cdot)$ with respect to p_2 simply yields the world market equilibrium condition for good 2. This reflects the fact that there are no other distortions. However, as explained before, this is not the case if the pattern of foreign factor ownership is exogenous in the short run.

Differentiating the indirect trade utility function partially with respect to p_2 we obtain:

$$\frac{\partial U^I(\cdot)}{\partial p_2} = -\frac{\partial U^I}{\partial Y^I}\left(\alpha_1^* \tilde{y}_{2,K_1} + \alpha_2^* \tilde{y}_{2,K_2}\right)\left(p_1^* \frac{\partial x_1^*}{\partial Y^{II}} + p_2 \frac{\partial x_2^*}{\partial Y^{II}}\right) \tag{17}$$

Expression (17) gives rise to the following proposition II.

Proposition II

Assume that a second best (foreign income minimising) optimal tariff exists in a simple Ricardo-Viner model with foreign factor ownership. Then the sum of the outputs of good 2 (produced in the home country and) imputed to the foreign country is zero if all goods are normal in demand in the foreign country.

Proposition II follows directly from expression (17). Q.E.D.

The optimal tariff or subsidy on good 2 is obtained by solving:

$$\overset{*}{\alpha}_1 \tilde{y}_{2,K_1} + \overset{*}{\alpha}_2 \tilde{y}_{2,K_2} = 0 \tag{18}$$

for p_2 and then substituting p_2 into the world goods market equilibrium condition, expression (9), and solving the latter for $\overset{*}{p}_2$.

The rationale underlying the second best optimal tariff is clear. If foreigners own domestic factors the income of foreigners depends upon the home price of good 2 and by choosing an appropriate p_2, the income of foreigners can be minimised (and the income of home households increased).

The following observations are now in order:

(1) The analogue of the standard optimal tariff is not an optimal tariff in the sense that $dU^I = 0$ if foreigners own factors in the home country. This can be seen from:

$$dU^I = \frac{\partial U^I}{\partial p_2} dp_2 + \frac{\partial U^I}{\partial \overset{*}{p}_2} d\overset{*}{p}_2 \tag{19}$$

The analogue of the standard optimal tariff was obtained by setting the coefficient of $d\overset{*}{p}_2$ equal to zero and solving the resulting equation in conjunction with the goods market equilibrium condition for p_2 and $\overset{*}{p}_2$. But if foreigners own factors in the home country the coefficient of dp_2 in (19) generally is nonzero, hence $dU^I = 0$.

(2) The second best optimal tariff is not an optimal tariff in the sense that $dU^I = 0$ if the home country can affect its terms of trade. This follows also from expression (19).

(3) Probably the most important result of the analysis so far is that neither the analogue of the standard nor the second best optimal tariffs can guarantee a welfare improvement relative to the free trade equilibrium *even if all the first and second order conditions are satisfied globally.* This is a straightforward

implication of the standard theory of the second best. Imposition of the analogue of the standard optimal tariff may entail such a rise in income flows from the home country that the terms of trade gains are more than offset by income losses. Similarly, imposing a second best optimal tariff, even if it minimises the income earned by foreigners in the home country, may lead to an overall welfare loss because of a deterioration in the terms of trade (taking into account imputed trading patterns).

2.3 The general optimal tariff

The general optimal tariff is derived by first differentiating the world market equilibrium condition, expression (9). This yields:

$$dp_2 = \gamma \, dp_2^* \tag{20}$$

where γ is a coefficient which may be positive or negative. If γ is evaluated in a free trade equilibrium without foreign factor ownership and substitution effects dominate income effects it is generally negative. But this cannot be guaranteed in a model with foreign factor ownership. The reason for this is that there are now new income effects associated with factor income flows between countries.

Substituting expression (20) into expression (19), we arrive at the following first order condition for a general optimal tariff:

$$\frac{\partial U^I}{\partial p_2}\gamma + \frac{\partial U^I}{\partial p_2^*} = 0 \tag{21}$$

where: $\frac{\partial U^I}{\partial p_2}$ is equal to expression (17)

and $$\frac{\partial U^I}{\partial p_2^*} = \alpha_1 \tilde{y}_{2}^*,_{K_1} + \alpha_2 \tilde{y}_{2}^*,_{K_2} + X_2^* \frac{(p_2 - p_2^*)}{p_2^*} E_x^* - X_2^* \tag{22}$$

see expression (10).

The general optimal tariff is therefore obtained by solving:

$$\alpha_1 \tilde{y}^*_{2,K_1} + \alpha_2 \tilde{y}^*_{2,K_2} + X^*_2 \frac{(p_2 - p^*_2)}{p_2} E^*_x - X^*_2 = -\frac{\partial U^I}{\partial p_2} \gamma \tag{23}$$

and the world market equilibrium condition, expression (9).

Rearranging expression (23) it is easy to see that the following proposition III follows.

Proposition III

Assume that a general optimal tariff exists in a simple Ricardo-Viner model with foreign factor ownership. Then the general optimal tariff is negative if trade pattern reversals occur and foreigners do not own factors in the home country. Generally trade pattern reversals are neither necessary nor sufficient for a negative general optimal tariff.

Proposition III follows directly from a rearrangement of expression (23). Q.E.D.

It should be noted that in order to obtain the general optimal tariff the indirect trade utility function has to be maximised with respect to p_2 and p^*_2 subject to the world's goods market equilibrium condition for good 2. In a more comprehensive analysis it would be instructive to solve also for the Lagrangean multiplier associated with the constraint. This may lead to additional insights with regard to the possibility of a negative optimal tariff even if the foreign country owns factors in the home country.

Another aspect of the analysis which deserves more careful consideration is the relationship between our analysis and the theory of transfer paradoxes in distorted economies when the transfers are endogenous [see e.g. Schweinberger (1990)]. To achieve this, one would have to solve for γ in expression (20) explicitly. Due to the many income effects this is relatively involved.

At this point it should be mentioned that all the results can readily be generalized to models with any finite number of goods and factors (provided that all the relevant functions are differentiable). It is easy to see from expressions (13) to (15) that the concept of imputing economy outputs to factors of production is completely general. It is very well known that if there are more than two goods, the standard optimal tariff structure(without foreign factor ownership) may contain negative elements, i.e.: the trade of a good may be subsidized rather than taxed. However, trade taxes have to predominate in the sense that governmental revenue is positive. The latter is not the case with foreign factor ownership. This can easilybe shown. As in the two good case the occurrence or non-occurrence of trade pattern reversals as well as the pattern of foreign factor ownership play a key part in this context.

Finally, another caveat seems appropriate: the informational requirements for calculating a general optimal tariff are formidable. In the light of the complexity involved it may be more practical to determine halfspaces in p_2 and p_2^* such that *locally* starting from a free trade equilibrium the home country achieves a welfare improvement. Fortunately, it is straightforward to relate the incremental analysis to the welfare optimum (see Motzkin's theorem).[7]

3. Summary and Conclusions

Many forms of internationalisation (globalisation) of economic activity are associated with foreign factor ownership (for example, foreign joint ventures, multinational corporations). The aim of this paper has been to examine the causal link between foreign factor ownership and tariff policy. There are many ways in which tariff policy can be endogenised. The choice made by us is a very simple one but the main ideas would carry over to much more complex settings such as social welfare functions or political support functions which consider distribution as well as efficiency.

In the presence of foreign factor ownership it is important to understand that generally (even if distributional issues are ignored) the analogue of the standard optimal tariff is not the same as a general optimal tariff. The reason for this is the presence of a distortion if, as in the short run, foreign factor ownership patterns are

---

7 For Motzkin's theorem, see Mangasarian (1969), p. 28.

exogenous. One of our main results is that the analogue of the standard optimal tariff is equal to the general optimal tariff if foreigners do not own factors in the home country. In this case the optimal tariff is negative if and only if trade pattern reversals occur. However, the general optimal tariff may be negative or positive. In fact trade pattern reversals are neither necessary nor sufficient for the general optimal tariff to be negative.

Imposition of the general optimal tariff guarantees a welfare improvement if certain first and second order conditions are satisfied, where it should be carefully noted that the fulfillment of the second order conditions should not be taken for granted. This is a problem which is very familiar from the literature on optimal taxation. On the other hand, imposition of the standard or the second best (foreign factor income minimising) tariff cannot even guarantee that there is a welfare improvement relative to the free trade equilibrium. This is a straightforward implication of the theory of the second best and one of the main messages of the paper.

We conclude with the following two observations:

(1) The present paper should be seen only as a first step towards a comprehensive analysis of the relationship between the globalisation of economic activity and tariff policy. Foreign factor ownership is, of course, only one aspect of the globalisation of economic activity.

(2) All the results of the paper are based upon a simple Ricardo-Viner model; however, it is straightforward to generalise them in many directions. It is obvious, for example, that the concept of trade pattern reversals can be applied in production models with any finite number of factors and goods. The reader is referred to Lloyd and Schweinberger (1988) where it is shown that the concept of imputed outputs is readily generalised to many factors, goods and households. The latter is very relevant if one intends to introduce distributional considerations by means of a social welfare or political support function.[8]

---

8 It is, for example, extremely likely that all the results of political economy approaches to the determination of tariffs are significantly affected by the existence of foreign factor ownership, see e.g. Grossman and Helpman (1993) or Hillman and Moser (1992).

Tariff policy in the real world is certainly also influenced by the effects of tariffs on unemployment. Making use of modern duality techniques, see Schweinberger (1978) and Neary (1985), it is easy to incorporate employment effects à la Brecher, see Brecher (1974). Last but not least the assumption of perfect competition in goods markets should be relaxed. To achieve this in a general equilibrium framework it is best to model imperfect competition on the part of production agents as price manipulable output rationing [see Schweinberger (1993)]. The introduction of imperfect competition raises a new and very interesting issue: income flows between countries which are not based on factor ownership but ownership of firms, i.e.: entitlement to residual profits.

References

Batra, R.N. and N. Naqvi (1987), "Urban Unemployment and the Gains from Trade", *Economica*, 54, pp. 381-396.

Bhagwati, J.N. and R.A. Brecher (1980), "National Welfare in the Open Economy in the Presence of Foreign-Owned Factors of Production", *Journal of International Economics*, 10, pp. 103-115.

Brander, J.A. and B.J. Spencer (1981), "Tariffs and the Extraction of Foreign Monopoly Rents Under Potential Entry", *Canadian Journal of Economics*, 16, pp. 289-299.

Brander, J.A. and B.J. Spencer (1984), "Trade Warfare: Tariffs and Cartels", *Journal of International Economics*, 16, pp. 227-242.

Brander, J.A. and B.J. Spencer (1985), "Export Subsidies and International Market Share Rivalry", *Journal of International Economics,* 18, pp. 227-242.

Brecher, R.A. (1974), "Minimum Wage Rates and the Pure Theory of International Trade", *Quarterly Journal of Economics*, 88, pp. 98-116.

Brecher, R.A. and C. Diaz Alejandro (1977), "Tariffs, Foreign Capital and Immiserising Growth", *Journal of International Economics,* 7, pp. 317-322.

Corden, W. M. and R. E. Falvey (1985), "Quotas and the Second Best", *Economics Letters*, 18, pp. 67-70.

De Meza, D. (1979), "Commercial Policy Towards Multinational Monopolies - Reservations on Katrak", *Oxford Economic Papers,* 31, pp. 334-337.

Dixit, A. and V. Norman (1980), *The Theory of International Trade: a Dual General Equilibrium Approach*, Cambridge.

Grossman, G.M. and E. Helpman (1993), "*Trade Wars and Trade Talks*", paper presented at the Tel Aviv - Konstanz Conference on International Economics.

Harris, R.G. (1993), "Globalization, Trade, and Income", *Canadian Journal of Economics*, No. 4, pp. 756-776.

Hillman, Arye L. and P. Moser (1992), *"Trade Liberalization as Politically Optimal Exchange of Market Access"*, mimeo.

Mangasarian, O.L. (1969), *Nonlinear Programming*, McGraw-Hill, New York.

Johnson, H.G. (1967), "The Possibility of Income Losses from Increased Efficiency or Factor Accumulation in the Presence of Tariffs", *Economic Journal,* 77, pp. 151-154.

Jones, R.W. (1987), "Trade Taxes and Subsidies With Imperfect Competition", *Economic Letters,* 23, pp. 375-379.

Jones, R.W. and S. Takemori (1989), "Foreign Monopoly and Optimal Tariffs for the Small Open Economy", *European Economic Review,* 33, pp. 1691-1707.

Levinson, J.A. (1989), "Strategic Trade Policy When Firms Can Invest Abroad: When Are Tariffs And Quotas Equivalent?", *Journal of International Economics*, 27, pp. 129-146.

Neary, J.P. (1985), "International Factor Mobility, Minimum Wage Rates and Factor Price Equalisation: A Synthesis", *Quarterly Journal of Economics*, pp. 550-570.

Schweinberger, A. (1989), "Foreign Capital Flows, Tariffs, and Welfare: a Global Analysis", *Canadian Journal of Economics* XXII, No.2, May 1989, pp. 310-327.

Schweinberger, A. and P.J. Lloyd (1988), "Trade Expenditure Functions and the Gains from Trade", *Journal of International Economics*, 24, pp. 275-297.

Schweinberger, A.G. (1978), "Employment Subsidies and the Theory of Minimum Wage Rates in General Equilibrium", *The Quarterly Journal of Economics*, Vol. XCII, No. 3, pp. 361-374.

Schweinberger, A.G. (1990), "On the Welfare Effects of Tied Aid", *International Economic Review*, Vol. 31, No. 2, pp. 457-463.

Schweinberger, A.G. (1993), *"Procompetitive Gains from Trade and Comparative Advantage"*, University of Konstanz, Discussion Paper No. 155.

Woodland, A.D. (1982), *"International Trade and Resource Allocation"*, North Holland.

Indirect Taxation in an Integrated Europe: Is There a Way of Avoiding Trade Distortions without Sacrificing National Tax Autonomy?*

Bernd Genser,
Andreas Haufler and
Peter Birch Sørensen**

Abstract

The paper discusses the main arguments for destination- versus origin-based commodity taxation in the European Community's Internal Market. Destination-based solutions distort commodity trade in the Community because cross-border purchases by final consumers can only be taxed in the origin country. On the other hand, an origin-based general consumption tax is neutral in a European context and it can be combined with destination-based taxation in third countries in a non-distortionary way. Furthermore, it is shown that the introduction of capital mobility does not affect the neutrality of an origin-based consumption tax. Finally, the paper addresses the administrative and political implications of a switch to the origin principle in the European Community.

---

* Reprinted from *Journal of Economic Integration*, Vol. 10 (2), June 1995, pp. 178-205.

** We thank Sijbren Cnossen, Michael Keen, Friedrich Schneider and two referees for helpful comments and suggestions. Financial support by the Deutsche Forschungsgemeinschaft through the Sonderforschungsbereich 178 „Internationalisierung der Wirtschaft" is gratefully acknowledged.

1. Introduction

In the literature on international taxation there has been a long-standing debate on the relative merits of the origin principle and the destination principle of commodity taxation[1]. Under the origin principle, goods are taxed in the country where they are produced, whereas the destination principle implies taxation in the country of final consumption.

While the origin principle has found several supporters in academic circles, the destination principle has so far won out in practice and is also the commodity tax principle codified by the GATT. However, because administration of the destination principle has traditionally relied on so-called border tax adjustments, the recent years have witnessed a renewed interest in the origin principle. The debate has focused on the European Community where internal border controls have been abolished in 1993. However, with the recent or planned introduction of value-added taxes in countries as diverse as Canada, Argentina, India, and Vietnam - many of them federal economies - the appropriate method of taxing goods that cross fiscal jurisdictions seems to be of increasing relevance in other parts of the world as well.

Against this background, the present paper discusses the possibilities of accommodating cross-country differentials in indirect tax rates without distorting international resource allocation in a world without economic borders. In discussing this issue, we attempt to provide a brief and non-technical overview of the existing knowledge of the allocative effects of alternative commodity tax principles, and to

---

1 Some of the classical references on this topic are the Tinbergen Committee [1953], the Neumark Committee [1963], Shibata [1967], and Biehl [1969]. More recent contributions include, among others, Whalley [1979 and 1981], Berglas [1981], Peffekoven [1983], Andel [1986], Cnossen and Shoup [1987], Siebert [1990], Sinn [1990], Krause-Junk [1990 and 1992], Haufler [1992], Bovenberg [1994] and Lockwood, de Meza and Myles [1994]. The close links that exist to the taxation of international factor flows are stressed, for example, by Sørensen [1990], Frenkel, Razin and Sadka [1991, Ch. 2], Genser [1992], and Keen [1993].

analyse within a simple framework whether conventional neutrality results based on pure trade models will carry over to a world with international capital mobility[2].

We start out in section 2.1 by briefly considering why the neutrality properties of the destination principle cease to hold under the conditions of the Internal Market where direct cross-border consumer trade will effectively be taxed under the origin principle. Sections 2.2 and 2.3 then present the argument that a switch to a suitable variant of an origin-based VAT in Europe is able to eliminate the distortions to international trade in a single market without border controls. Section 2.4 proceeds to discuss how domestic tax wedges such as differentiated tax rates on different commodities may cause international trade distortions and how such distortions might be neutralized under an origin-based commodity tax regime.

In section 3 the standard framework of most of the existing literature on international commodity taxation is extended by switching from pure trade models to models with international factor mobility. A simple intertemporal model is developed to investigate whether a general single-rate VAT remains non-distortionary in the presence of international capital flows. We find that an origin-based consumption tax will indeed lead to an efficient international resource allocation even with mobile capital, provided prices or exchange rates are flexible.

While our theoretical analysis thus poses the origin principle in a rather favourable light, section 4 briefly considers some practical and administrative arguments which tend to favour the destination principle over the origin principle. Finally, we sum up our main conclusions in section 5.

---

[2] Throughout this paper, we will distinguish sharply between „allocative neutrality“ which implies the absence of relative price distortions, and „distributional neutrality“ which refers to the absence of income effects. Most of the discussion will focus on issues of allocative neutrality.

2. Commodity Taxes in Standard Trade Models

2.1 Destination Principle

To discuss the effects of alternative tax principles in models with commodity trade only, we initially assume an „idealized" value-added tax, which is levied at a uniform rate on all produced goods and services while factors of production, notably labor, are in fixed supply[3]. With fixed factor supplies it is intuitive that a general commodity tax is equivalent to a lump sum tax in a closed economy. Furthermore, the lump sum character of the tax is maintained in an open economy when all internationally traded goods are taxed under the destination principle. Let p_i^k be the producer prices of an arbitrary number of final consumer goods i in countries $k \in [A,B]$ and let t^k be the general commodity tax rate in country *k*. Under the destination principle, the tax rate of the importing country applies equally to domestic and foreign products so that, from the perspective of country *A*'s consumers, the following arbitrage condition must hold:

$$\left(1+t^A\right) p_i^A = \left(1+t^A\right) p_i^B \Rightarrow p_i^A = p_i^B \quad \forall i . \tag{1}$$

Thus, in the absence of transportation costs, consumer arbitrage will equalize producer prices across countries, and relative producer prices will be left undistorted, coinciding with relative consumer prices. Furthermore, changes in the national VAT rate will not shift tax revenues between countries because the tax base under the destination principle is the value of domestic consumption. Together, these constitute the well-known neutrality properties of the destination principle.

---

[3] These assumptions will be relaxed in section 2.4.

The problem in the European Community's Internal Market is, however, that the destination principle cannot be administered for all consumer goods. In the absence of border controls, cross-border purchases by final consumers can only be taxed in the country of origin[4]. While, e.g., Cnossen [1990, p. 477] holds that „(...) the abolition of frontier controls may have less effect on revenue and resource allocation than is generally thought", others consider these effects to be more severe. They argue that if the destination principle is maintained for trade between registered traders, as is the case under both the transitional deferred payment system adopted by the Community until (at least) the end of 1996, and the international tax credit system envisaged for the period thereafter, a mixed tax principle emerges which does not have the desirable neutrality properties of the destination principle (Sinn [1990], Krause-Junk [1990])[5]. Similar effects can be expected from the increasing volume of intra-Community trade in services, which in many cases must be taxed in the country of origin. To show these effects let good 1 be a good (or service) purchased directly by final consumers whereas good 2 denotes a good purchased by VAT-registered traders. In the absence of transportation costs, arbitrage yields

---

4 The Community has, however, taken several measures to reduce the scope of origin taxation in the Internal Market: (a) purchases by tax-exempt entities in excess of ECU 35,000 are taxable as self supplies in the member state of destination, (b) mailorder firms with intra-Community exports exceeding 1 million ECU per annum are legally required to charge and remit the VAT of the member state of destination, (c) cars not purchased through registered dealers are taxed in the destination country upon registration.

5 Under the deferred payment system, border tax adjustments are maintained despite the abolition of border controls and the zero-rating of exports is based on the proof that goods have been sold to a trader registered in another member state. Under the international tax credit system, the tax liability for imports is based on the origin country's tax rate but the recouping effect of the tax credit at subsequent processing stages ensures that the effective tax rate is that of the destination country. The economic effects of the deferred payment and the international tax credit system are thus equivalent if, under the latter scheme, a clearing mechanism restores the allocation of tax revenues according to the countries' final consumption (cf. Cnossen [1983], and Haufler [1992], pp. 251-253).

$$\left(1+t^{A}\right) p_1^{A} = \left(1+t^{B}\right) p_1^{B} ,$$
$$p_2^{A} = p_2^{B} \tag{2}$$

so that for $t^{A} \neq t^{B}$ relative producer prices in the two countries differ and trade is distorted under the tax regime chosen by the Community.

Tax bases in each country also differ from the case with border controls, redistributing tax revenues from the importer to the exporter of the good which is purchased through cross-border shopping and is thus taxed in the country of origin. This issue is most serious when the possibility of (legal and illegal) tax avoidance schemes is taken into account[6]. If the effect on tax revenues induced by this kind of arbitrage activities is sufficiently strong, policy makers in each country have an incentive to lower the domestic tax rate in order to attract foreign cross-border shopping and increase the national tax base (cf. Sinn [1990]).

2.2 The General Origin Principle

Given the difficulties of administering a general destination principle in the European Internal Market, there has been a renewed interest in the question whether the Community should switch to the origin principle for taxing its internal trade. Under the origin principle, goods bear the tax rate of the producer country, and for any good *i*, arbitrage thus yields

$$\left(1+t^{A}\right) p_i^{A} = \left(1+t^{B}\right) p_i^{B} \quad \forall \ i . \tag{3}$$

---

6 This may occur through commercial „carriers" providing re-import services or through mail order firms which are split into separate legal entities, thus avoiding the requirement to charge the VAT rate of the destination country (cf. Sinn [1990] and Krause-Junk [1990], pp. 258-261).

Clearly, it is crucial for the allocative neutrality of a general origin-based consumption tax that condition (3) holds for *all* categories of goods. While this is fairly obvious for final consumer goods it is less obvious for internationally traded intermediate goods and capital inputs since these purchases are deductible from the base of a value-added tax of the consumption type. To ensure that (3) is indeed enforced by arbitrage for inputs as well as outputs the origin-based VAT must be administered by an international subtraction method or by a notional tax credit method (cf. Cnossen and Shoup [1987], p.71, and Krause-Junk [1990], pp. 262-264). The exposition here will focus on the latter scheme.

Under the notional tax credit method, for a producer in country A purchasing intermediate inputs from a domestic supplier there is no difference from the conventional tax credit method. If he buys inputs I at a producer price of p_I^A and sells final output C at a producer price of p_C^A he would have a VAT bill of

$$VAT = t^A p_C^A C - t^A p_I^A I \ , \tag{4}$$

and would earn a net cash flow of

$$p_C^A\left(1+t^A\right)C - p_I^A\left(1+t^A\right)I - VAT = p_C^A C - p_I^A I \ . \tag{5}$$

However, if the producer were to purchase his intermediate inputs from a supplier in country B at a tax-inclusive price of $p_I^B\left(1+t^B\right)$, the notional credit method requires that this purchase should be treated for VAT-purposes as if it had borne the domestic rate t^A rather than the foreign rate (hence the term „notional“). The tax credit is calculated by applying the domestic tax rate to the gross-of-tax import expenditure $p_I^B\left(1+t^B\right)I$, deflated by the domestic tax factor $\left(1+t^A\right)$, and the domestic VAT liability becomes

$$VAT = t^A p_C^A C - t^A p_I^B \frac{\left(1+t^B\right)}{\left(1+t^A\right)} I \;, \tag{6}$$

implying that the producer's net cash flow is equal to

$$p_C^A\left(1+t^A\right)C - p_I^B\left(1+t^B\right)I - VAT = p_C^A C - p_I^B \frac{\left(1+t^B\right)}{\left(1+t^A\right)} I \;. \tag{7}$$

Comparing equations (5) and (7), we see that producers will not be indifferent between purchasing their inputs at home or abroad, unless the condition $p_I^A\left(1+t^A\right) = p_I^B\left(1+t^B\right)$ holds for all intermediates and capital goods. Thus, under the notional credit method, condition (3) will indeed be enforced for all goods by international arbitrage[7]. Therefore, *relative* producer and consumer prices are unaffected by international differences in tax rates and the international pattern of production will be efficient under a general origin-based consumption tax. In each country, producer prices and thus factor returns fall by the level of the domestic tax, implying a real devaluation in the high-tax country. Consumers are compensated for the lower factor incomes through the lump sum government transfers financed by the consumption tax. Therefore, no income effects arise and the general origin principle is equivalent to the destination principle in a setting with commodity trade only.

---

7 Alternatively, an origin-based value-added tax can be administered through the international subtraction method (e.g. Sinn [1990], p. 496). Under this method gross-of-tax imports would be deducted from the tax base and the VAT liability would be calculated as

$$VAT = \frac{t^A}{\left(1+t^A\right)}\left[p_C^A\left(1+t^A\right)C - p_I^B\left(1+t^B\right)I\right] \;,$$

where the tax rate is discounted by the domestic tax factor to express it as a percentage of consumer prices. This reduces to equation (6), demonstrating that the notional tax credit and the international subtraction method lead to identical arbitrage conditions. A brief discussion of the administrative differences between these two schemes of origin taxation is given in section 4.

The sensitivity of these results to the opening of international factor markets will be analysed in section 3.

2.3 The Restricted Origin Principle

The above discussion has been restricted to a two-country setting, which has ignored trade relations with non-member states. It is obvious that the neutrality of the origin principle carries over to a many-country world when the origin principle is applied world-wide. In current practice, however, the destination principle is the general scheme of international commodity taxation, which is also implicitly codified by GATT rules. Since non-EC countries have no motive to move away from the destination principle, a world-wide switch to the origin principle is beyond the reach of the European Community and is therefore hardly a realistic alternative. In the policy debate and in the academic literature it has therefore traditionally been assumed that the feasible alternative from an EC perspective is the *restricted origin principle* where intra-Community trade is taxed in the country of production but all trade between EC members and the rest of the world is taxed in the destination country.

To discuss the role of intra-Community tax differentials under the restricted origin principle, assume a trade structure where A and B are the members of a tax union while country C represents the rest of the world. Country A exports good 1 to both other countries, country B exports good 2, and country C exports good 3. Arbitrage equalizes consumer prices in the trading countries if an international transaction is taxed under the origin principle. If the destination principle is applied instead, international differences in tax rates are irrelevant for the choice between imported and domestically produced goods and producer prices are equalized between the trading nations. The following set of arbitrage conditions must then hold in equilibrium:

$$p_1^A = \frac{\left(1+t^B\right)}{\left(1+t^A\right)} p_1^B = p_1^C ,$$

$$\frac{\left(1+t^A\right)}{\left(1+t^B\right)} p_2^A = p_2^B = p_2^C ,$$

$$p_3^A = p_3^B = p_3^C .$$

Forming relative prices, these equations imply that

$$\frac{p_1^A}{p_3^A} = \frac{\left(1+t^B\right)}{\left(1+t^A\right)} \frac{p_1^B}{p_3^B} = \frac{p_1^C}{p_3^C},$$

$$\frac{\left(1+t^A\right)}{\left(1+t^B\right)} \frac{p_2^A}{p_3^A} = \frac{p_2^B}{p_3^B} = \frac{p_2^C}{p_3^C} . \tag{8}$$

Thus, unless tax rates are harmonized within the union, relative producer (and consumer) prices will differ both within the union and between union countries and the rest of the world, and international trade will therefore be distorted (cf. Berglas [1981], p. 382).

Furthermore, two routes of trade deflection arise under the restricted origin principle when tax rates differ between union countries: consumers in the high-tax country have an incentive to channel their imports from the rest of the world through the low-tax union partner whereas producers in the low-tax country receive higher tax rebates if they export to the rest of the world via a subsidiary in the high-tax union country (Shibata [1967], p. 212). When transaction costs for deflected trade are negligible (or linear but lower than the intra-Community tax differential) trade is fully deflected and tax collections in the high-tax country will be zero (Georgakopoulos and Hitiris [1992], pp. 119-121).

Even if trade deflection can be controlled by tax authorities, tax revenues are redistributed from the country which runs a deficit in its bilateral trade balance with the union partner to the country with an intra-union trade surplus (Berglas [1981], pp. 383-385). By lowering its tax rate, each of the union countries can systematically improve its intra-union trade balance and expand the domestic tax base. Therefore, a process of downward tax competition becomes a possible scenario under the traditional version of the restricted origin principle, which has been discussed so far (cf. Haufler [1994]).

However, as recently demonstrated by Lockwood, de Meza and Myles [1994], it is possible to combine the destination principle and the origin principle in a non-distortionary way: EC members could apply an origin-based VAT for trade with *all* their trading partners (i.e., tax all exports and exempt all imports) whereas non-EC countries employ a destination-based VAT (i.e., exempt exports to and tax imports from both EC and non-EC countries). A general tax principle is then applied from the perspective of each country and the neutrality properties of the world-wide destination and origin principles carry over to this international tax scheme[8].

Since EC countries levy no tax on imports, this solution implies that exports from the rest of the world to each of the union countries remain tax-free. Arbitrage conditions are thus given by

$$\left(1+t^{A}\right)p_i^{A}=\left(1+t^{B}\right)p_i^{B}=p_i^{C}\quad\forall\ i\in[1,2,3]\,. \tag{9}$$

On the other hand, exports from EC member states to the rest of the world are taxed in *both* the exporting and the importing country since the rest of the world applies a

---

[8] Lockwood, de Meza and Myles [1994, p. 315] label this tax scheme „non-reciprocal restricted origin principle“ in contrast to the „reciprocal restricted origin principle“ pioneered by Shibata [1967]. The crucial difference is that union countries tax-exempt their exports to, and tax their imports from, third countries under Shibata's version of the restricted origin principle whereas these border tax adjustments are not made under the tax principle proposed by Lockwood, de Meza and Myles.

uniform tax on both imported and domestically produced goods. Consumer prices in country C are thus given by

$$\left(1+t^{C}\right)p_i^{C}=\left(1+t^{C}\right)\left[\left(1+t^{A}\right)p_i^{A}\right]=\left(1+t^{C}\right)\left[\left(1+t^{B}\right)p_i^{B}\right]\quad\forall\, i\in[1,2,3]\qquad(10)$$

which reduces to (9) because the tax factor $(1 + t^{C})$ cancels out. Hence, relative producer (and consumer) prices will be unaffected by taxes in all parts of the world.

While the neutrality property of this scheme may not be intuitive at first sight, its economic rationale is fully in line with our earlier discussion: the double taxation of EC exports to the rests of the world ensures that factor returns in each member state fall by the full amount of the domestic tax so that border prices are equalized world-wide[9]. Since country C levies VAT on both domestic and foreign goods, consumer prices remain unchanged and the import decision is not distorted after a switch to the new tax scheme. The same is true in EC countries where the fall in factor prices equalizes the consumer prices of domestically produced goods on the one hand and of untaxed imports from EC partners and the rest of the world on the other. Real income effects also do not arise because the tax base for each union country is the value of domestic production, which equals the value of domestic consumption by the condition of multilaterally balanced trade.

2.4 The Role of Domestic Distortions

The above discussion has abstracted from existing domestic distortions which clearly play an important role in the indirect tax systems of EC member states. Two types of distortions have to be distinguished: if factor supplies - notably labor - are endogenous, a general commodity tax distorts the individual's trade-off between the

---

9 Border prices refer to the price of a good when it enters the destination country, prior to the imposition of VAT or other duties.

consumption of goods and leisure. Under both the general destination and the general origin principle the disposable real wage rate (i.e., the price of leisure relative to the aggregate consumption good) falls as a result of the general commodity tax, and this tax wedge is larger in the high-tax country. International tax differentials will thus lead to cross-country differences in the marginal rate of substitution between leisure and commodity consumption, but they will *not* prevent the cross-country equalization of relative commodity prices and thus will not distort import and export decisions at the margin (cf. Frenkel, Razin, and Sadka [1991], p. 39).

The second type of distortions concerns non-uniform commodity taxation, implying that different groups of commodities are taxed at different rates. A split VAT rate structure can be observed in most EC countries and a reduced rate is still permitted on a specified list of goods in the Internal Market, just as excise taxes continue to play an important role in the tax structure of EC member states. Again, a domestic distortion is introduced but the distortion now applies to traded goods as well if tax rates differ between countries. Under the destination principle, relative producer prices in equation (1) are still equalized across countries, even if country *A* levies different tax rates on goods 1 and 2. Therefore, even though marginal rates of substitution differ across countries, world output is still efficiently produced if the destination principle is applied. In contrast, it can be inferred from the arbitrage conditions (3) that relative producer prices are distorted by non-uniform national VAT structures if tax rates differ across countries and the origin principle is applied (Frenkel, Razin and Sadka [1991], pp. 35-39).

By the aggregate production efficiency theorem (Diamond and Mirrlees [1971]), the equalization of marginal rates of transformation across countries is a necessary condition for a second-best optimum so that the destination principle is to be preferred over the origin principle in this second-best framework[10]. Furthermore, the destination and the origin principle will provide different incentives for strategic tax setting if taxation is non-uniform (Lockwood [1993]).

It can be shown, however, that harmonizing the *relation* between the tax-inclusive prices of the goods bearing the standard and the reduced VAT rates, respectively, is sufficient to restore aggregate production efficiency under the origin principle (Fratianni and Christie [1981], pp. 414-419). Let t^A and t^B be the standard VAT rates in the two countries, which are applied to good 2. The tax-inclusive price of good 1, which bears the reduced tax rate, should then be $h\left(1+t^k\right)p_1^k$ in each country where the fraction h must be identical across countries. Arbitrage conditions are then given by

$$h\left(1+t^A\right)p_1^A = h\left(1+t^B\right)p_1^B,$$

$$\left(1+t^A\right)p_2^A = \left(1+t^B\right)p_2^B, \qquad (11)$$

and it is obvious that relative producer prices are equalized internationally when these conditions are met[11].

Our discussion of international commodity tax principles in a setting with international factor immobility may therefore be summarized as follows: under the current mixed tax principle, intra-European trade will be distorted unless EC members are willing to harmonize both the level and structure of indirect tax rates. On the other hand, if European countries unilaterally adopt a consistent origin principle in their trade with both EC members and non-members, and if they are still

---

10 The same argument applies to the choice between the residence principle and the source principle of factor taxation; see Frenkel, Razin, and Sadka [1991], pp. 100-105.

11 The illustrative example used by Fratianni and Christie [1981], p. 415 assumes that commodity tax rates in country *A* are 8% and 20%, respectively, as compared to 5.3% and 17% in country *B*. This implies a common value for *h* equal to 0.9 in both countries.

willing to harmonize their *structures* of indirect taxation (a rather strong requirement indeed), each country can choose its tax *level* independently without interfering with free trade.

One limitation of the literature surveyed above is that it tends to abstract from international factor mobility despite the fact that factors (in particular capital) are becoming increasingly mobile internationally. The following section will therefore investigate whether the neutrality of the origin principle carries over to a more realistic setting with international capital mobility.

3. Introducing International Capital Mobility

3.1 A Simple Two-Period Model with Commodity Taxes

We consider a small open economy producing a single internationally traded good which is used for consumption as well as investment[12].

This domestic good is a perfect substitute for foreign goods, so under the origin principle commodity price arbitrage implies that the domestic producer price p will be governed by

$$p(1+t) = Ep^*(1+t^*) \equiv 1, \tag{12}$$

where t and t^* are the domestic and the foreign commodity tax rates, p^* is the foreign-currency price of foreign goods, E is the exchange rate, and we have normalized the foreign tax-inclusive price level at unity. Recall from our discussion of equation (3) above that this arbitrage condition holds for both consumer and

---

[12] Note that the one-good assumption made here is not incompatible with international trade in commodities. Rather, the one-good assumption implies that commodity trade nets out in the aggregate when international capital flows are absent.

capital goods if either the notional credit method or the international subtraction method are applied under an origin-based consumption tax.

The representative domestic consumer lives for two periods and maximizes a well-behaved utility function of the form

$$U = U(C_1, C_2), \tag{13}$$

where C is consumption during the first period of his life and C_2 is consumption during the second period. The consumer is the owner-manager of a domestic competitive firm. At the beginning of period 1, this firm is endowed with a pre-determined, non-depreciable initial stock of capital K_1, but during period 1 the consumer can spend part of his earnings on physical investment (or sell part of his initial capital stock) so that he may enter period 2 with a different capital stock K_2.

On the other hand, since the consumer's life ends after period 2, he may finance part of his consumption during this period by the proceeds from the sale of his capital stock at the end of the period. Production in any period is a function of the physical capital stock existing at the beginning of the period and of the consumer's fixed labor supply, which is subsumed in the production function $f(\cdot)$. In addition to his earnings from the firm, the consumer receives a lump sum government transfer T in each period. In the *absence* of international capital mobility, the consumer must thus maximize (13) subject to the two budget constraints

$$p(1+t)C_1 = [p\,f(K_1) - p(K_2 - K_1)] + T_1, \tag{14}$$

$$p(1+t)C_2 = [p\,f(K_2) + pK_2] + T_2, \tag{15}$$

where the terms in square brackets represent the net cash flows from the firm after payment of commodity taxes. The term $p(K_2 - K_1)$ in (14) indicates expenditure on physical investment during period 1. This is valued at producer prices because investment expenditure is deductible from the base of a general origin tax of the consumption type (cf. equation (5)). Similarly, the term pK_2 in equation (15) is the revenue from the sale of the capital stock at the end of period 2. Since this revenue is taxable, the net cash flow to the consumer is again determined by the producer price p. Note that even though only the domestic producer price enters the budget constraint (14), the arbitrage condition (12) ensures that (14) will in fact hold regardless of whether the firm purchases its capital goods from domestic or foreign suppliers, given that VAT liabilities are calculated according to the notional credit method or the international subtraction method described in section 2.2.

To complete the description of our simple model, we must specify the lump sum government transfers which are financed by the commodity tax. As mentioned in section 2.2, an origin-based commodity tax of the consumption type will exempt investment expenditure but tax the proceeds of the sales of all goods, including investment goods, so the tax revenue and hence the transfer payments in the two periods will be given by

$$T_1 = t\left[pf(K_1) - p(K_2 - K_1)\right],$$

$$T_2 = t\left[pf(K_2) + pK_2\right]. \qquad (16)$$

Let us first employ the model to reproduce the conventional neutrality properties of an origin-based general commodity tax in the absence of capital mobility. Maximizing the utility function (13) with respect to C_1, C_2, and K_2, subject to the two budget constraints (14) and (15), and using (16) to eliminate T_1 and T_2 from the resulting first-order conditions[13], one finds that the consumer's optimum conditions in the absence of capital mobility can be written as

---

[13] Note that the transfer payments in each period are exogenous from the viewpoint of the representative consumer so that their values must be inserted only *after* the optimization problem has been solved.

$$\frac{\partial U / \partial C_1}{\partial U / \partial C_2} = 1 + f'(K_2), \tag{17}$$

$$C_1 = f(K_1) - (K_2 - K_1) \qquad C_2 = f(K_2) + K_2 \ . \tag{18}$$

Since the tax rate does not appear anywhere in these equations, it follows that the tax is completely neutral, having neither substitution nor income effects on resource allocation. Equation (17) reproduces the standard Pareto condition for a first best optimum that the marginal rate of substitution between consumption in the two periods must equal the marginal rate of transformation, while equations (18) simply restate the economy's overall resource constraints for the two periods.

We turn now to the case where an international capital market exists. In the *presence* of international capital mobility, the consumer may use part of his cash inflow in period 1 to purchase an internationally traded financial asset S which pays the exogenous world interest rate r^* in period 2. Allowing for the resale of this asset at the end of period 2, the consumer then faces the constraints

$$p(1+t)C_1 + S = \left[pf(K_1) - p(K_2 - K_1)\right] + T_1$$

$$p(1+t)C_2 = \left[pf(K_2) + pK_2\right] + T_2 + (1+r^*)S \ .$$

Eliminating S yields

$$p(1+t)\left[C_1 + \frac{C_2}{(1+r^*)}\right] = pf(K_1) - p(K_2 - K_1) + T_1 + \frac{\left[pf(K_2) + pK_2 + T_2\right]}{(1+r^*)}. \tag{19}$$

When he has access to an international capital market, the consumer may reallocate his consumption over time along the international capital market line, and his budget equations collapse into a single intertemporal constraint stating that the present value of his (tax-inclusive) consumption expenditure must equal the present value of the payments received from the firm and from the government.

The consumer now maximizes the utility function (13) with respect to C_1, C_2, and K_2, subject to the intertemporal budget constraint (19), recalling from (12) that $p(1 + t) = 1$. Again, we may use (16) to eliminate T_1 and T_2 from the first-order conditions, and we then find that the equilibrium of our market economy will be characterized by the optimum conditions

$$\frac{\partial U / \partial C_1}{\partial U / \partial C_2} = 1 + r^*, \qquad f'(K_2) = r^*, \tag{20}$$

$$C_1 + \frac{C_2}{(1+r^*)} = f(K_1) - (K_2 - K_1) + \frac{[f(K_2) + K_2]}{(1+r^*)}. \tag{21}$$

Again we see that the tax rate has dropped out from the equilibrium conditions, implying complete neutrality of the origin principle under international capital mobility as well. According to (20) the consumer will reallocate consumption over time until his marginal rate of substitution between present and future consumption equals the (constant) marginal rate of transformation $(1 + r^*)$ offered by the international capital market, and the firm will carry physical investment to the point where the marginal product of capital equals the exogenous return on international financial assets. Equation (21) shows that the value of consumption equals the value of output, net of investment, in present value terms. Therefore, it is intuitive that a switch to the origin principle has no effects on the international distribution of income.

We emphasize, however, that the neutrality of the origin principle depends crucially on the assumption that the general commodity tax is of the consumption type. In contrast, if the commodity tax is of the *income* type, investment expenditure is not deductible from the tax base and the sale of investment goods is not included in the base. The price of capital goods is then given by the *consumer* price of output, and the consumer's budget constraints (14) and (15) change to

$$p(1+t)C_1 = \left[pf(K_1) - p(1+t)(K_2 - K_1)\right] + T_1 , \tag{22}$$

$$p(1+t)C_2 = \left[pf(K_2) + p(1+t)K_2\right] + T_2 . \tag{23}$$

Tax revenues are altered accordingly and (16) changes to

$$\begin{aligned} T_1 &= t\, p\, f(K_1) , \\ T_2 &= t\, p\, f(K_2) . \end{aligned} \tag{24}$$

In the absence of capital mobility, maximizing (13) subject to the budget constraints (22) and (23) yields the following first-order condition for K_2:

$$\frac{\partial U / \partial C_1}{\partial U / \partial C_2} = 1 + \frac{f'(K_2)}{(1+t)} . \tag{25}$$

In contrast to equation (17), the commodity tax rate enters the first-order condition (25), demonstrating that intertemporal resource allocation is distorted by a commodity tax of the income type. This result is familiar from the analysis of an income tax: since savings (investment) cannot be deducted from the tax base in period 1 while the return to savings (investment) is taxed in period 2, future consumption is discriminated by the tax and the marginal rate of substitution (of C_2 for C_1) will fall below the marginal rate of transformation. It is easy to show that this distortion is also present under an origin-based commodity tax of the income type when international capital mobility is introduced.

Of course, our model can also be utilized to investigate the effects of a destination-based general consumption tax. In that case, goods arbitrage will imply that

$$p(1+t) = Ep^*(1+t) \Rightarrow p = Ep^* \equiv 1 , \tag{26}$$

where we may now set the foreign producer price at unity. Both the temporal budget constraints (14) and (15) and the intertemporal constraint (19) will remain unaffected by the switch from an origin-based to a destination-based consumption tax, but tax revenues and hence transfer payments will be given by

$$T_1 = tC_1 , \qquad T_2 = tC_2 . \tag{27}$$

Following an optimization procedure similar to the one indicated above, the reader may easily convince herself that a destination-based general consumption tax likewise implies complete neutrality, whether capital is mobile or not. As in the case of pure commodity trade, uniform consumption taxes levied under the destination and the origin principle are equivalent in this two-period setting with capital mobility.

3.2 Discussion of Long-Run Efficiency

At a closer look, it is not really surprising that the neutrality of an origin-based consumption tax survives the introduction of capital mobility. International capital mobility simply allows an intertemporal reallocation of consumption, but when the general consumption tax rate is constant over time, it will not affect the relative price of present versus future consumption and hence will not influence the economy's saving-investment balance. To put it differently, consumption in different periods may be seen as separate commodities which are taxed at a uniform rate when the commodity tax rate is time-invariant, and the consumer's intertemporal budget constraint is then equivalent to a static budget constraint linking the consumption of the two commodities 'present consumption' and 'future consumption'. With this translation of the consumer's intertemporal problem, it should be intuitively clear that the neutrality of the origin principle derived in a static many-commodity setting without capital mobility will carry over to the intertemporal setting with international borrowing and lending.

Notice that the validity of this result does not hinge on our small-economy assumption. In a general equilibrium model of two large, interdependent open economies, the optimum conditions derived above would still characterize the equilibrium of each individual country, and one would only have to add the overall resource constraint for the world economy as a whole (which would obviously not include any taxes) to close such a model. Notice also that our aggregation of all goods into a single commodity is quite innocent, as long as trade in all categories of goods (including intermediates and capital goods) enforces the general arbitrage condition (3). In that case all producer prices of inputs and outputs will adjust proportionally to a change in the general commodity tax rate. As we have seen, fulfilment of (3) for all types of goods requires that a multi-stage tax like the value-added tax should be administered according to either the notional credit method or the international subtraction method.

Some further insights can be obtained by looking at the results derived from the above two-period model in an alternative way: in long run equilibrium, no capital flows occur and the current account of each country must be balanced. If the value of net foreign assets measured in domestic currency is denoted by V, and if one assumes that the physical quantities of exports X and imports M depend on the relative price of domestic goods (thereby allowing for imperfect substitutability of traded goods), the current account equation for the domestic economy under the origin principle will read

$$p(1+t)X\left(\frac{p(1+t)}{Ep^*(1+t^*)}\right)-Ep^*(1+t^*)\,M\left(\frac{p(1+t)}{Ep^*(1+t^*)}\right)+r^*V=0\,.$$

Division by $Ep^*(1+t^*)$ yields

$$\frac{p(1+t)}{Ep^*(1+t^*)}X\left(\frac{p(1+t)}{Ep^*(1+t^*)}\right)-M\left(\frac{p(1+t)}{Ep^*(1+t^*)}\right)+\frac{r^*V}{Ep^*(1+t^*)}=0. \quad (28)$$

In the absence of capital mobility we have $V = 0$. It is then obvious that if relative producer prices p/Ep^* flexibly adjust by the factor $(1 + t^*)/(1 + t)$, relative consumer prices and hence trade flows will be unaffected by taxes, and trade will still be balanced despite international differences in the origin-based commodity tax rate.

With capital mobility, where V generally differs from zero, the proportional adjustment of the prices of all goods is still the key to the allocative neutrality of the origin principle[14]. In particular, the general adjustment of all prices (including the prices of capital goods) explains why the deflated net foreign asset term in equation (28) will be unaffected - so that the current account will remain in equilibrium - even though producer prices adjust to the imposition of an origin tax. To illustrate, consider a net debtor country where foreign investors own a fraction α of the domestic capital stock K. In long-run equilibrium, the market value of the physical capital stock must equal its replacement value. With p_k denoting the producer price of domestic capital goods, foreigners will therefore have to inject a capital inflow of $\alpha p_k (1 + t) K$ into the domestic economy in order to acquire a fraction α of the domestic capital stock[15]. In the current account equation (28) we then have $V = - \alpha p_k (1 + t) K$, and the equation may therefore be written as

$$\frac{p(1+t)}{Ep^*(1+t^*)} X\left(\frac{p(1+t)}{Ep^*(1+t^*)}\right) - M\left(\frac{p(1+t)}{Ep^*(1+t^*)}\right) - r^* \alpha \frac{p_k(1+t)}{Ep^*(1+t^*)} K = 0, \qquad (29)$$

---

[14] This long-run equilibrium setting also underlies Krause-Junk's [1992, pp. 149-151] discussion of the efficiency of the origin principle in a model with international trade in capital goods, but without savings and capital accumulation.

[15] Note that even though a business investor may deduct the VAT paid on his purchase of investment goods from the total VAT liability *in his home country* and will therefore base his calculations of profitability on the net-of-tax price of capital goods p_k, the amount of foreign exchange injected into the domestic economy by a foreign investor will of course still be equal to the tax-inclusive price $p_k(1 + t)$ at which capital goods are traded in the domestic market.

where p^* should now be interpreted as the foreign price of consumer goods. This equation makes clear that if domestic producer prices of capital goods (p_k) as well as the producer prices of consumer goods (p) adjust by the factor $1/(1 + t)$, or if the exchange rate E adjusts by the factor $(1 + t)$, there is no need for trade and capital flows to adjust to a change in the tax rate, and the current account will remain in balance.

Alternatively, we may say that even though a higher origin-based domestic commodity tax rate implies a higher tax burden on output produced by means of domestically located capital, there is no incentive to shift part of this capital abroad, because investors attempting to liquidate domestic capital goods for the purpose of capital exports would end up with a correspondingly lower after-tax revenue from the liquidation and hence would face a higher relative price of foreign (physical) assets which would eliminate the incentive for additional capital exports.

Thus, under the origin principle, cross-country tax differentials are capitalized in the after-tax prices of physical assets and give rise to asset-price differentials which are proportional to the differentials in not-of-tax output prices. Hence, with the ratio of input (asset) to output prices being unaffected by the tax differentials, there is no tax incentive to shift production and investment from one country to another.

3.3 Short-Run Effects and Income Distribution

As already suggested, the allocative neutrality of the origin base should be interpreted as a long run equilibrium phenomenon. In the short run and perhaps also in the medium term, the capitalization effects and the price adjustments just described can be expected to work imperfectly, due to the existence of nominal rigidities, including contracts fixed in nominal terms. In particular, if nominal exchange rates are fixed, so that the neutralization of a domestic tax increase requires a downward adjustment of nominal wages and prices, there may be considerable real effects of the tax increase for quite a long time.

Furthermore, even though neither a general origin-based consumption tax nor a general destination-based tax will distort relative prices in the long run, the two types of taxes differ in their distributional effects, including the distribution across different generations and the distribution between domestic and foreign citizens. As to the international effects, if foreigners own part of the domestic capital stock initially, a switch to the origin principle will reduce the real rate of return to investment from the perspective of foreigners. If tax proceeds are distributed entirely to residents of the home country this will cause an international redistribution of real income which is absent under the destination principle (cf. Bovenberg [1994]).

The same point can be stated in an alternative way by observing that the home country will run a trade surplus in long-run equilibrium under this scenario. Therefore, a switch from the destination to the origin base increases the tax base of the home country. Note that this effect did not appear in the two-period model of section 3.1 because it was assumed there that trade was balanced in present value terms for the home country.

In an overlapping generations framework, additional redistributive effects occur across different generations in the home country under both the origin and the destination base. These distributional effects - which have recently been thoroughly analyzed by Bovenberg [1994] - are in the nature of income effects, and via their impact on savings, they will tend to affect the long-run equilibrium magnitude of the net foreign asset term as well as the trade flows in equation (28). Thus, in so far as intergenerational and international distribution effects are of quantitative importance, the general commodity taxes analyzed here will have real effects and hence will be neutral only in the sense that they will not interfere with international efficiency.

4. Administrative and Political Aspects

The above discussion has focused on the allocative neutrality of a general consumption tax levied under the origin principle in a simple macroeconomic model. On the other hand, administrative and political arguments have always figured prominently in the discussion of alternative tax principles and, in view of the immediate policy relevance of the topic, a brief review of the most relevant arguments will be included here.

Our discussion in section 2.2 has shown that a *notional* tax credit for imports is compatible in principle with the tax credit scheme that is currently implemented for domestic transactions in all EC member states [cf. equation (6)]. If the foreign tax rate is lower (higher) than the domestic one, this implies that imports are subsidized (taxed) in the destination country in anticipation of the recouping effect which occurs at subsequent production stages (cf. Krause-Junk [1990], pp. 262-264).

Alternatively, the subtraction method could be used to exclude intermediate goods from the commodity tax base. Two variants of this tax scheme can be distinguished: one option would be to apply the subtraction method exclusively to international transactions while domestic transactions would still be taxed according to the tax credit method (cf. Sinn [1990], p. 496, fn. 13). The problem with this solution is that the recouping effect would simply be postponed by one stage and imported goods would not effectively bear the tax rate of the origin country if there are two or more further processing stages in the destination country. Therefore, to preserve the origin taxation of imported goods it would be necessary to distinguish between imported and domestic value added throughout the further chain of processing in the destination country. The substantial practical difficulties of this procedure have been stressed by Andel [1986].

The second option would be the consistent use of the subtraction method for international as well as domestic purchases. The drawback is here that the tax laws of the Community and each of its member states would have to be changed in order to reverse the decision in favour of the tax credit method, which has been made by EC member states in the Second VAT Directive of 1967. Given the difficulties of applying either the one or the other variant of the subtraction method, the notional tax credit seems to be the preferred choice of implementing the origin principle.

It should also be stressed that no additional administrative complications arise for the taxation of trade with third countries if EC members systematically exempt all imports from tax while third countries levy VAT on all their imports (cf. section 2.3). Trade flows from the rest of the world to the Community would be tax-exempt in the origin country but EC members still grant a notional tax credit based on their domestic tax rates in order to neutralize the recouping effect which occurs at later stages of production.

In contrast, EC exports to the rest of the world would leave the origin country at their tax-inclusive prices but no tax credit would be granted in the country of destination, which simply adds the domestic tax rate on the (tax-inclusive) price of imported goods.

Nevertheless, a number of problems remain under each of the alternatives of implementing the origin principle in the European Community. Perhaps the most serious one, put forward by Cnossen and Shoup [1987, p.73], is that both the notional tax credit and the subtraction method give rise to transfer-pricing when tax rates differ between EC members.

Since tax credits or deductions from the tax base are based on the *value of imports* and the effective tax rate on the final product is a weighted average of the statutory tax rates in the exporting and importing countries, there is an incentive for internationally integrated firms to overstate (understate) the import value if the tax rate in the destination country is higher (lower) than the rate of the origin country. Given the world-wide experience with transfer pricing in the field of capital income taxation and the increasing importance of multinational firms operating in the Community, this form of commodity tax evasion must be considered as a serious practical disadvantage of the origin principle[16].

Another point which has long been emphasized in the discussion of alternative tax principles is that the neutrality of the origin principle must also be *perceived* by economic agents. It is often argued that producers in high-tax member states are unlikely to be convinced by the analysis of exchange rate adjustments that they are *not* put at a disadvantage in comparison to producers in low-tax countries (e.g. Cnossen and Shoup [1987], p.71). This argument becomes even stronger if the Community's exports to the rest of the world are subject to double taxation whereas trade in the other direction remains untaxed. This will most likely be perceived as non-neutral by producers throughout the Community and even if this tax scheme were adopted by policy makers, it may be challenged before the European Court of Justice on the grounds that it violates fundamental rules of reciprocity.

5. Conclusions

The purpose of this paper was to provide an overview of the main arguments for destination- versus origin-based commodity taxation in the European Internal Market. One option is to maintain the destination principle for trade between VAT-registered traders while allowing final consumer purchases to be taxed in the country of origin. This system inevitably distorts intra-Community trade although the distortion need not weigh heavily from a macroeconomic perspective when the volumes of tax-induced cross-border shopping are low. Alternatively, a tax scheme can be implemented where EC members adopt the origin principle for their internal

---

[16] Note that with non-uniform VAT rates within individual EC countries, the same transfer pricing argument applies equally to *domestic* transactions if a consistent subtraction method were to be implemented in the Community.

and external trade whereas non-members consistently use the destination principle. In a setting with commodity trade only, the latter tax scheme is neutral if the commodity tax is completely general. With a split VAT structure, however, the origin principle violates production efficiency unless indirect tax structures are harmonized between countries.

The paper has further shown that the introduction of international capital mobility does not affect the allocative neutrality of a general consumption tax levied under the origin principle. The intuition for this result is that a general consumption tax affects neither aggregate savings nor - through the deductibility of investment expenditures from the tax base - the real return to domestic investment. Therefore, no international capital movements are induced by tax rate changes and commodity trade will thus be undistorted. Finally, it has been argued that a notional tax credit scheme allows to switch to the origin principle while maintaining the convenient tax credit method for domestic transactions in the Community. Implementation problems remain, however, because this method may lead to tax evasion through transfer-pricing, and it is likely to stir political opposition because its neutrality is not perceived by EC producers.

A switch to the origin principle also requires that either prices or exchange rates are flexible. Because of the serious short-run difficulties involved in a process of domestic wage and price deflation, the only practicable way for the EC countries to switch to the origin principle would be to adjust exchange rate parities. Thus, each member country would have to adjust its exchange rate in proportion to the level of its indirect tax rates (cf. Siebert [1990], pp. 60-62). Since the planned transition to a common currency offers an opportunity to undertake a final exchange rate realignment, it might seem natural to consider a switch to the origin principle at that time. This timing could also be motivated by the fact that the transition to a monetary union will reduce the transaction costs of direct consumer purchases across intra-European borders, thereby exacerbating the distortions associated with the current EC system. On the other hand, the anticipation of an exchange rate realignment prior to the transition to monetary union could induce speculative capital flows which might create some short-run instability in financial markets.

Summing up these arguments, no clear-cut choice emerges between the different commodity tax regimes which are feasible and desirable under the conditions of the European Community's Internal market. Given the present fairly limited amount of distortionary direct cross-border consumer trade, maintaining the destination principle for purchases by registered traders may be preferable on practical and political grounds. However, if direct consumer trade assumes increasing importance as economic integration proceeds, the option of switching to the origin principle and the notional tax credit scheme seems to deserve serious attention by policy makers.

References

Andel, N. (1986), „Sollte man in der EG im Rahmen der Mehrwertsteuer zum Ursprungslandprinzip übergehen?“, *Finanzarchiv 44*, pp. 484-488.

Berglas, E. (1981), „Harmonization of Commodity Taxes“, *Journal of Public Economics 16,* pp. 377-387.

Biehl, D. (1969), *„Ausfuhrland-Prinzip, Einfuhrland-Prinzip und Gemeinsamer-Markt-Prinzip. Ein Beitrag zur Theorie der Steuerharmonisierung“*, Heymanns, Köln.

Bovenberg, L.A. (1994), „Destination- and Origin-based Taxation under International Capital Mobility“, *International Tax and Public Finance 1*, pp. 247-273.

Cnossen, S. (1983), „Harmonization of Indirect Taxes in the EEC“, *British Tax Review 4,* pp. 232-253.

Cnossen, S. (1990), „The Case for Tax Diversity in the European Community“, *European Economic Review 34,* pp. 471-479.

Cnossen, S. and C.S. Shoup (1987), „Coordination of Value-added Taxes“, in: S. Cnossen (ed.), *Tax Coordination in the European Community,* Kluwer, Deventer, pp. 59-84.

Diamond, P.A. and J.A. Mirrlees (1971), „Optimal Taxation and Public Production I: Production Efficiency", *American Economic Review 61*, pp. 8-27.

Europäische Gemeinschaft für Kohle und Stahl - Hohe Behörde (1953), (Tinbergen Report), *Bericht über die durch die Umsatzsteuer aufgeworfenen Probleme auf dem Gemeinsamen Markt.*

European Communities-Commission (1963) (Neumark-Report), *The EEC Reports on Tax Harmonization, The Report of the Fiscal and Financial Committee and the Reports of the Sub-groups A, B and C,* Unofficial Translation by H. Thurston, International Bureau of Fiscal Documentation, Amsterdam.

Fratianni, M. and H. Christie (1981), „Abolishing Fiscal Frontiers within the EEC", *Public Finance 36*, pp. 411-429.

Frenkel, J., A. Razin and E. Sadka (1991), *International Taxation in an Integrated World*, MIT Press, Cambridge/Mass.

Genser, B. (1992), „Tax Competition and Tax Harmonization in Federal Economies", in: H.J. Vosgerau (ed.), *European Integration in the World Economy,* Springer Verlag, Heidelberg, pp. 200-237.

Georgakopoulos, T. and T. Hitiris (1992), „On the Superiority of the Destination over the Origin Principle of Taxation for Intra-union Trade", *The Economic Journal 102*, pp. 117-126.

Haufler, A. (1992), „Indirect Tax Policy in the European Community: An Economic Analysis", in: H.J. Vosgerau (ed.), *European Integration in the World Economy*, Springer Verlag, Heidelberg, pp. 243-270.

Haufler, A. (1994), „Unilateral Tax Reform under the Restricted Origin Principle", *European Journal of Political Economy 10*, pp. 511-527.

Keen, M. (1993), „The Welfare Economics of Tax Co-ordination in the European Community: a Survey", *Fiscal Studies 14*, No. 2, pp. 15-36.

Krause-Junk, G. (1990), „Ein Plädoyer für das Ursprungslandprinzip", in: F.X. Bea und W. Kitterer (ed.), *Finanzwissenschaft im Dienste der Wirtschaftspolitik*, Mohr, Tübingen, pp. 253-265.

Krause-Junk, G. (1992), „Die europäische Mehrwertsteuer und das Ursprungslandprinzip", *Finanzarchiv 49*, pp. 141-153.

Lockwood, B. (1993), „Commodity Tax Competition under Destination and Origin Principles", *Journal of Public Economics 52*, pp. 141-162.

Lockwood, B., D. de Meza and G. Myles (1994), „The Equivalence between Destination and Non-reciprocal Restricted Origin Tax Regimes", *Scandinavian Journal of Economics 96,* pp. 311-328.

Peffekoven, R. (1983), „Probleme der Internationalen Finanzordnung", in: F. Neumark (ed.), *Handbuch der Finanzwissenschaft*, Bd. 4, 3. Aufl., pp. 219-268.

Shibata, H. (1967), „The Theory of Economic Unions: A Comparative Analysis of Customs Unions, Free Trade Areas and Tax Unions“, in: C.S. Shoup (ed.), *Fiscal Harmonization in Common Markets*, Columbia University Press, New York, pp. 145-264.

Siebert, H. (1990), „The Harmonization Issue in Europe: Prior Agreement or a Competitive Process?“, in: H. Siebert (ed.), *The Completion of the Internal Market,* Mohr, Tübingen, pp. 53-75.

Sinn, H.W. (1990), „Tax Harmonization and Tax Competition in Europe“, *European Economic Review 34,* pp. 489-504.

Sørensen, P.B. (1990), „Tax Harmonization in the European Community: Problems and Prospects“, *Bank of Finland Discussion Papers* No. 3/90.

Whalley, J. (1979), „Uniform Domestic Tax Rates, Trade Distortions and Economic Integration“, *Journal of Public Economics 11*, pp. 213-221.

Whalley, J. (1981), der Adjustment and Tax Harmonization: Comment on Berglas“, *Journal of Public Economics 16*, pp. 389-390.

ADDRESSES OF THE AUTHORS

Prof. Gil BUFMAN
Department of Economics
Tel Aviv University
Ramat-Aviv
Tel Aviv 69 978
Israel

Prof. Alex CUKIERMAN
The Eitan Berglas School of Economics
Tel Aviv University
Ramat Aviv
Tel Aviv 69 978
Israel

Prof. Dr. Bernd GENSER
Fakultät für Wirtschaftswissenschaften
und Statistik
Universität Konstanz
Postfach 55 60
78434 Konstanz
Germany

Prof. Gene M. GROSSMAN
Woodrow Wilson School
Princeton University
Princeton, New Jersey 08540
USA

Dr. Andreas HAUFLER
Fakultät für Wirtschaftswissenschaften
und Statistik
Universität Konstanz
Postfach 55 60
78434 Konstanz
Germany

Prof. Elhanan HELPMAN
Department of Economics
Tel Aviv University
Ramat-Aviv
Tel Aviv 69 978
Israel

Prof. Arye L. HILLMAN
Department of Economics
Bar-Ilan University
Ramat Gan 52900
Israel

Manuel HINDS
The World Bank
Department of Research
1818 A. Street N.W.
Washington, D.C. 20433
USA

Prof. Dr. Nikolaus K.A. LÄUFER
Fakultät für Wirtschaftswissenschaften
und Statistik
Universität Konstanz
Postfach 55 60
78434 Konstanz
Germany

Prof. Leonardo LEIDERMAN
Department of Economics
Tel Aviv University
Ramat-Aviv
Tel Aviv 69 978
Israel

Branco MILANOVIC
The World Bank
Department of Research
1818 A. Street N.W.
Washington, D.C. 20433
USA

Prof. Assaf RAZIN
Department of Economics
Tel Aviv University
Ramat Aviv
Tel Aviv 69 978
Israel

Prof. Efraim SADKA
Department of Economics
Tel Aviv University
Ramat-Aviv
Tel Aviv 69 978
Israel

Prof. Dr. S. SUNDARARAJAN
National Institute of Bank Management
Kondhwe Khurd
NIBM Post Office
Pune 411 048
India

Prof. Dr. Albert SCHWEINBERGER
Fakultät für Wirtschaftswissenschaften
und Statistik
Universität Konstanz
Postfach 55 60
78434 Konstanz
Germany

Prof. Dr. Heinrich URSPRUNG
Fakultät für Wirtschaftswissenschaften
und Statistik
Universität Konstanz
Postfach 55 60
78434 Konstanz
Germany

Prof. Peter Birch SØRENSEN
Institute of Economics
Copenhagen Business School
Nansensgade 19, 5th floor
DK-1366 Kopenhagen K
Denmark

Prof. Dr. Hans-Jürgen VOSGERAU
Fakultät für Wirtschaftswissenschaften
und Statistik
Universität Konstanz
Postfach 55 60
78434 Konstanz
Germany

Druck: Strauss Offsetdruck, Mörlenbach
Verarbeitung: Schäffer, Grünstadt